The Campus History Series

Columbia State Community College

Tennessee's First

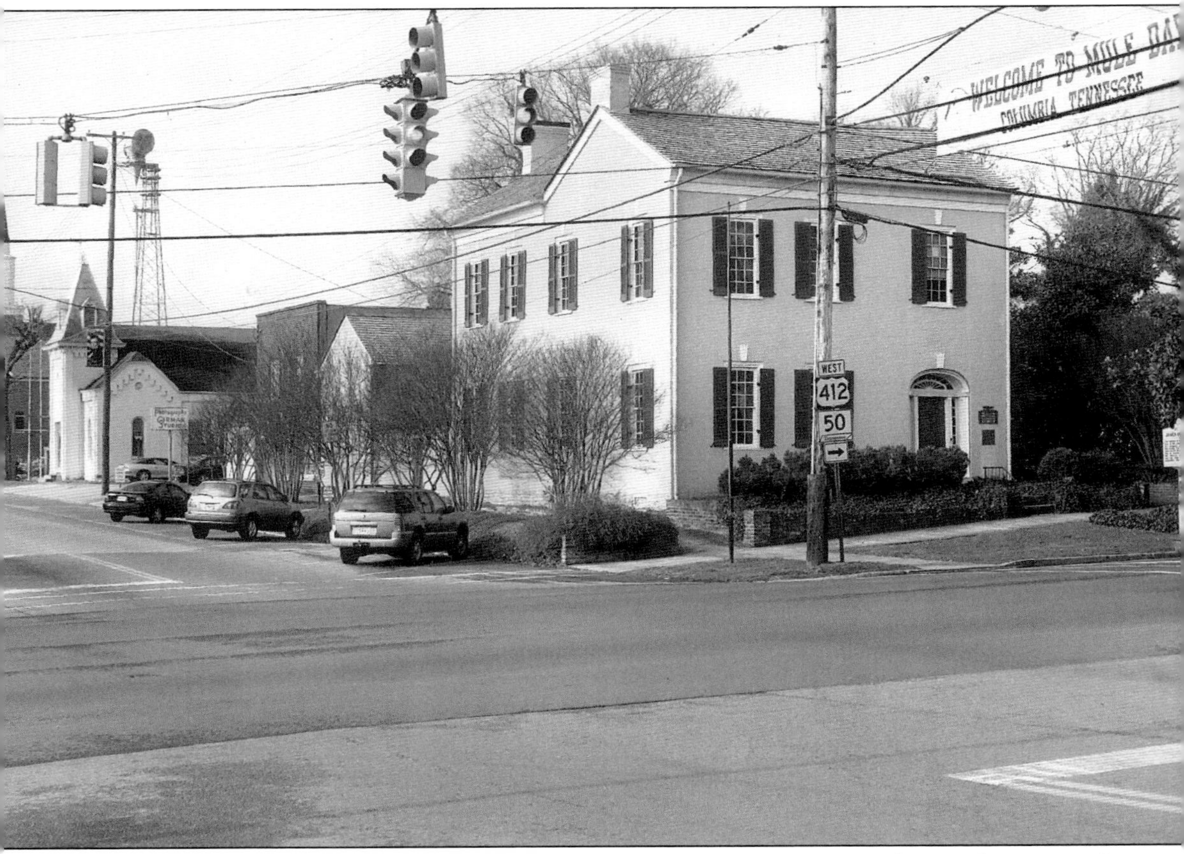

The original campus of Columbia State Community College sits just four miles west of downtown Columbia, Tennessee. Columbia is the ancestral home of the 11th United States president, James Knox Polk. Columbia is also known as the "Mule Capital of the World." Pictured is the Polk Home, which sits on the corner of West 7th and High Streets. To the far left is the steeple of the First Baptist Church, where most of the classes were held during the college's first year of operation, 1966–1967. The sign welcomes visitors to "Mule Day 2004."

The Campus History Series

Columbia State Community College

Tennessee's First

Carolyn R. Allred-Winnett, Monte Bayless,
Fred Behrens, and Lewis E. Moore Jr.

ARCADIA
PUBLISHING

ISBN 978-0-7385-1659-2

Published by Arcadia Publishing
Charleston, South Carolina

Printed in the United States of America

Library of Congress Catalog Card Number: 2004103399

For all general information contact Arcadia Publishing at:
Telephone 843-853-2070
Fax 843-853-0044
E-mail sales@arcadiapublishing.com
For customer service and orders:
Toll-Free 1-888-313-2665

Visit us on the Internet at www.arcadiapublishing.com

We dedicate this history to all our students, past and present. Most have made us extremely proud. We hope that as you peruse this book, fond memories of your days at Columbia State are rekindled.

CONTENTS

ACKNOWLEDGMENTS

We gratefully acknowledge the enthusiastic support of President Hawkins and the Columbia State Community College Foundation for this project. In addition, we are grateful to Elaine Kelsey for coordinating the project with the publisher and performing other tasks indispensable to its success.

Our research would not have been possible without the cooperation of the staff of the John Finney Learning Resources Center. We are especially grateful to Martha Briscoe of the Center staff. We also wish to thank Freda McClain, Karen Kendall-Fite, Bonnie Sealy-Mosley, and Columbia Photo.

We are most grateful for the collective memory of alumni, faculty, staff, and members of the community from which we have drawn to chronicle the story of Columbia State's relatively brief yet significant history. We ask the forgiveness of any individual or group that we might have overlooked because of page and picture limitations. Although we perused thousands of images, there were some we desired that were just not available. Those images, therefore, must forever remain fond memories.

Introduction

Perhaps the most exciting day in the history of Columbia, Tennessee, was March 15, 1967. The First Lady, Lady Bird Johnson, came with her husband, President Lyndon Johnson, to dedicate Columbia State Community College "forever to the service of the people and to the progress of the nation." Among the special guests who accompanied them were United States Secretary of Health, Education, and Welfare John Gardner; Tennessee Gov. Buford Ellington, and Tennessee Commissioner of Education J. Howard Warf. Dr. James Clark, dean and acting president, presided over the ceremonies, which included his remarks in addition to those of the First Lady, the President, Secretary Gardner, and Governor Ellington.

Just months earlier, Columbia State had opened as the state's first community college in facilities "all over town." Major facilities included offices that were located in a converted residence next to the West 7th Street Church of Christ. Most classes were held in the First Baptist Church, science classes were held in lab facilities on the Columbia Military Academy campus, and the Memorial Building served as the student center. Buses, driven by teachers and other college personnel, transported students between various locations.

An initial student body of 363 registered on September 23, 1966. Three days later the college's first convocation was held downtown in the Polk Theater. Gov. Frank Clement was the featured speaker. "Because of this school," he said prophetically, "young people, who otherwise would have to terminate their academic careers at the high school level, will here find a way into higher education."

The history of Tennessee community colleges goes back at least as far as recommendations made by the Pierce-Albright report in 1957. Maury County citizens formed a committee of some 600 persons to seek a college. On December 12, 1963, the state board of education's Junior College Committee visited Maury County to view prospective sites. On December 17, 1964, the committee adopted a resolution calling for the establishment of three community junior colleges, one in each of the state's three grand divisions.

The Maury County group made a presentation to the board's Junior College Committee on June 4, 1965. On June 22, at a meeting called by the board, the committee recommended that junior colleges be placed in the Columbia, Cleveland, and Jackson areas, with the exact locations to be chosen by Commissioner Warf. These sites were in the southern half of the state, which was underserved by public higher education institutions.

On June 30, 1965, Commissioner Warf toured sites in Maury County and selected the 204-acre Hickman farm located four miles west of downtown Columbia on Highway 99. On July 12, the Maury County Quarterly Court unanimously approved, per state requirements, purchase of the property and pledged an additional $250,000 toward construction costs of the new campus. Governor Clement and Commissioner Warf broke ground at enthusiastic public ceremonies on October 20, 1965.

Plans were formulated for opening the college in the fall of 1966 before the expected construction completion date in the fall of 1967. Columbia State would serve as a prototype for those to follow. Work began in the spring of 1966. Dr. Hal Ramer, assistant commissioner for higher education, and Dr. Archie Rushton, the newly appointed executive dean for community colleges, directed the effort from the state level. Dr. James Clark was appointed dean of instruction and acting president to lead the establishment of the college at the local level. New staff and faculty began arriving almost daily as efforts intensified to be ready for a fall quarter opening. Securing physical facilities, hiring appropriate personnel, developing a curriculum and schedule of classes, writing a catalog, and taking student applications were just some of the tasks to complete.

This new innovation within Tennessee's public higher education systems raised several questions. The general public did not understand where the two-year colleges fit. Would they provide the first two years of higher education or two additional grades of high school? Would they be governed by state or local boards? Would they threaten senior college enrollments? Would they be resident or commuter colleges? Would students have difficulties transferring to senior colleges? And, the question that never seems to die—would Columbia State ever become a four-year college?

Rushton and Clark were committed to two years of rigorous college-level work. Anyone with a high school diploma or GED would be eligible to attend. The decision was made that they would not be junior colleges but more comprehensive community colleges. The state would maintain fiscal and administrative control. As a concession to senior colleges, the new schools would be commuter, non-resident colleges. There would be ease of transfer from community colleges to senior institutions. The question about four-year status still arises periodically.

The process of creating Columbia State during the middle months of 1966 occurred in the time frame of other momentous events in the country. Racial violence and civil rights marches, increasing troop strength in Vietnam, the first successful artificial heart pump, and the beginning of Medicare were important issues of the time.

Over the college's 40-year history, there have been many changes, but the one chief goal for which it was created has been consistently pursued: making higher education available to more and more people in the college's service area. Even in the beginning, regular on-campus classes were augmented by continuing education classes at night and at off-campus locations. Developmental classes have always been available for those who need more preparation for college success. The college has moved from off-campus classes in leased or donated space to classes offered at centers in Lawrence and Williamson Counties and sites in Clifton and Lewisburg. Classes are also made available through Interactive Television and the Internet. Past success stimulates Columbia State to provide access to higher education to more and more people in the service area.

One

In The Beginning

Efforts began in the spring of 1966 to create Columbia State as a prototype for the other Tennessee community colleges that were to follow. In a brief span of 18 months, the college was conceptualized, personnel were hired, temporary quarters were secured, classes were scheduled, and three full quarters of instruction were provided while a new campus with six buildings was completed and readied for occupancy by the fall of 1967. An air of excitement permeated the community. New college personnel were welcomed and lavishly feted. The enthusiasm of the students was contagious.

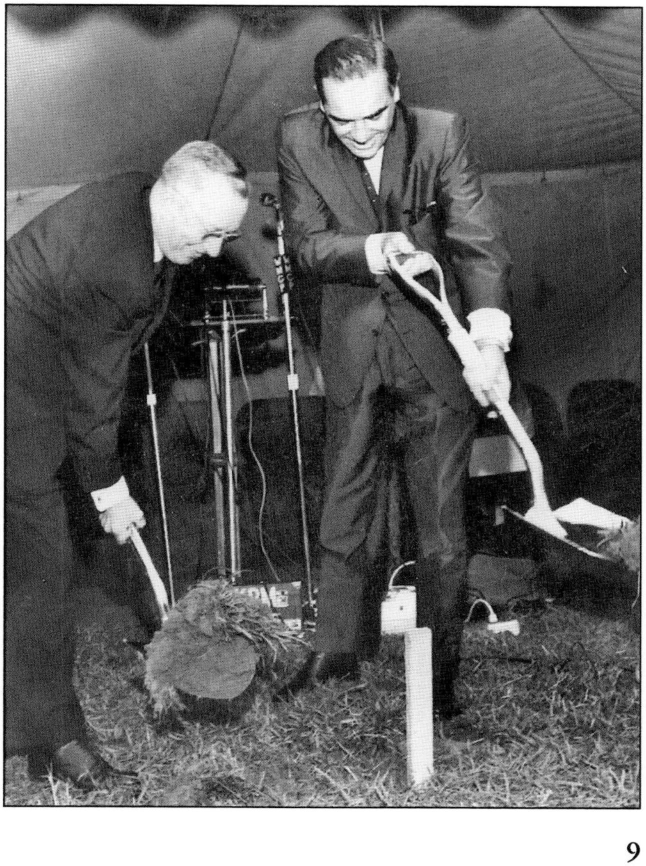

Comm. of Education Howard Warf personally toured prospective sites for the college and selected the 204-acre Hickman farm just west of the city. He and Gov. Frank Clement turned the first spades of dirt at the groundbreaking ceremonies on October 20, 1965.

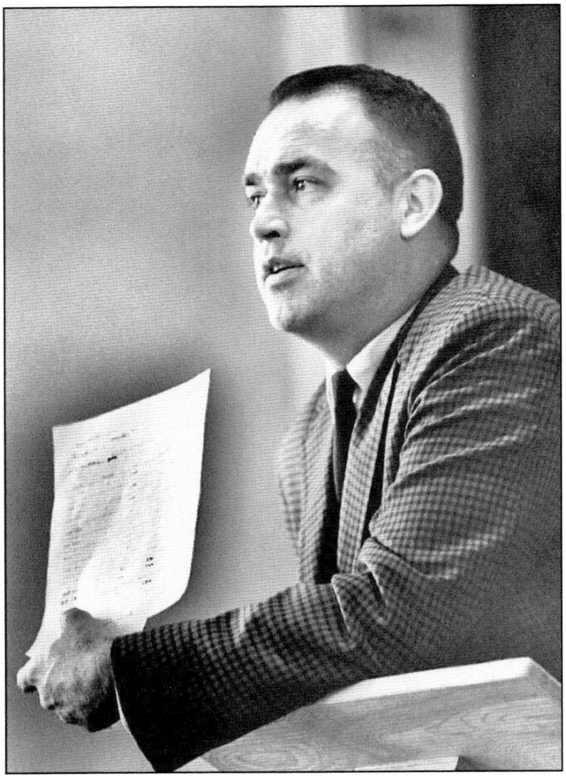

William O. "W.O." Johnson was the first employee hired in the community college system. He served as the director of admissions from 1966 until his retirement.

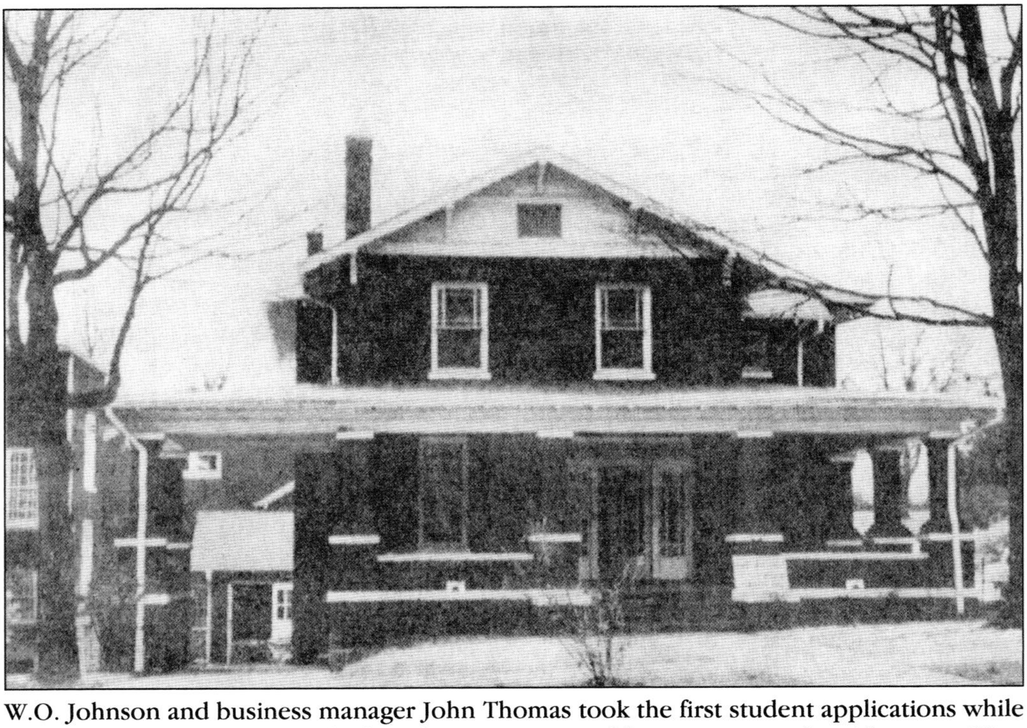

W.O. Johnson and business manager John Thomas took the first student applications while sitting on the sidewalk outside the Administration Building, a converted residence on West 7th Street. The office furniture had not yet arrived.

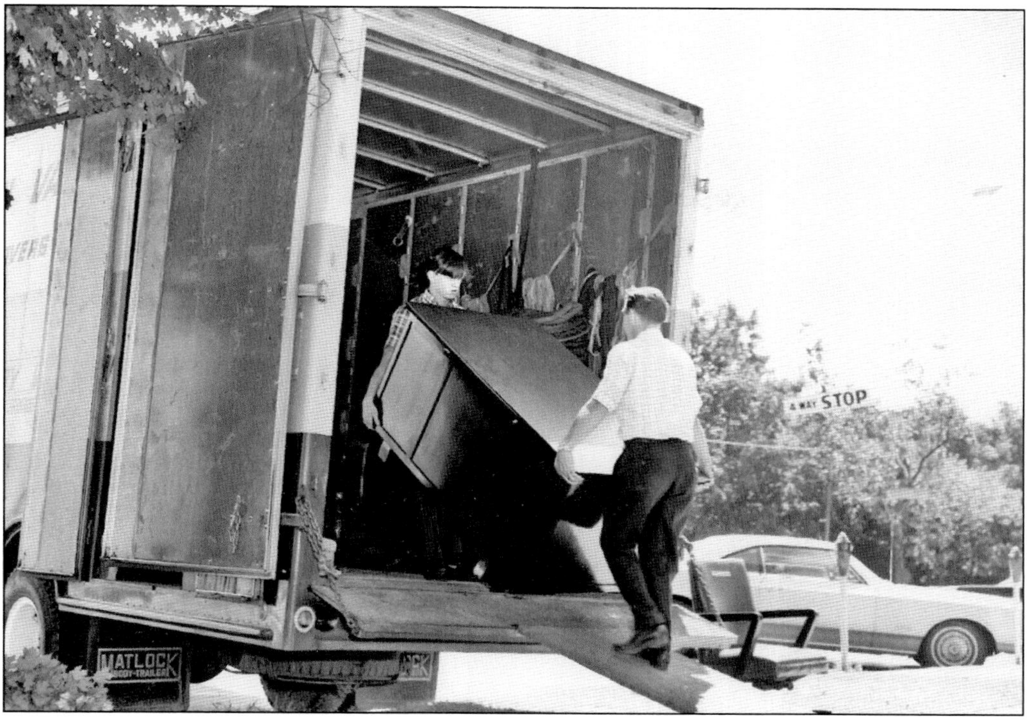

Furniture and equipment were secured, moved into the temporary quarters, and only months later moved to the new campus.

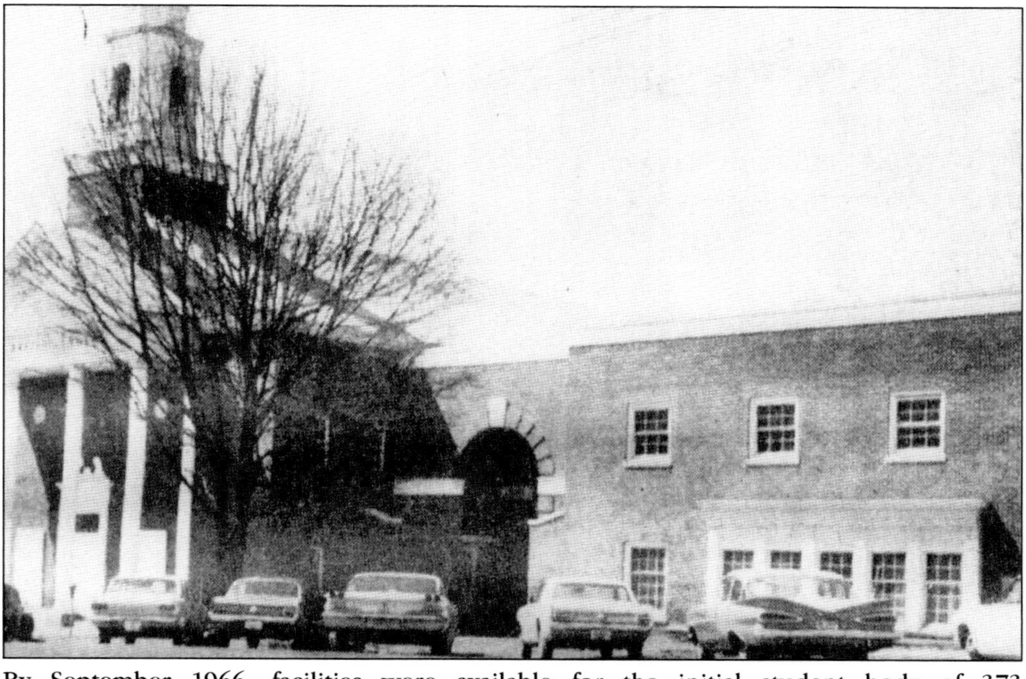

By September 1966, facilities were available for the initial student body of 373 students. Classes were scheduled in almost a dozen locations, most in the First Baptist Church. The church housed classrooms and faculty offices, and the Fellowship Hall was used as a lunchroom.

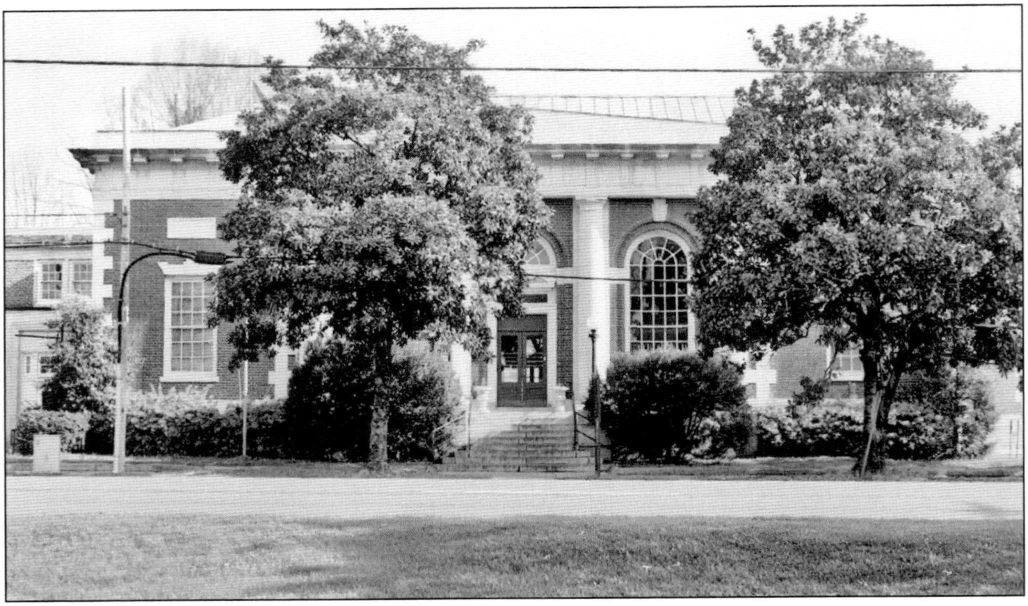

The Memorial Building, formerly an old post office, was used as a student center and as a location for registration, student assemblies, and special programs.

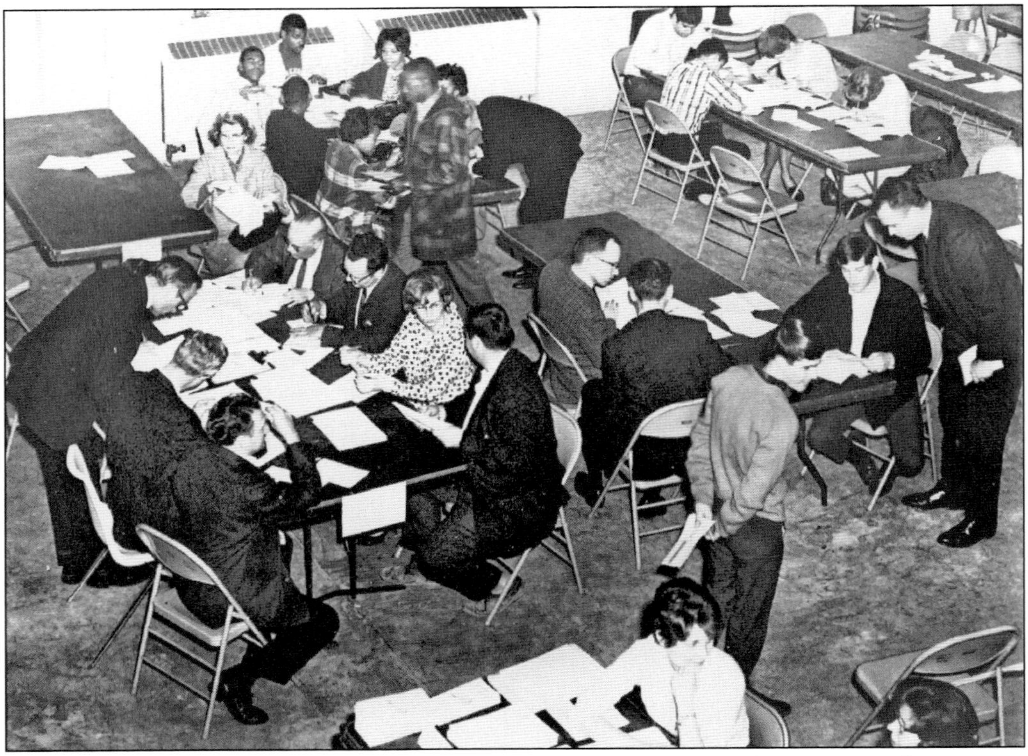

September 23, 1966, saw the first class walk through disorganized registration lines. Long lines, long waits, tired feet, and headaches marked the opening of that first quarter.

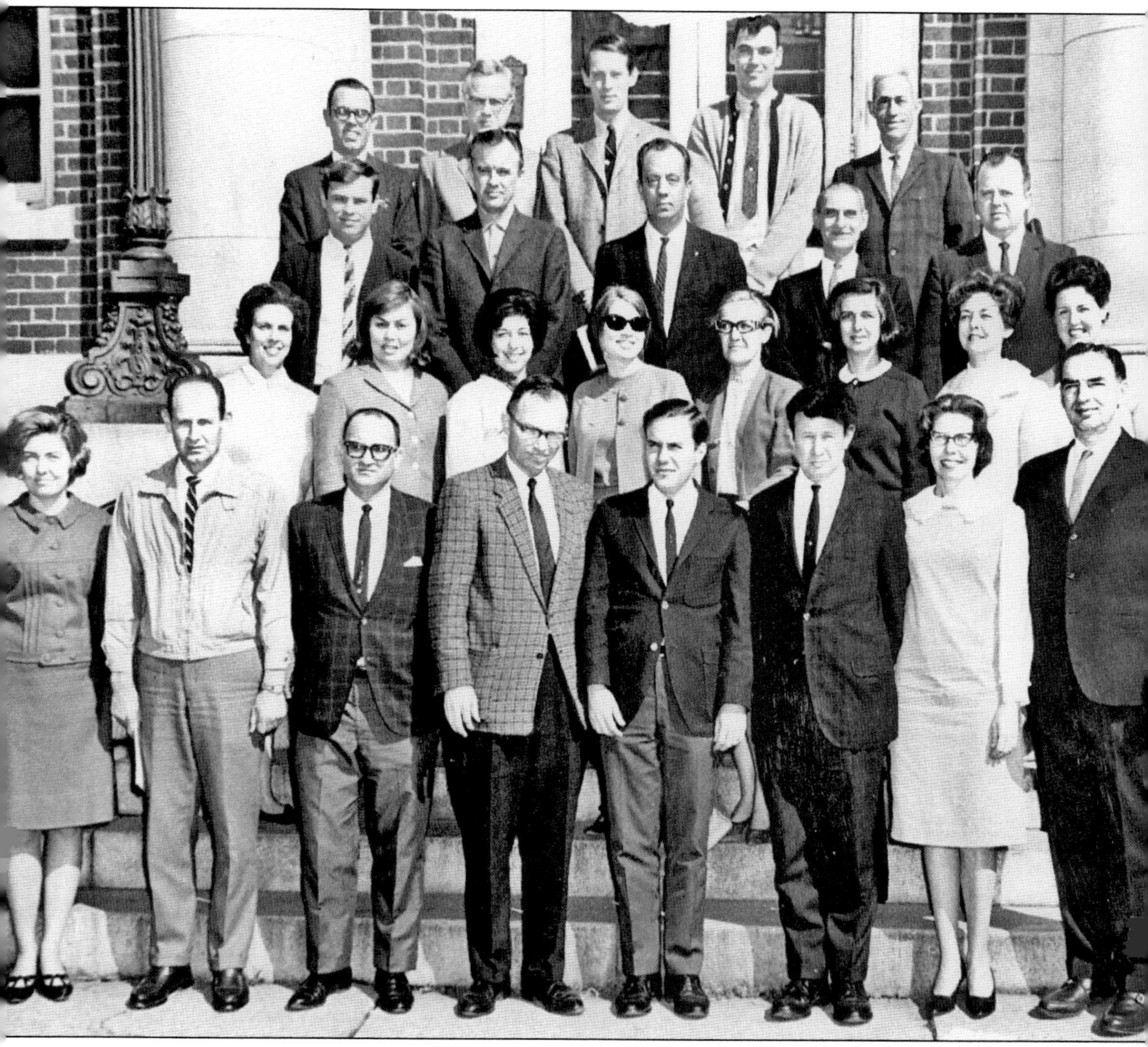

Standing on the front steps of the Memorial Building are the first faculty members and heads of departments. From left to right are (first row) Carolyn Allred, Eugene Durham, John Fort, Fred Eberhart, Dwight Gatwood, J.V. Guidry, Mary Mott McCampbell, and Dean James Clark; (second row) Doris Bernett, Charlene Black, Claudia Spence, Ann Cami, Beatrice Chesrown, Jane Ross, Winifred Clark, and Ava Eaton; (third row) Monte Bayless, John Mitchell, James Minatra, Leon van Leeuwen, and Lewis Moore; (fourth row) John Thomas, John Dillingham, Fred Behrens, Bennett Jent, and George Watson. Mildred Mitchell, Dorothy Powell, Hayward Bond, H.T. Breland, Sue Burkhart, W.O. Johnson, Paul Sands, Darrell Simmons, and J.E. Milton were not present.

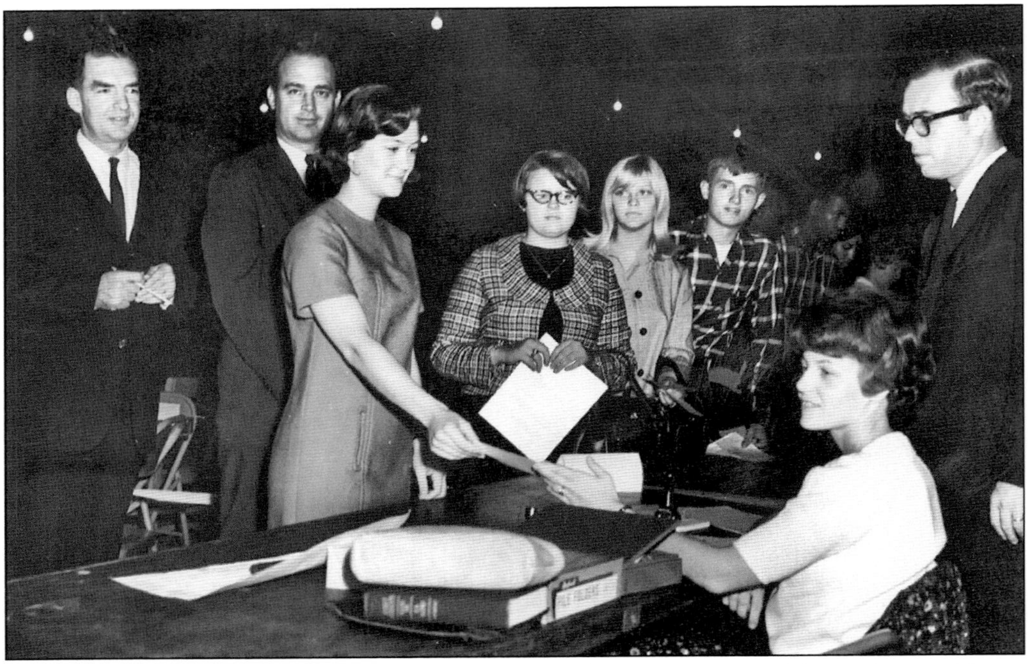

Mary Lou Harris, the first student to register, pays her fees to Jean Hurt of the Business Office as business manager John Thomas looks on. Dean Clark and W.O. Johnson are behind Harris.

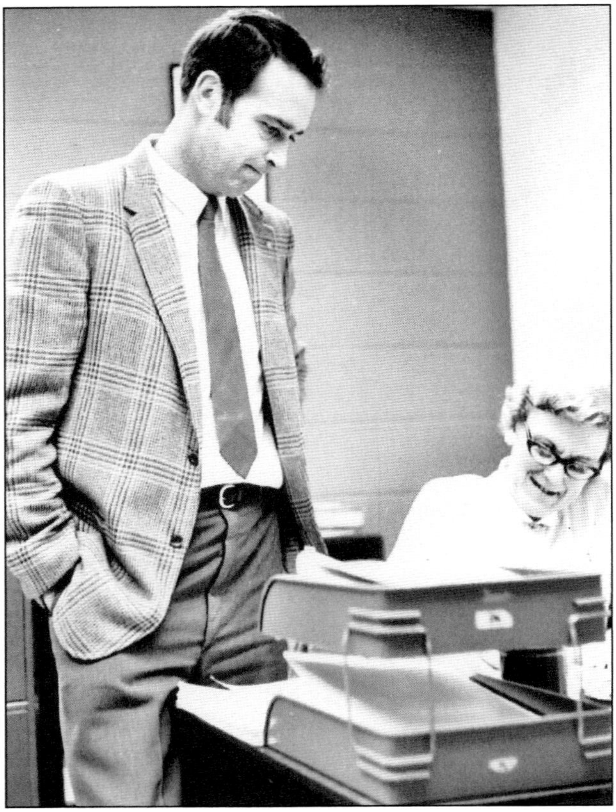

W.O. Johnson and Grace Alderson check the first class rolls.

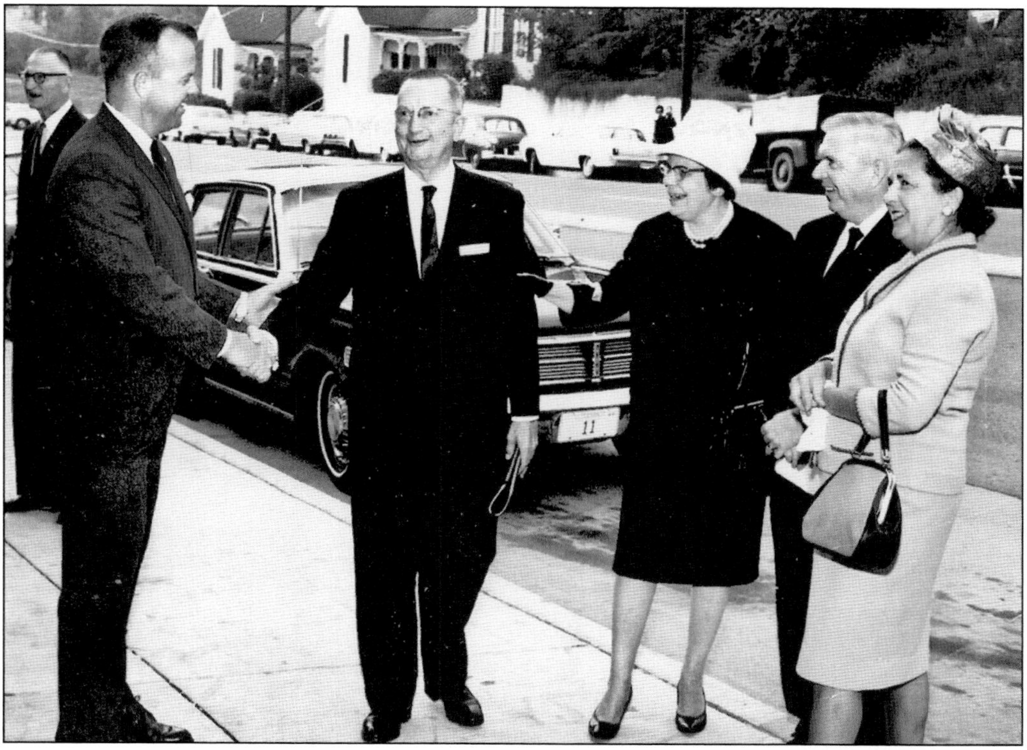

The first college convocation was held at the Polk Theater in downtown Columbia on September 26, 1966, with James H. Jones of Mt. Pleasant as master of ceremonies. Members of the state board of education attended. Lewis Moore welcomed Commissioner Warf and Mrs. Warf to the convocation.

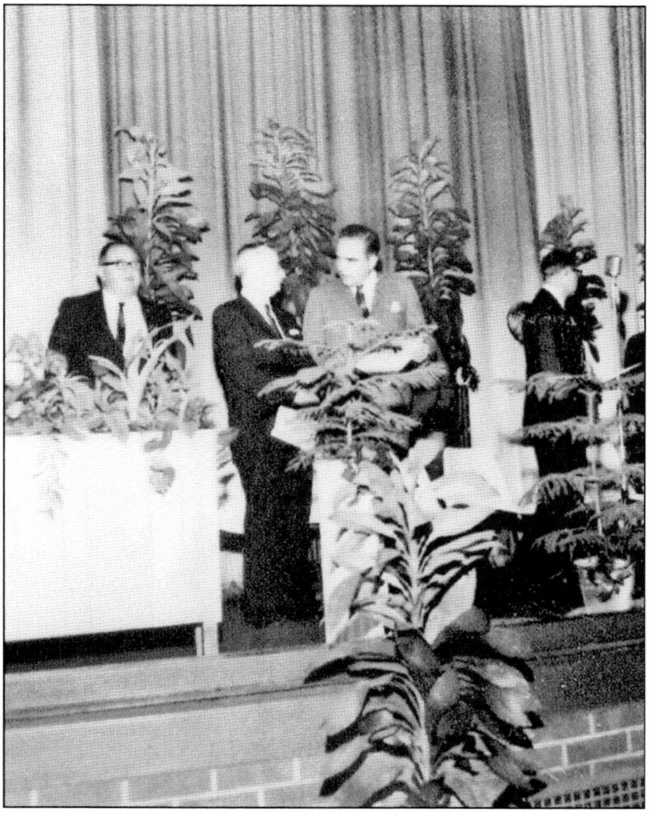

Commissioner Warf is shown with Gov. Frank Clement at the convocation. Governor Clement emphasized the importance of the occasion.

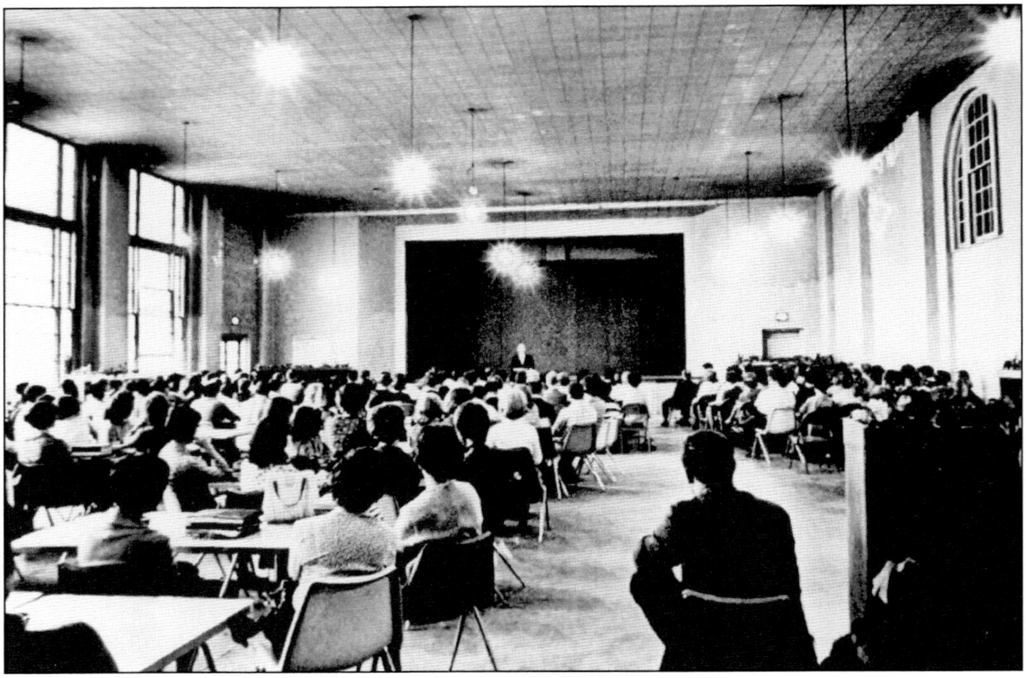

This was the first student assembly in the Memorial Building. It was during this first year that the students selected the Charger as the Columbia State mascot and green and white as the school colors.

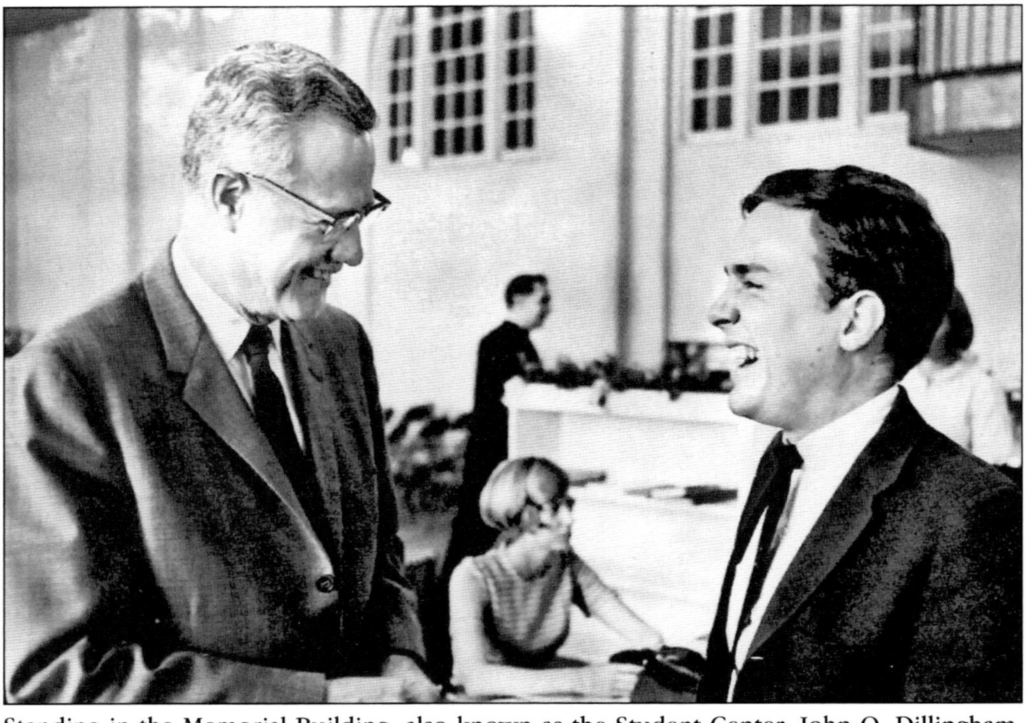

Standing in the Memorial Building, also known as the Student Center, John O. Dillingham, chairman of the social science division, is undoubtedly sharing wisdom with Dwight Gatwood, instructor of music. In the background are Dean James Clark and student Jane Quillen.

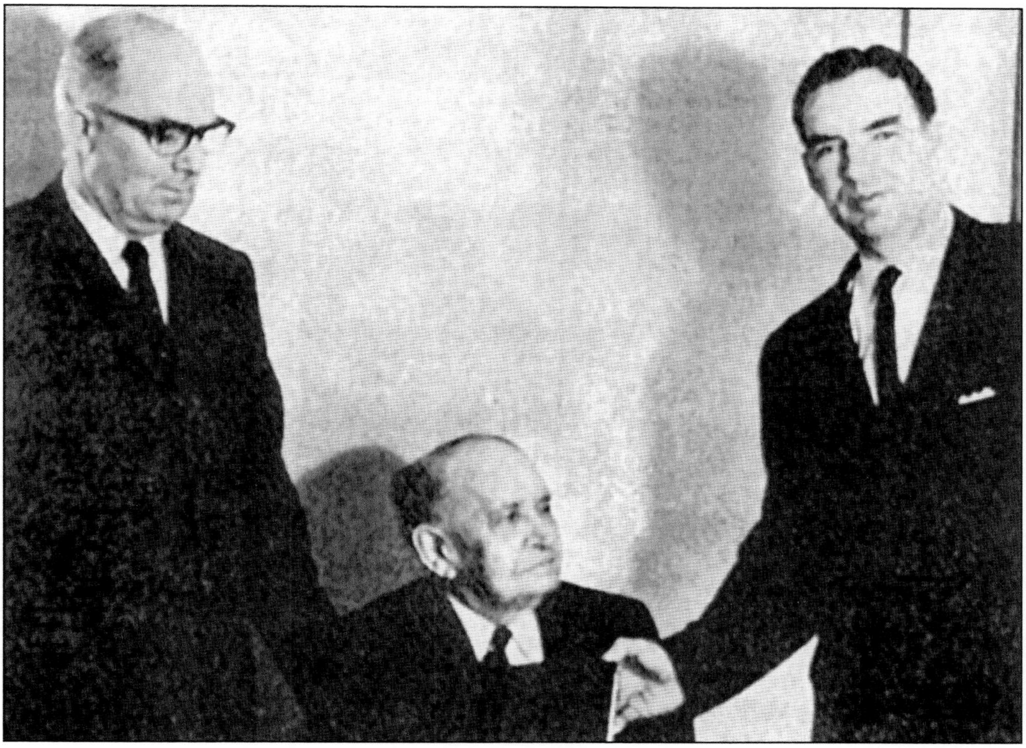

Judge W.B. Turner (center) presents a copy of his book, *Historic Maury County, Tennessee*, to Dr. James W. Clark for the Columbia State library. Pictured are Dr. Archie S. Rushton (left), Judge Turner, and Clark. A graduate of Auburn, Clark was appointed dean on March 29, 1966. He served Columbia State for three years as the dean of instruction in addition to serving as acting president for the first two years.

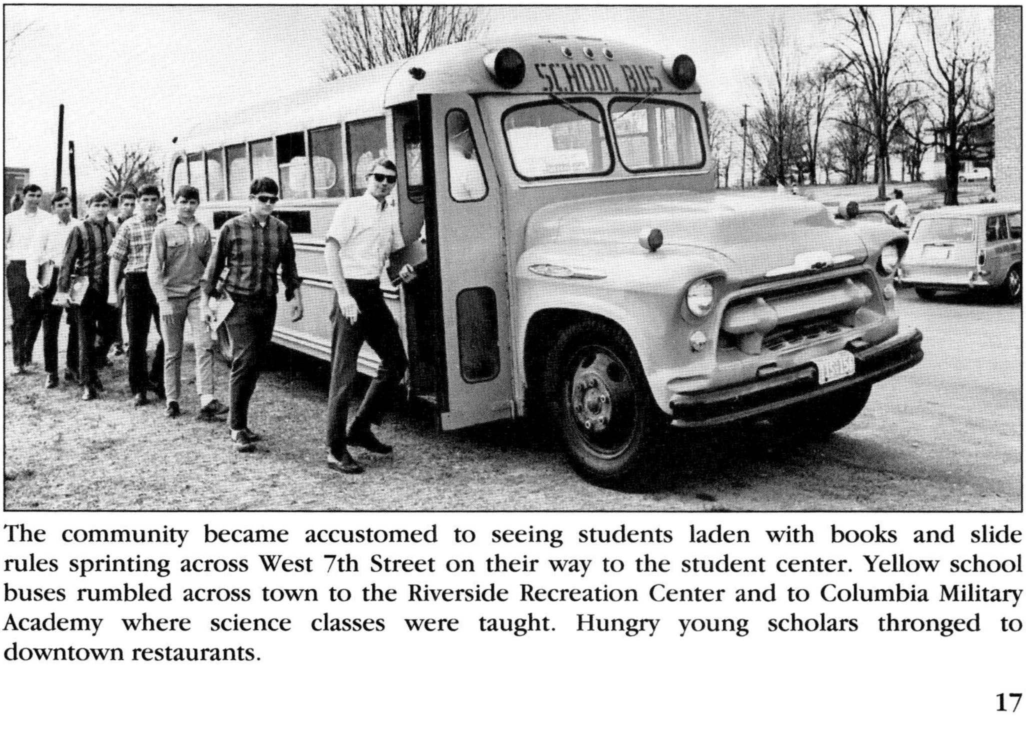

The community became accustomed to seeing students laden with books and slide rules sprinting across West 7th Street on their way to the student center. Yellow school buses rumbled across town to the Riverside Recreation Center and to Columbia Military Academy where science classes were taught. Hungry young scholars thronged to downtown restaurants.

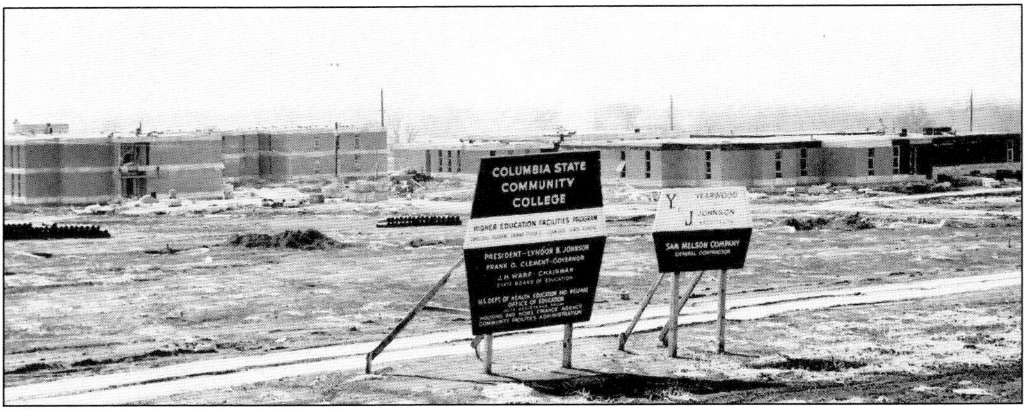

During the winter quarter of 1967, enrollment climbed to 538 and the permanent campus began to take shape along state Highway 99.

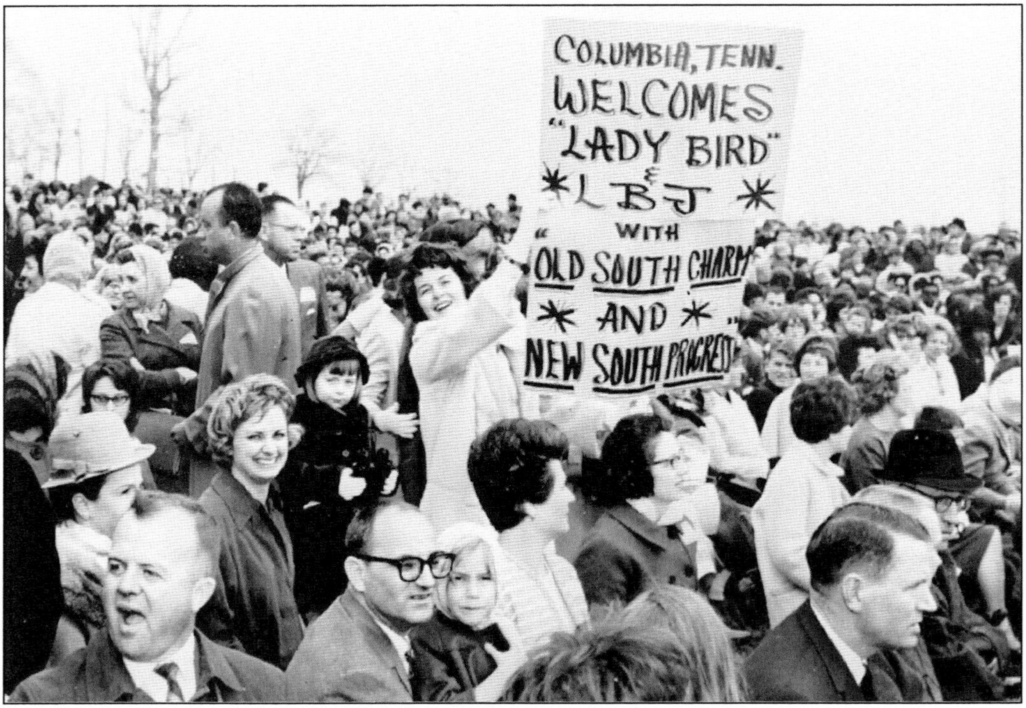

On March 15, 1967, over 8,000 supporters of the college braved the cold March wind to watch Lady Bird Johnson unveil the dedication plaque. Sydney McClain, a continuing supporter of the college, is holding the sign.

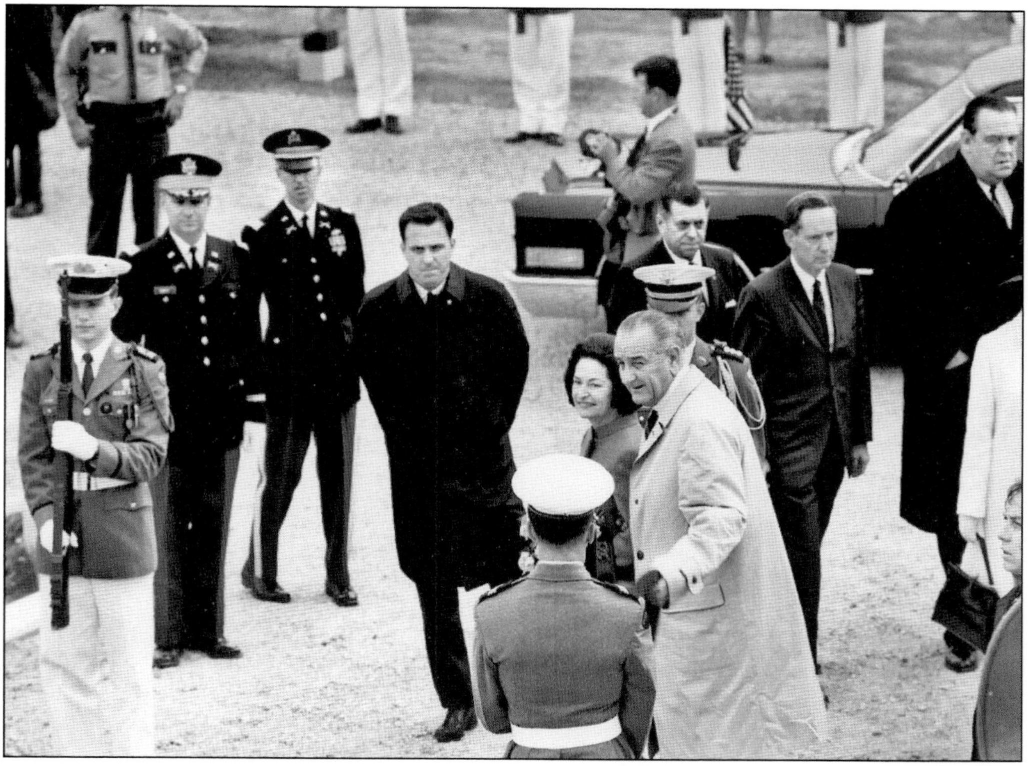

Excitement filled the air as the first visit of an American president in 150 years approached. The day was proclaimed by Mayor James Dowdy and County Judge John Stanton as "CSCC Dedication Day." Behind the Johnsons are Dowdy, Stanton, and commissioner of safety Greg O'Rear.

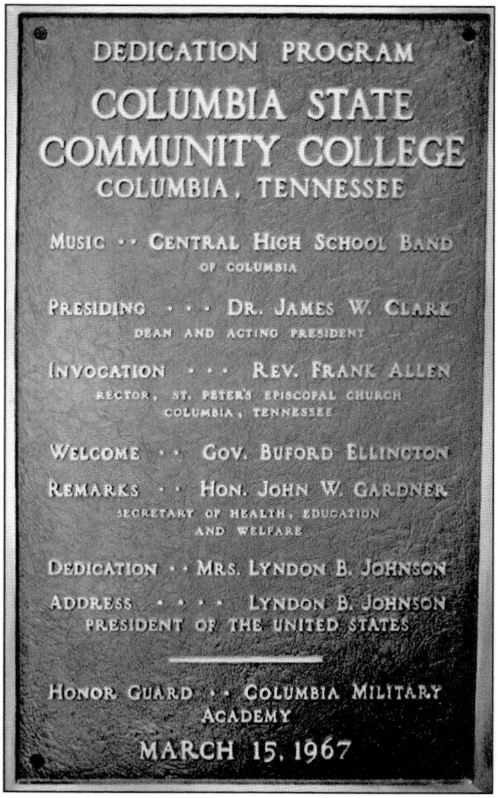

DEDICATION PROGRAM

COLUMBIA STATE COMMUNITY COLLEGE

COLUMBIA, TENNESSEE

MUSIC ·· CENTRAL HIGH SCHOOL BAND
OF COLUMBIA

PRESIDING ··· DR. JAMES W. CLARK
DEAN AND ACTING PRESIDENT

INVOCATION ··· REV. FRANK ALLEN
RECTOR, ST. PETER'S EPISCOPAL CHURCH
COLUMBIA, TENNESSEE

WELCOME ·· GOV. BUFORD ELLINGTON

REMARKS ·· HON. JOHN W. GARDNER
SECRETARY OF HEALTH, EDUCATION AND WELFARE

DEDICATION ·· MRS. LYNDON B. JOHNSON

ADDRESS ···· LYNDON B. JOHNSON
PRESIDENT OF THE UNITED STATES

HONOR GUARD ·· COLUMBIA MILITARY ACADEMY

MARCH 15, 1967

A copy of the dedication program was memorialized in a plaque that now hangs in the Pryor Administration Building along with the dedication plaque.

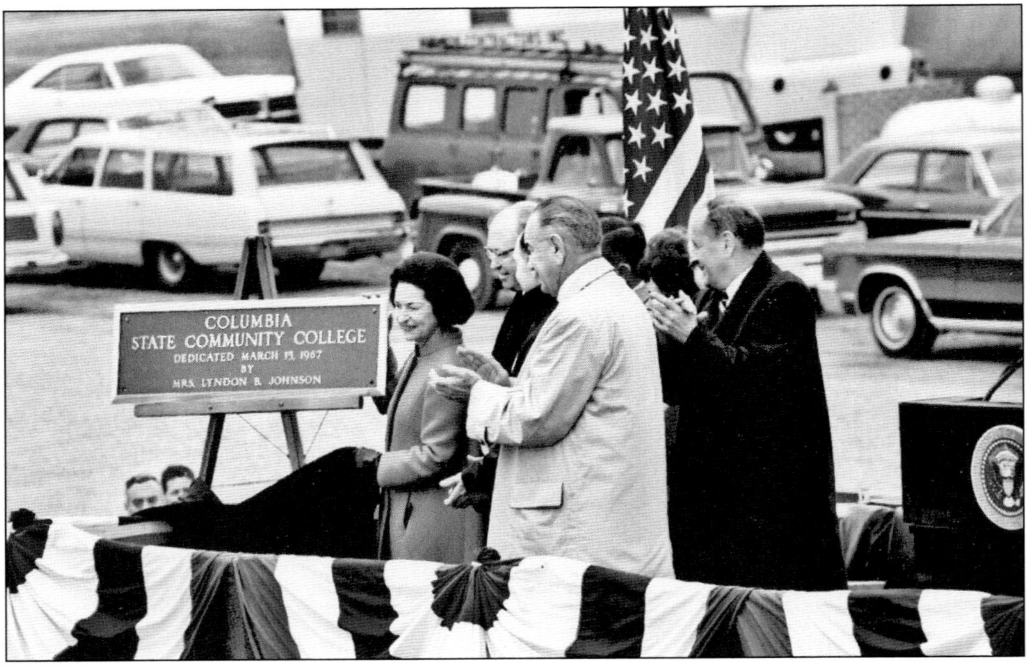

The First Lady officially dedicated the new campus and declared that Columbia State represented the "new beat and rhythm of our land. . . . when a Columbia Community College rises from a once empty field, the country expands not outward, but upward. . . . I am honored to dedicate this college."

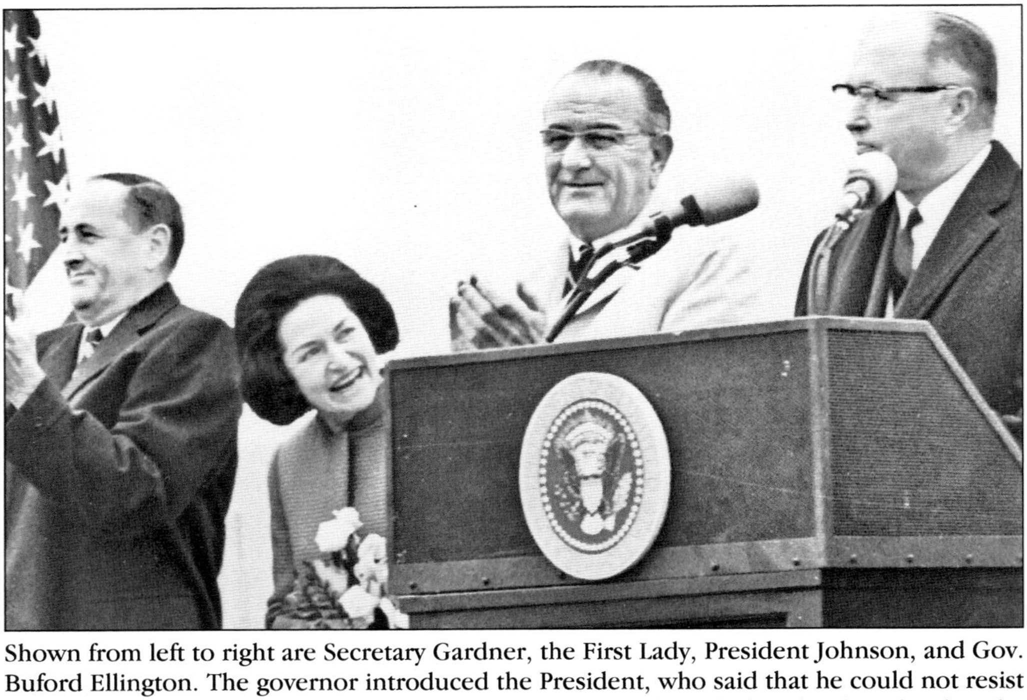

Shown from left to right are Secretary Gardner, the First Lady, President Johnson, and Gov. Buford Ellington. The governor introduced the President, who said that he could not resist coming to Columbia to congratulate the people who had worked so hard to develop the college. He added, "What you are doing here in Columbia is closer to my heart than anything else I deal with within the whole range of national policy."

Two

ACADEMICS

The goal of providing two years of quality coursework has always been the highest priority of the college. The curriculum has always followed the pattern set forth in the initial purpose of the college: to provide two years of university-parallel courses, to provide technical and pre-professional courses for those preparing to enter the work force, and to offer a program of continuing education.

The initial accreditation of the institution in December 1968 by the Southern Association of Colleges and Schools was achieved in the shortest time allowable. Full accreditation was granted in December 1972. The college's service area, composed of Maury, Lawrence, Lewis, Giles, Marshall, Perry, Hickman, Wayne, and Williamson Counties, was approved by the Tennessee Board of Regents on June 15, 1983.

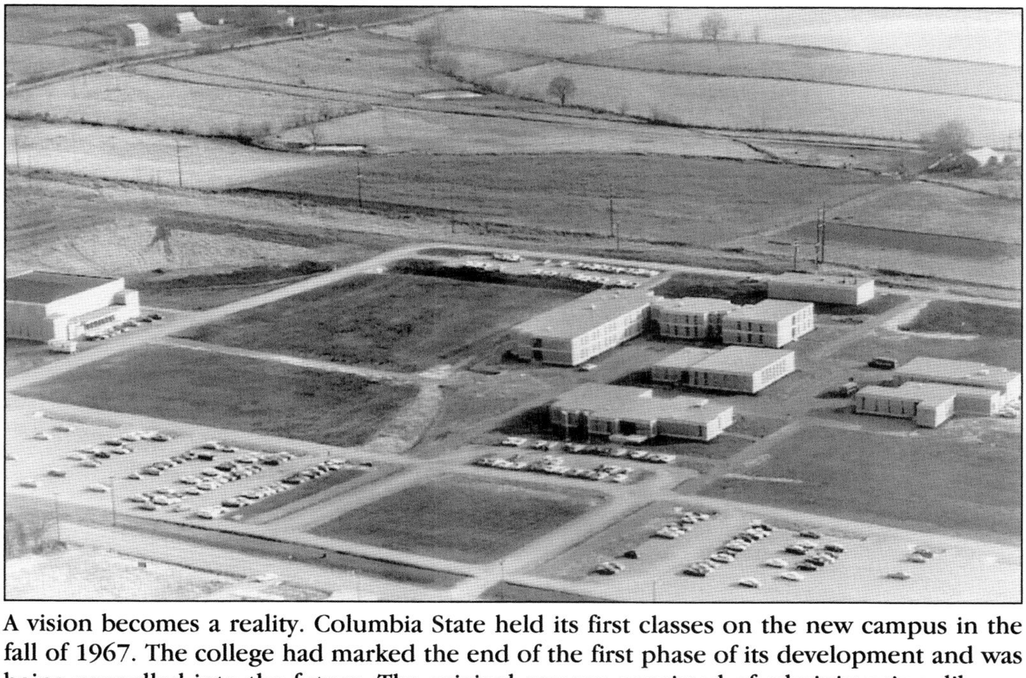

A vision becomes a reality. Columbia State held its first classes on the new campus in the fall of 1967. The college had marked the end of the first phase of its development and was being propelled into the future. The original campus consisted of administration, library, classroom (L-shaped), student center, gymnasium, and maintenance buildings.

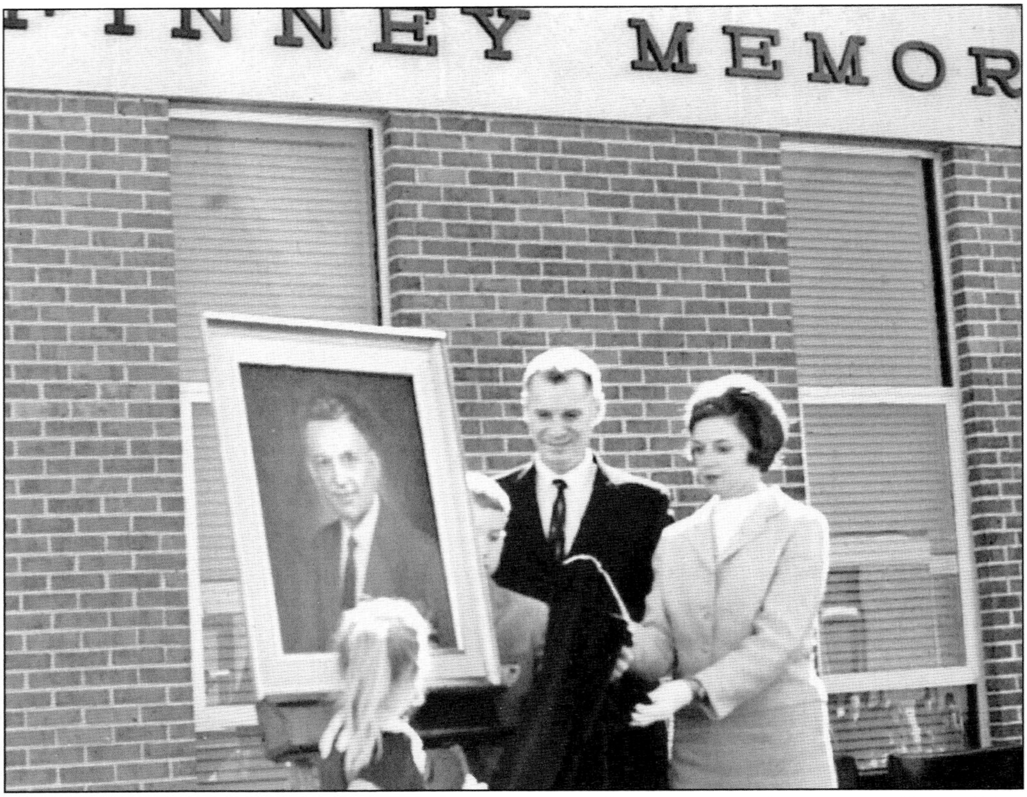

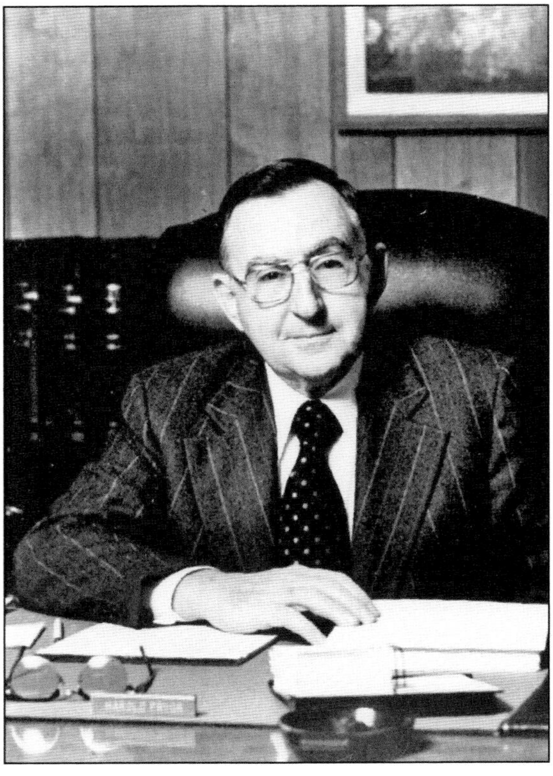

John W. Finney, long-time editor of the *Daily Herald*, devoted the last years of his life to the cause of a state college in the Columbia area. Mr. Finney did not live to see the realization of his dream. The original John W. Finney Memorial Library was dedicated in October 1967. Around the portrait of John Finney are, from left to right, Elizabeth and Delk Kennedy, grandchildren of Mr. Finney, Sam Kennedy, and Betty Finney Kennedy, daughter of Mr. Finney.

Dr. Harold S. Pryor, a native Tennessean, was named as Columbia State's president on February 9, 1968. He holds a doctorate in educational administration from the University of Tennessee. He came to Columbia State from Austin Peay State University where he was director of teacher education. Pryor served as president until retiring in 1984.

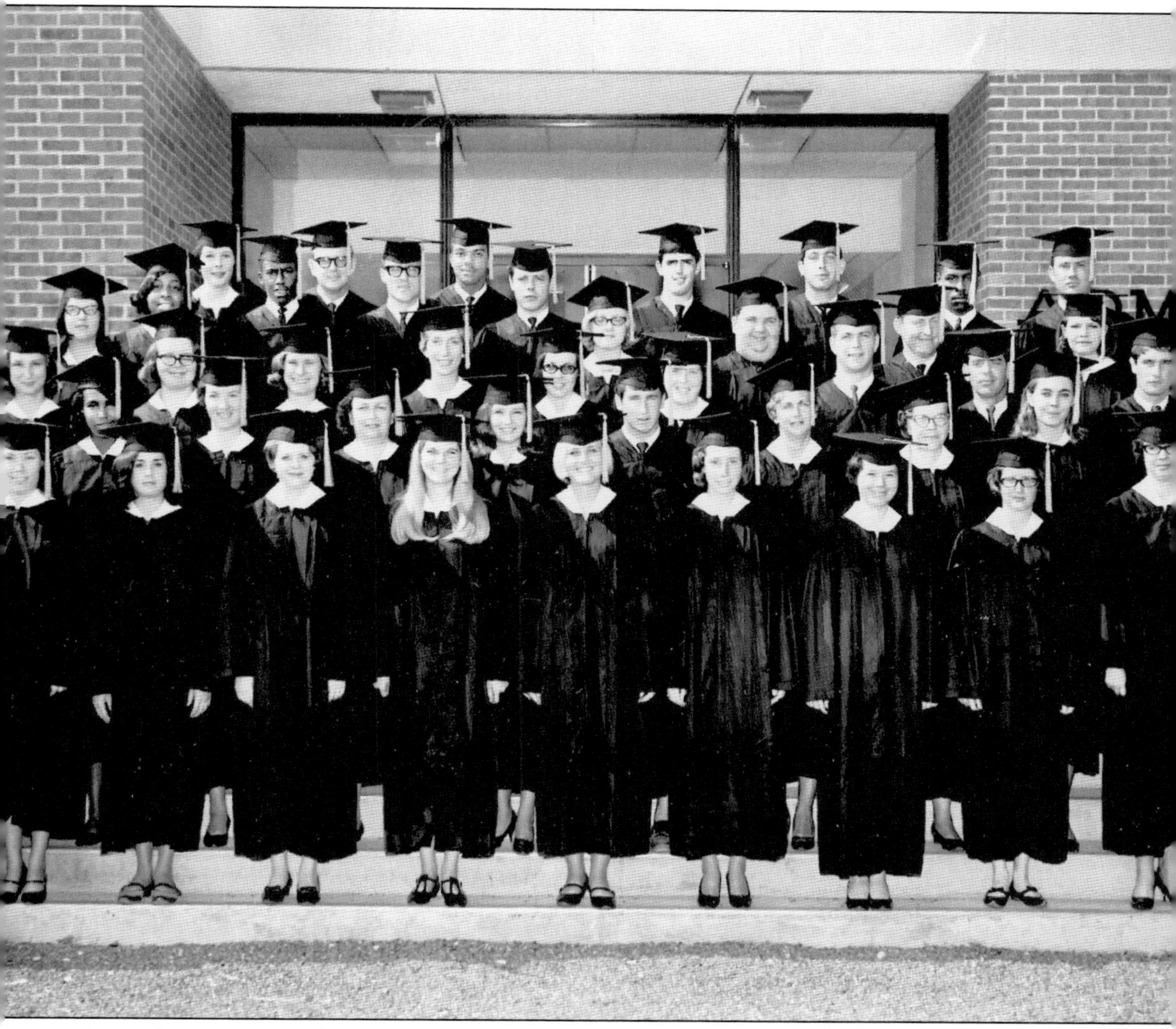

On Friday, June 7, 1968, at 7 p.m., the first 44 graduates of the new institution marched into the gymnasium to hear the commencement address by the Honorable J.H. Warf, chairman of the state board of education. President Pryor conferred the degrees, assisted by Dean Clark and W.O. Johnson. Dr. Pryor read a letter of congratulations from President Lyndon Johnson. The graduates, from left to right are (first row) Sara Kerr Fralix, Sharon Pogue Strange, Suzanne West Turner, Linda Garbarina, Sandra Jean Hines, Myra Perry, Sheila Mash, Susan Dillingham, and Linda Pigg; (second row) Martha Steele, Patricia Mayberry, Wilma Jean Sweeney, Sheila McNeese Alderson, Joseph William Wesche, Peggy Ruth Mullins, Evelyn Roberts Morton, and Janice Kaye Bell; (third row) Judith Ann Murphy, Wilma Kay York, Paula Voss Cox, Janice Shackelford Hollis, Mary Ellen Fly, Eloise Marlin, James Wilson Copley, Donald Ray Massey, and William Ray Jernigan; (fourth row) Alice Faye Brooks, Lillie Mae Mitchell, James Martin, Dennis Powers, Larry Wayne Chappell, Virginia Massey Davis, Wayne Domico, Harold "Moe" Grimes, and Susan Heller; (fifth row) Martha Woody, Jerry Gamble, Wilburn Hardison, Leonard Ray Potts, William F. Terry, Cyrus Brown, and Lloyd Burton Pruett.

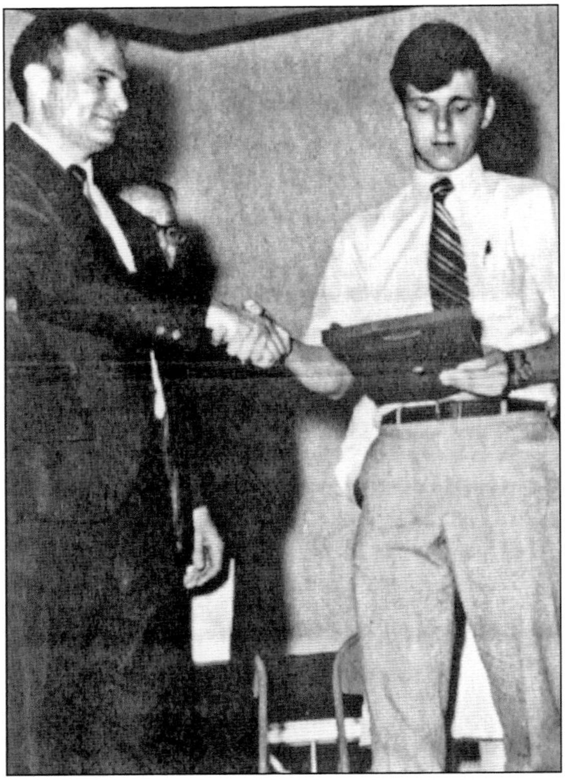

The first annual "Honors and Awards Day" was on Wednesday, May 14, 1969. John Dillingham opened the assembly, and Lewis Moore presided. The dean's list was recognized, and division awards and the Columbia State Women's Club award were presented. Pictured is Cuyler Dunbar, first dean of students, presenting the Faculty Award to SGA president John Knox.

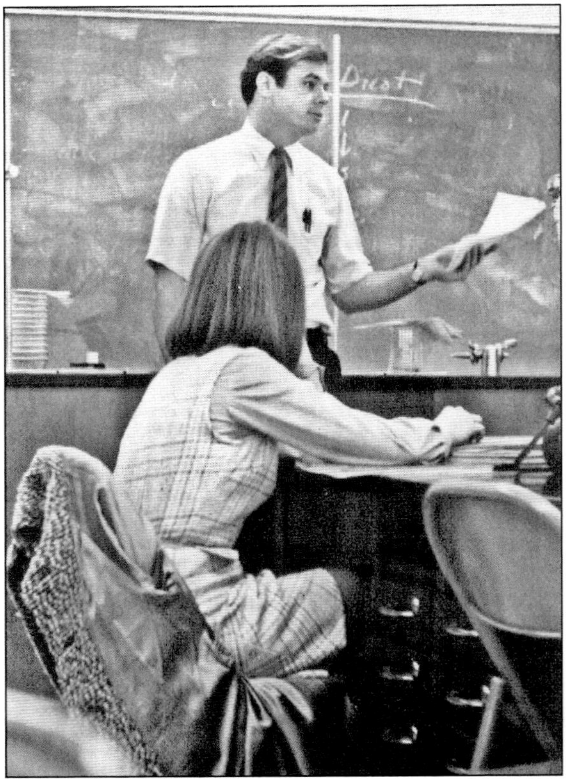

Monte Bayless, one of Columbia State's original faculty members, teaches a biology class in the J. Howard Warf Science Building, the first classroom building.

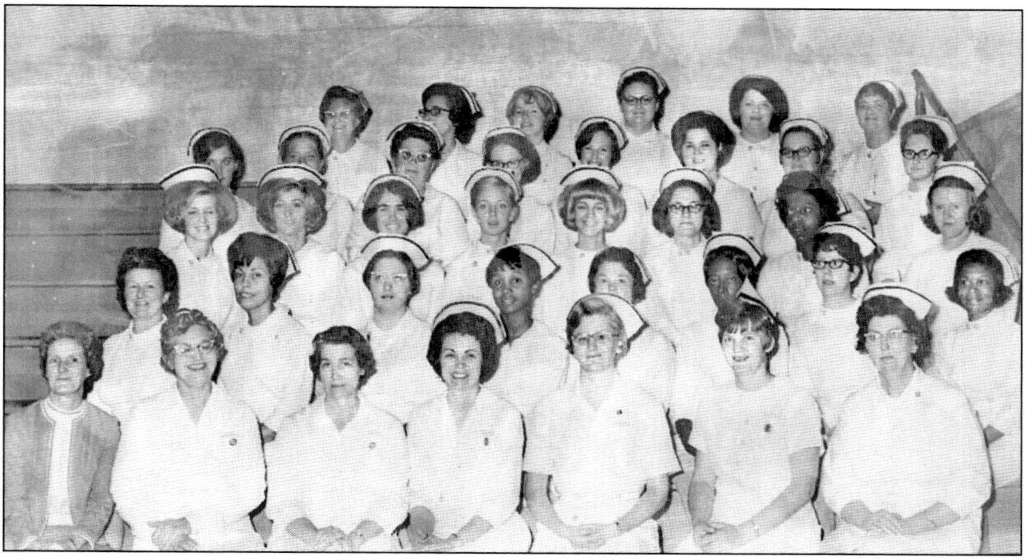

The class of 1969 included the first 30 graduates of the nursing program. These students are pictured with faculty members. Seated in the front row, from left to right, are Elaine Van Everen, Marie Jones, Susan Sloan, Doris White, Jene Holland, Deanna Naddy, and Dorothy Powell, the director of nursing.

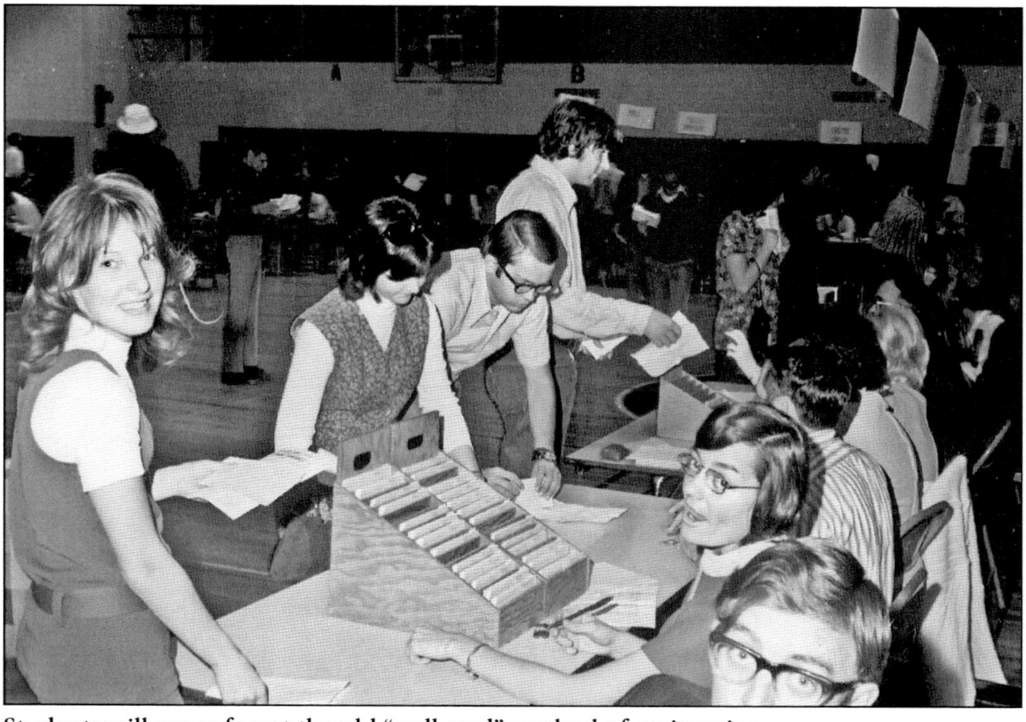

Students will never forget the old "pull card" method of registration.

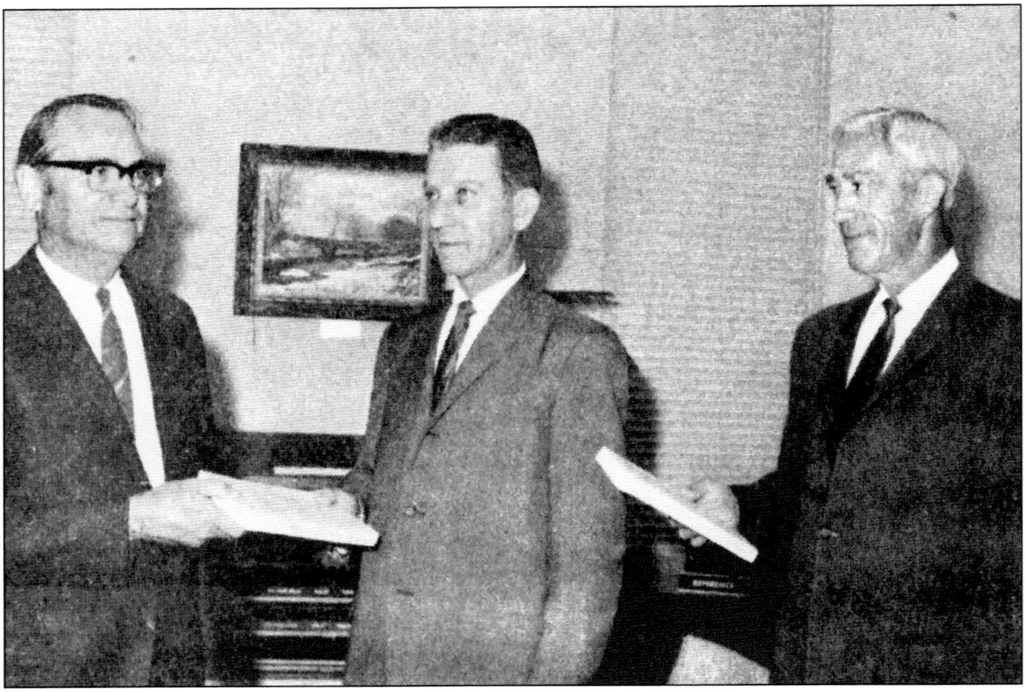

Truman Perry presents copies of a book about the Western Electric Company to Dr. Darrell Simmons, head of the Technology Division and George Watson, Columbia State's first librarian.

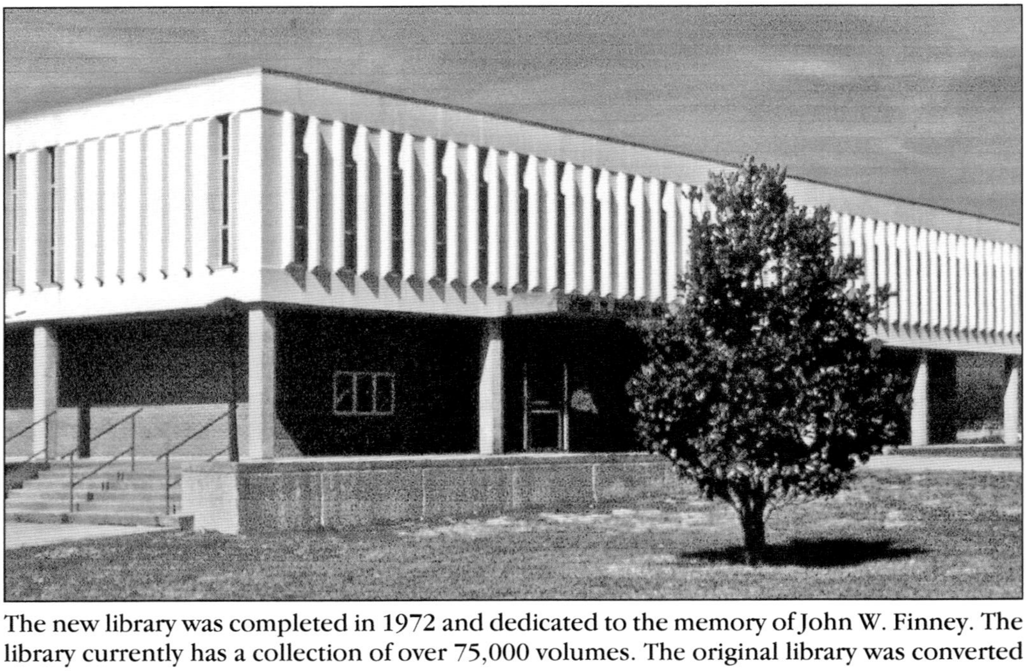

The new library was completed in 1972 and dedicated to the memory of John W. Finney. The library currently has a collection of over 75,000 volumes. The original library was converted into a nursing education building.

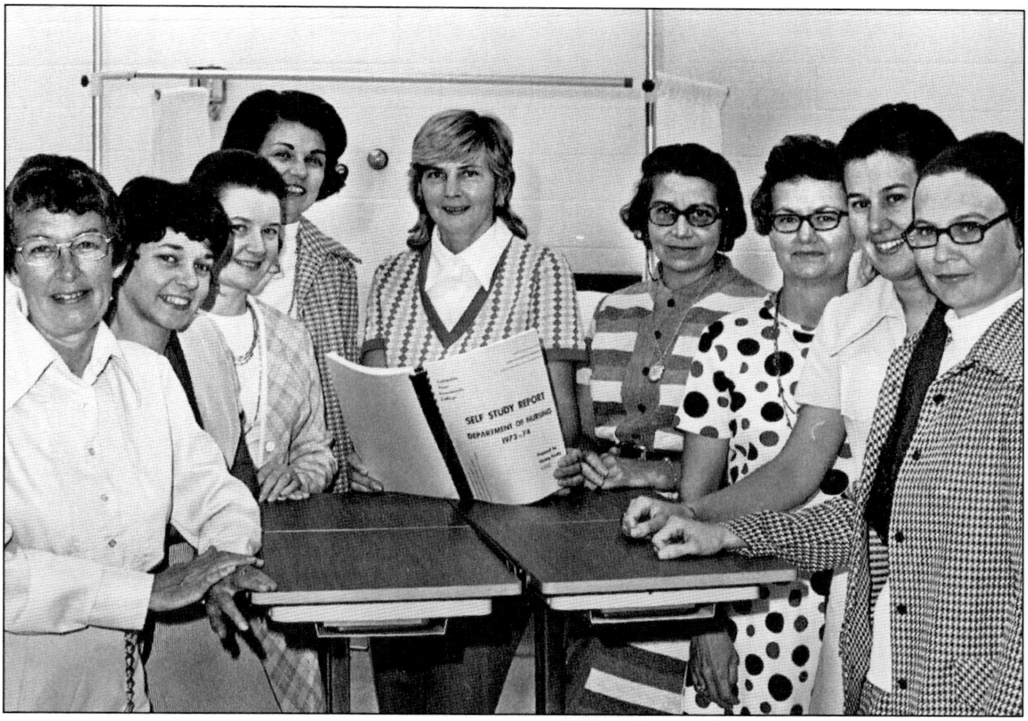

Faculty in the nursing department look over the results of the department's self-study report. Pictured from left to right are Roberta Patton, Sally Matthews, Janet Rogers, Doris White, Dir. of Nursing Deanna Naddy, Susan Sloan, Peggy Murphy, Diane Buchanan, and Gayle Larkin. The associate degree nursing program received accreditation from the National League of Nursing in 1974.

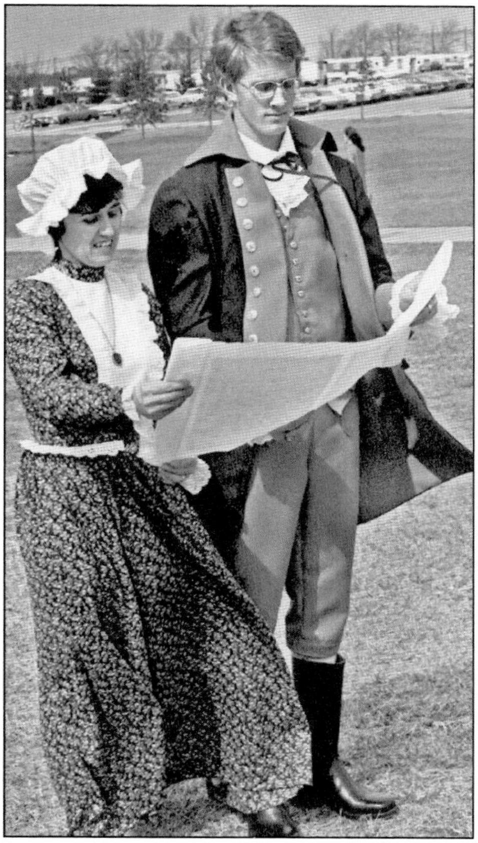

The college celebrated its 10th anniversary in the bicentennial year of 1976 and was designated an official bicentennial campus. Students dressed in styles of the 17th and 18th centuries and participated in social and sporting events of that period. Columbia State was also designated as an official campus of the bicentennial of the United States Constitution. Steve Beck and friend look over a document.

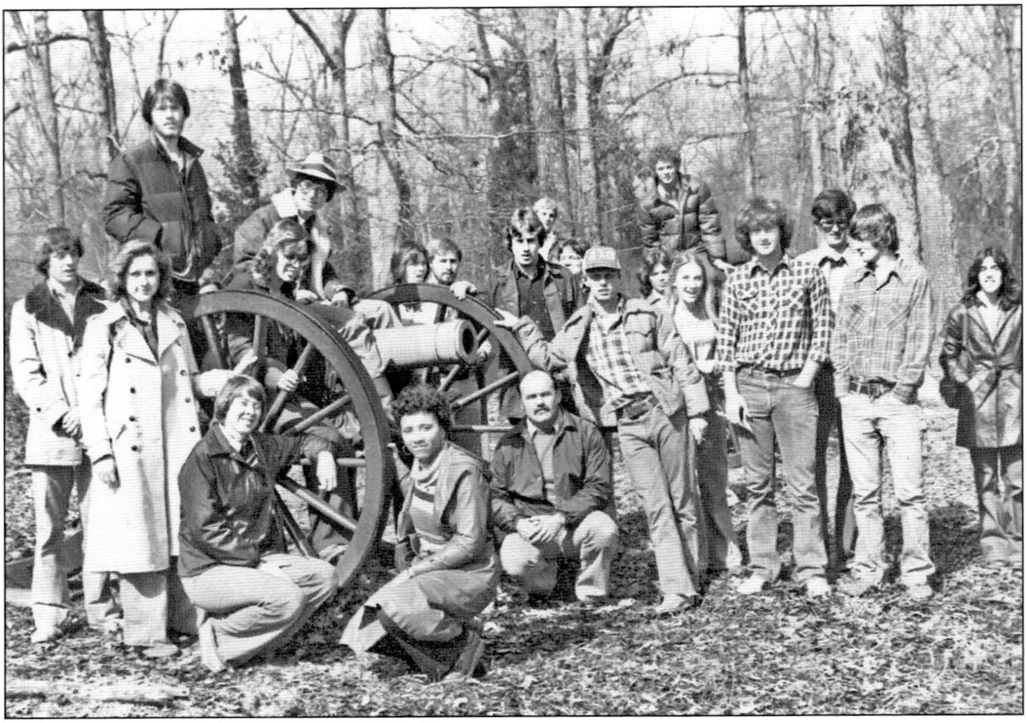

Bill Andrews took his class on a field trip to Shiloh Battlefield in 1976.

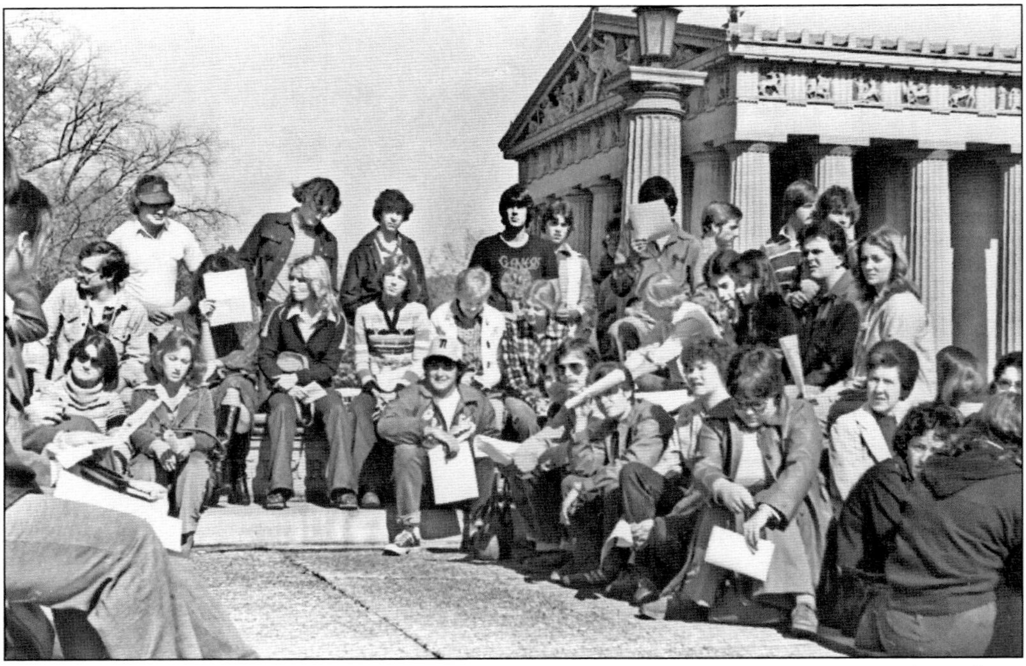

In 1978, funded by a grant from the National Endowment for the Humanities, the college instituted a humanities tutorial for all full-time freshmen. This series of one-credit-hour courses carried the student through the classical ages of Greece and Rome, the middle ages of Northern Europe, and the Renaissance Period. These students enjoyed a field trip to the Parthenon in Nashville.

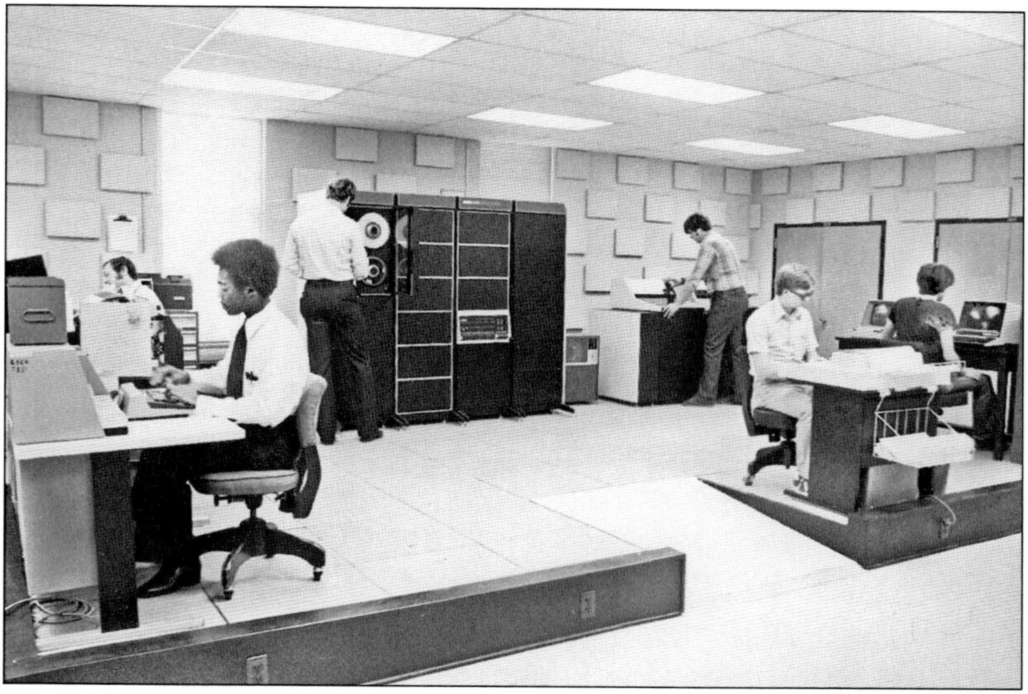

This is the computer center as it looked in 1978 with one of the college's first computers, a PDP 11/70. Pictured in the foreground are Wayne Watkins (left) and student worker Ricky Martin.

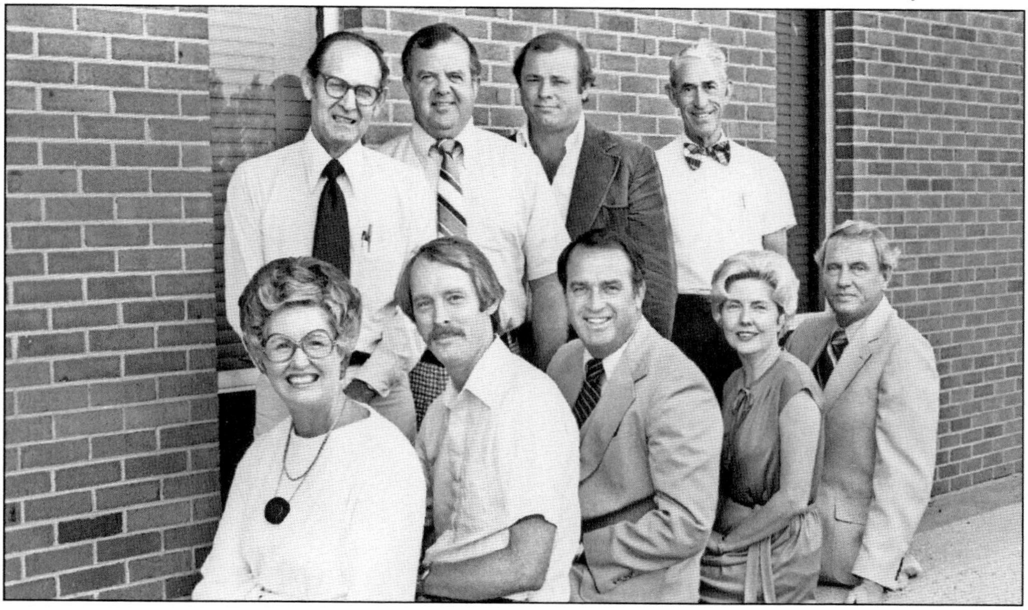

Five years after the opening of the college, faculty and staff who had been with the college since its inception met and organized themselves into the "Antediluvians," which to them meant "antiquated; before the great flood of students." Pictured about 1978 are the Antediluvians who were still at Columbia State. From left to right are (front row) Ava Eaton, Fred Behrens, W.O. Johnson, Carolyn Allred, and Paul Sands; (back row) Gene Durham, Lewis Moore, Monte Bayless, and George Watson. Antediluvians no longer at the college were Leon van Leeuwen, Sue Burkhart, John Fort, and John Dillingham.

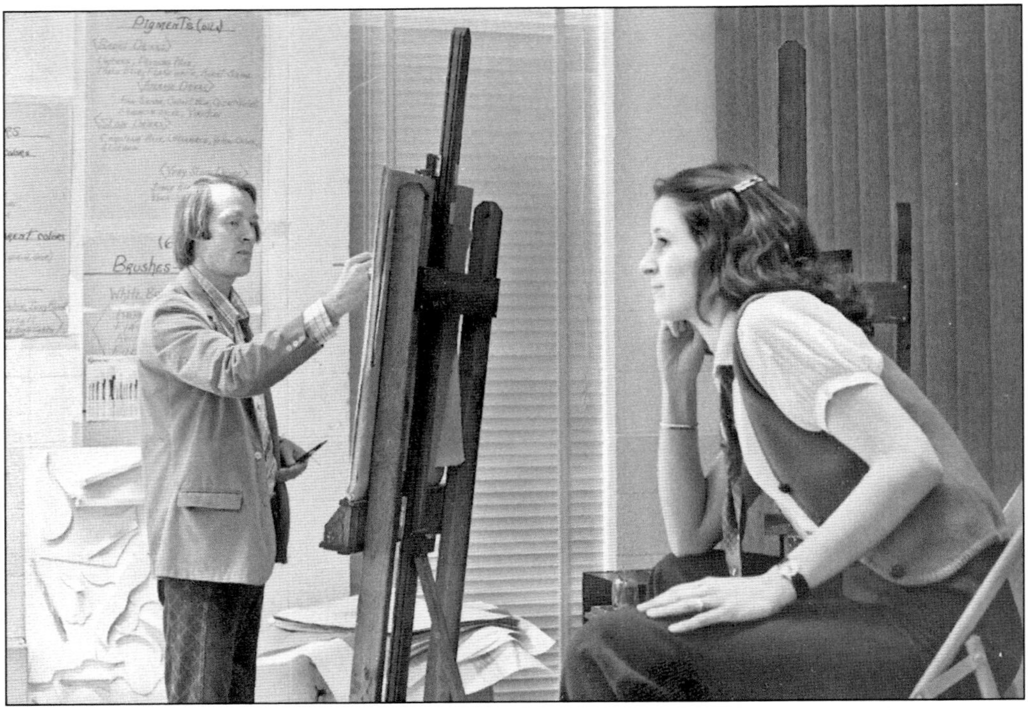

Fred Behrens, one of Columbia State's original faculty members, demonstrates portrait painting.

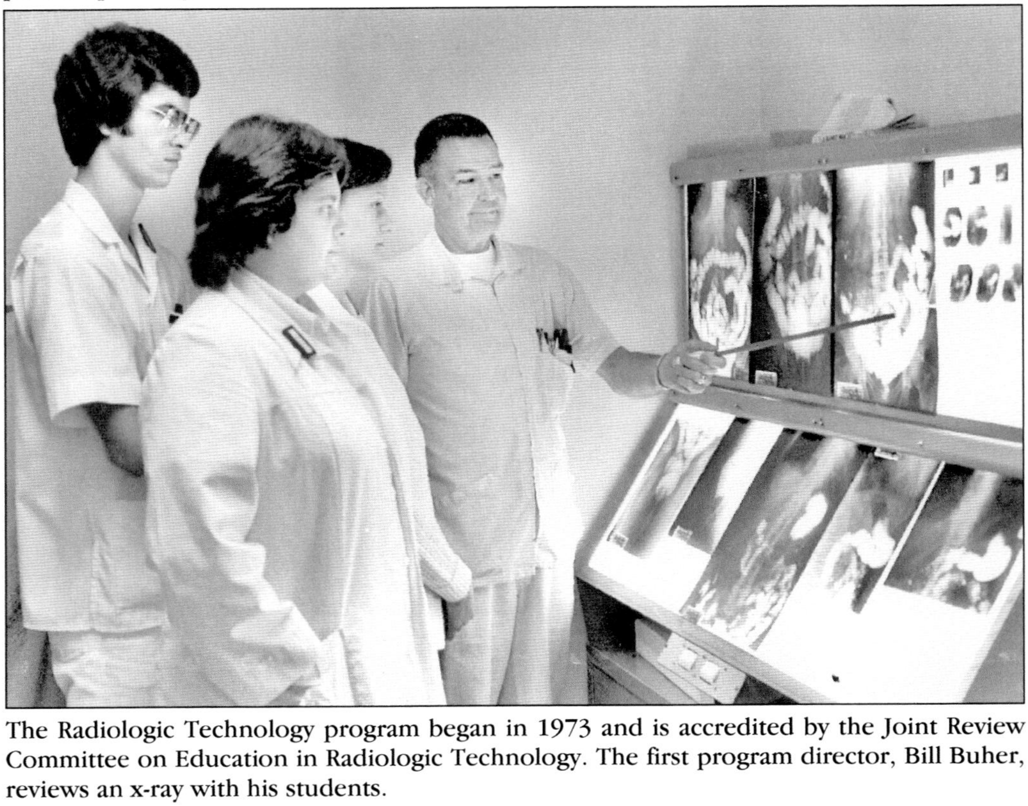

The Radiologic Technology program began in 1973 and is accredited by the Joint Review Committee on Education in Radiologic Technology. The first program director, Bill Buher, reviews an x-ray with his students.

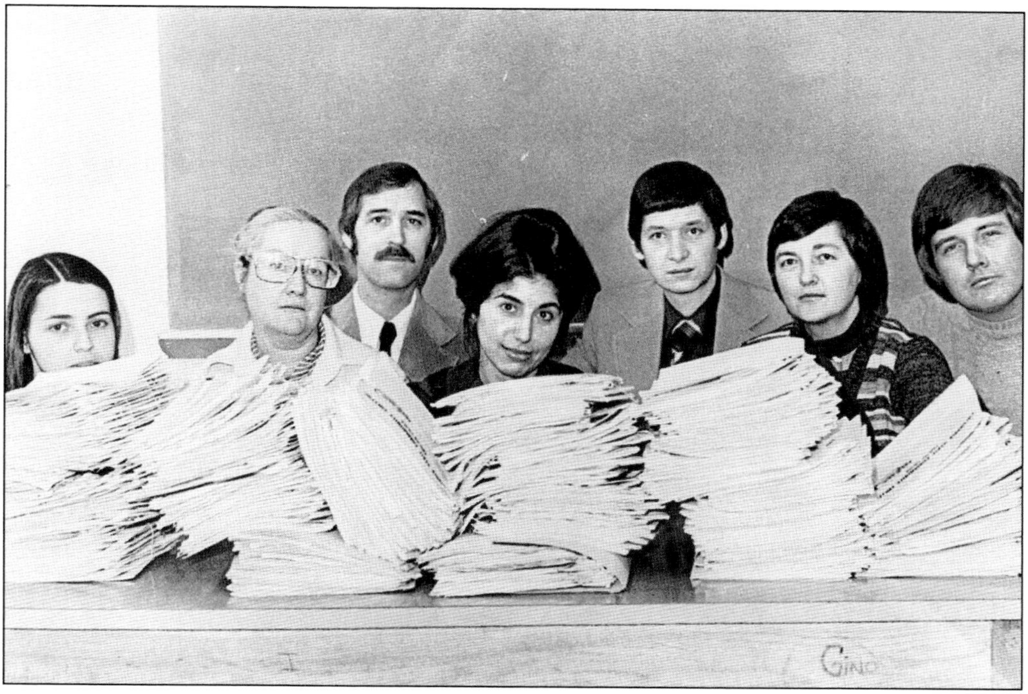

How many papers does one have to grade each week? Looking over these imposing stacks, from left to right, are English instructors Jean McCants, Bea Curry, Doug Eason, Joan Nucifora, Marvin Austin, Jean Jones, and Jim Spresser.

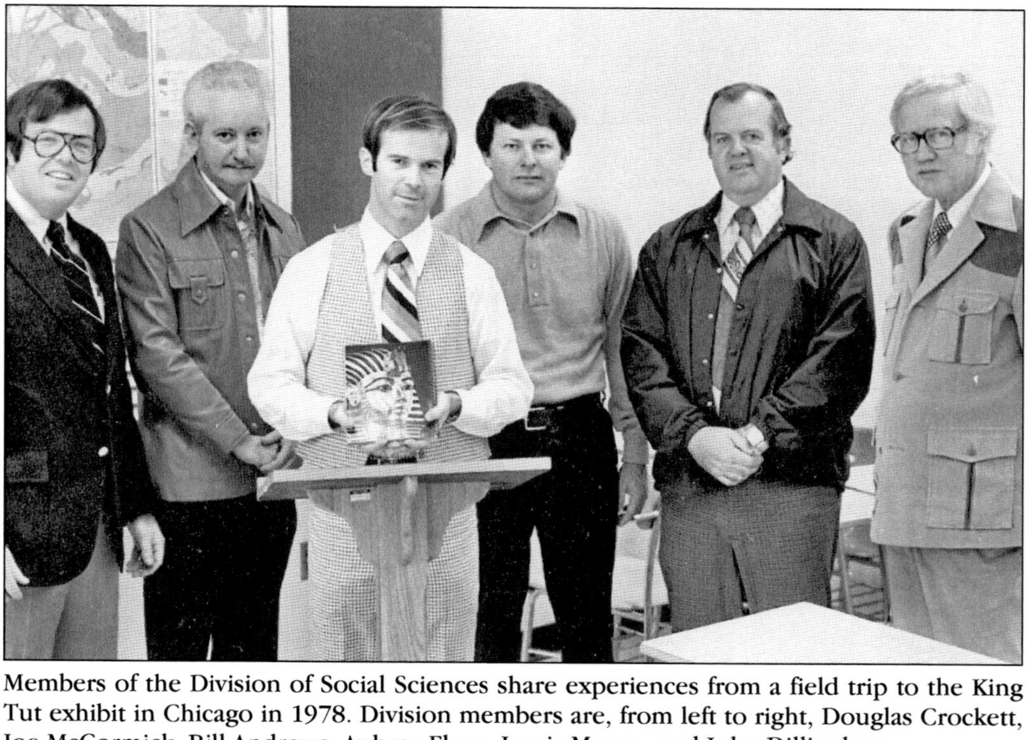

Members of the Division of Social Sciences share experiences from a field trip to the King Tut exhibit in Chicago in 1978. Division members are, from left to right, Douglas Crockett, Joe McCormick, Bill Andrews, Aubrey Flagg, Lewis Moore, and John Dillingham.

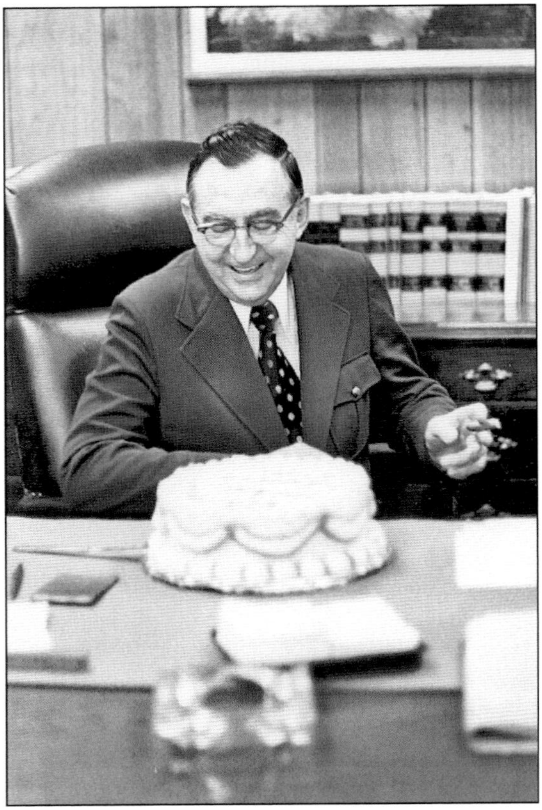

President Pryor celebrates a birthday with traditional cake and his "trademark cigar."

Faculty show traditional reactions to an in-service session in the library.

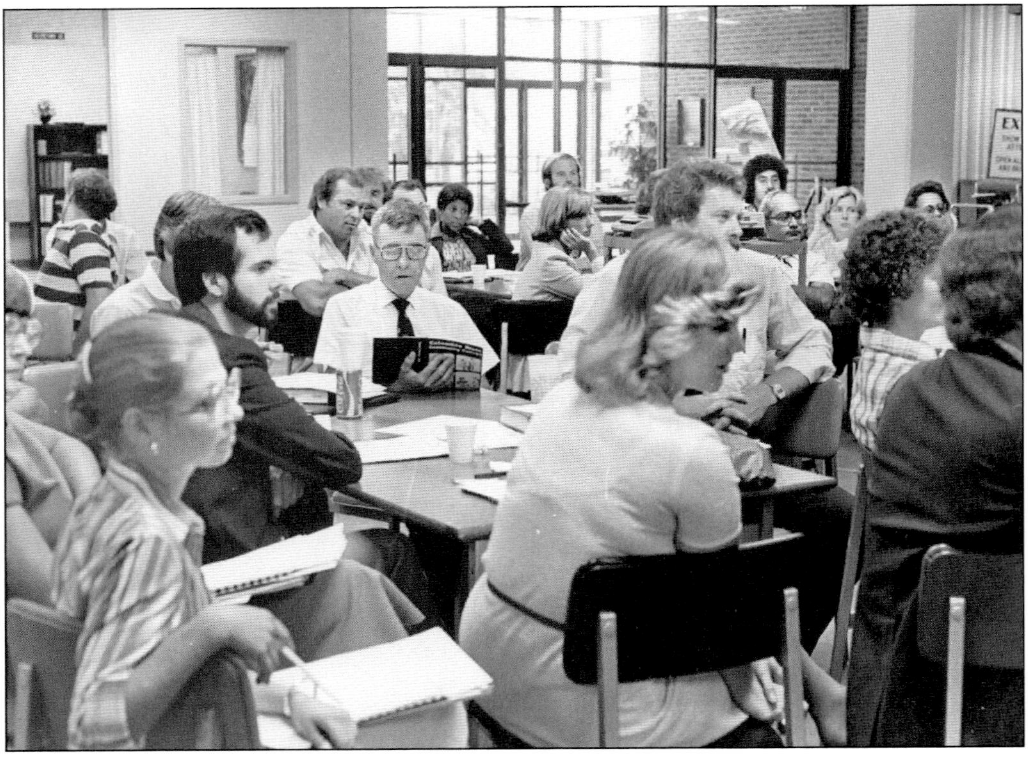

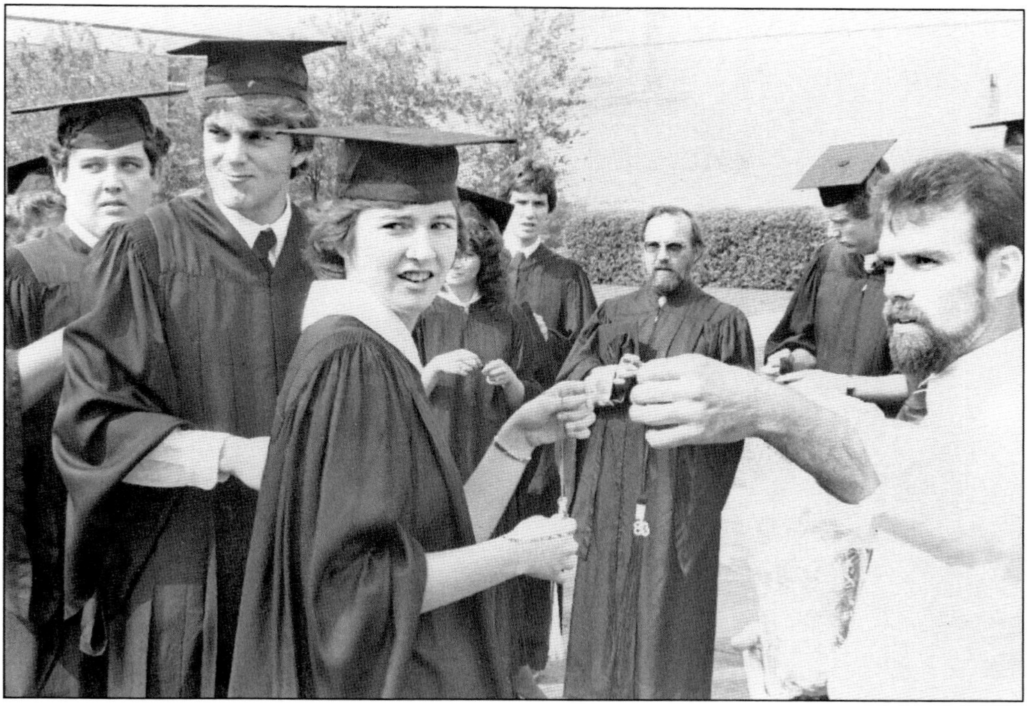

Sandra Bowman Serkownek waits for instructions from Ricky Martin in the 1983 graduation line. Sandra is currently an associate professor of industrial technology and the division chair of business and technology. Ricky is a 1977 graduate of Columbia State and is an instructor of physical education and aquatics.

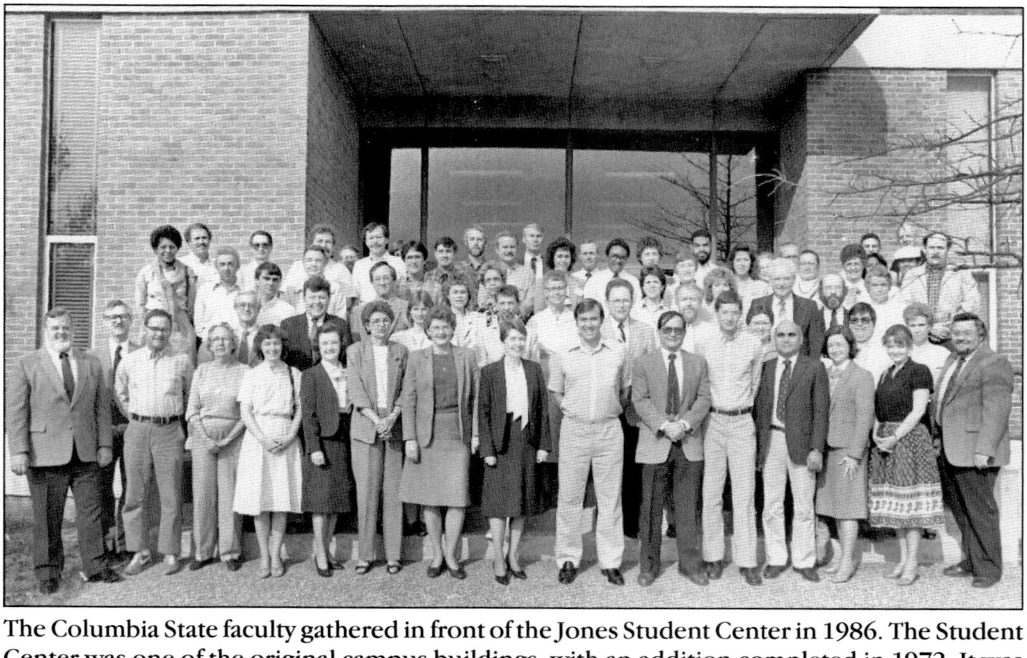

The Columbia State faculty gathered in front of the Jones Student Center in 1986. The Student Center was one of the original campus buildings, with an addition completed in 1972. It was dedicated to James H. Jones Jr., a local member of the state board of education.

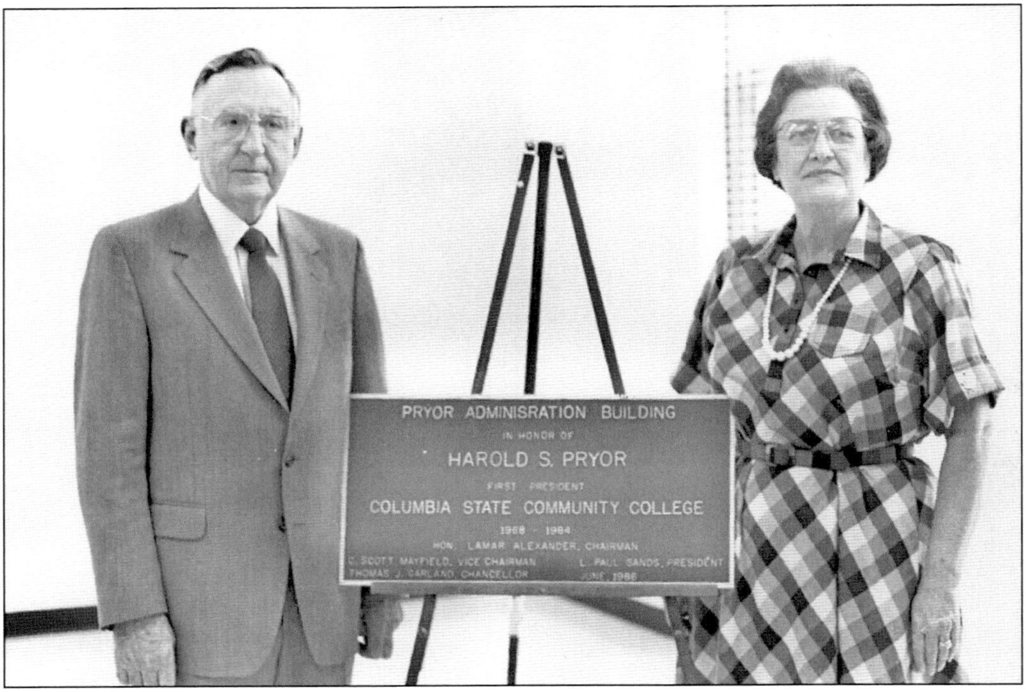

The Pryor Administration Building, one of the original campus buildings, was dedicated in 1986. Harold and LaRue Pryor stand by the dedication plaque.

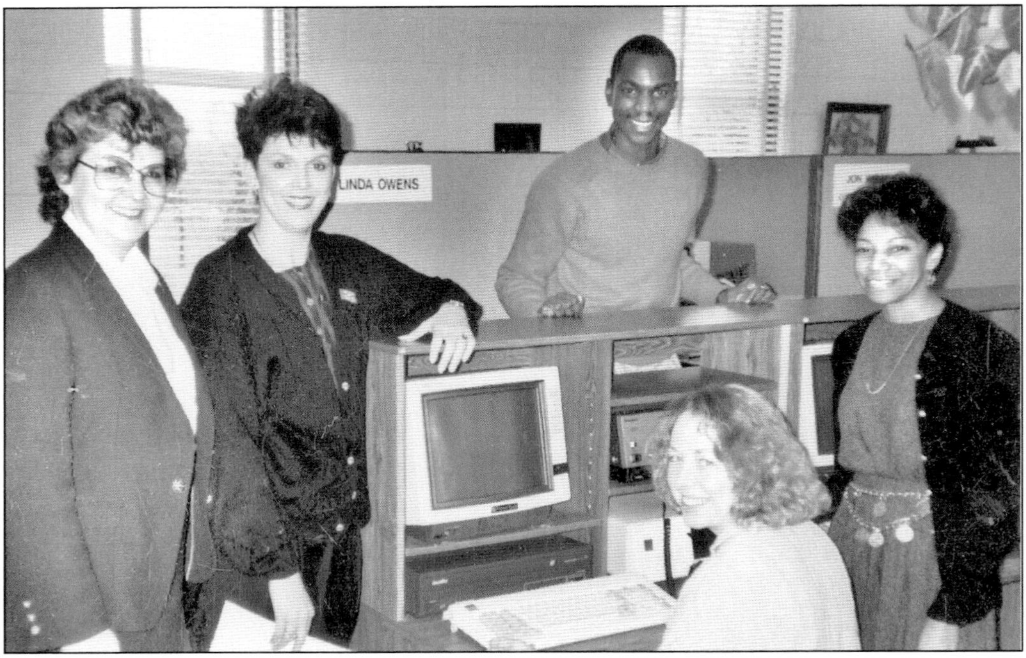

The Center of Emphasis was instituted in 1986 as a result of a grant from the Tennessee Board of Regents. The original grant was for a center in nursing and biology. It was later expanded to include programs for most disciplines. Here a student tries out new software while (from left to right) Dir. of Nursing Deanna Naddy, Dannylou Wilson, Jon Walton, and Linda Owens look on.

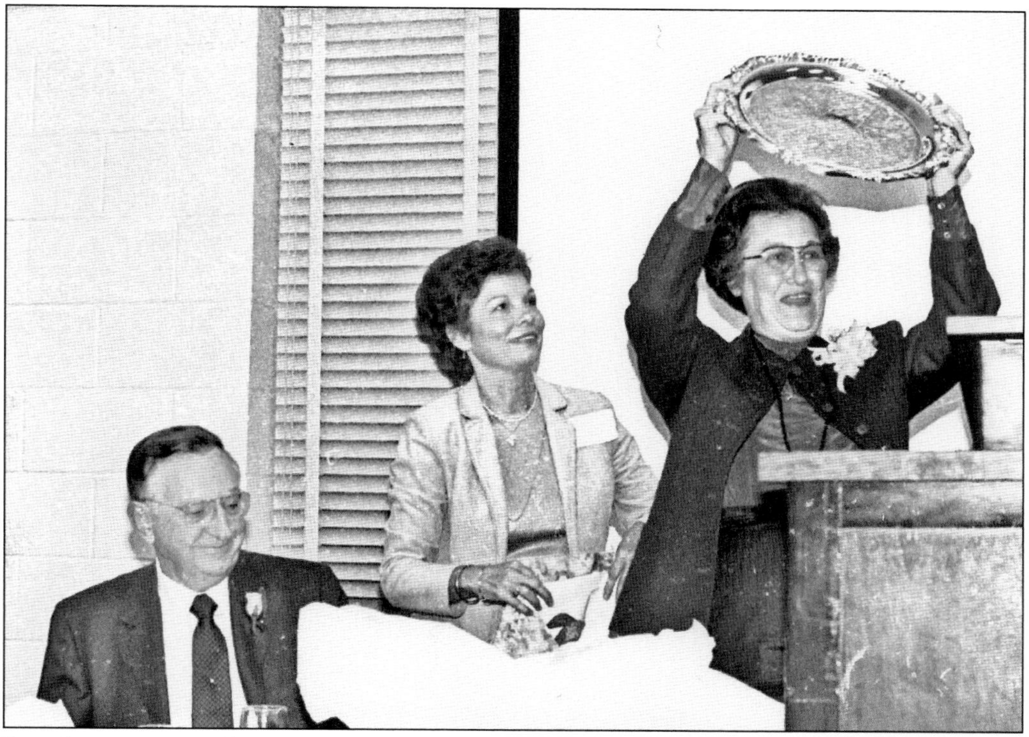

President Pryor's wife LaRue opens a gift from the college, presented by Jean Sands, wife of Paul Sands, at Pryor's retirement party.

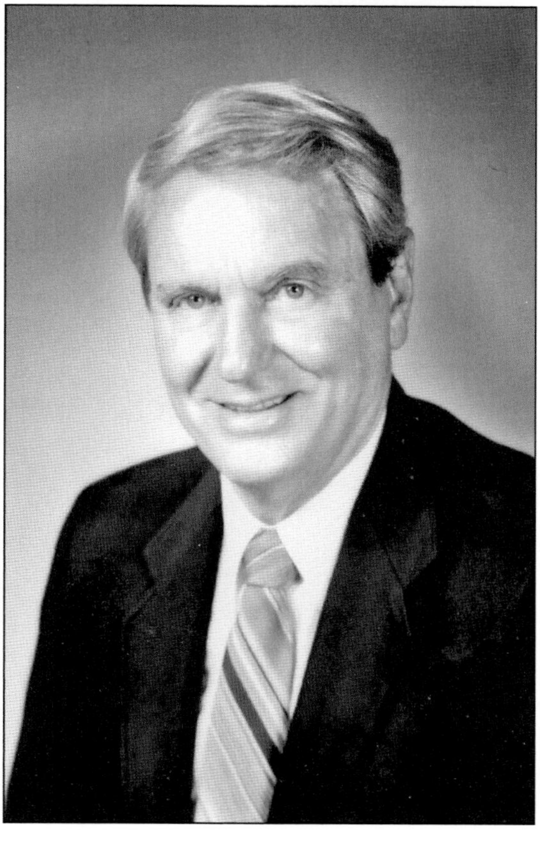

Dr. L. Paul Sands became Columbia State's second president in October 1984 and served in that capacity until November 1996. As head of the Division of Education, Dr. Sands was a member of Columbia State's first faculty. He was also the dean of instruction and executive dean before becoming president. He holds a doctorate in education from the University of Georgia.

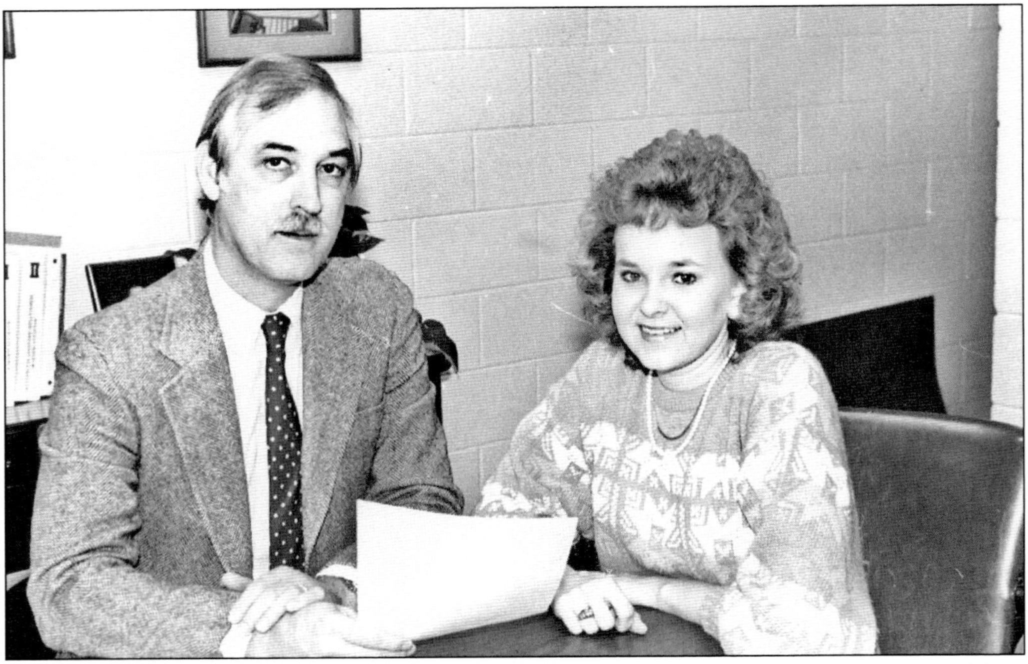

The Columbia State chapter of the Student Tennessee Education Association (STEA) celebrates American Education Week. Pictured is Dean of Instruction Douglas Eason and STEA president Amy Deavers. Dr. Eason is now president of Mitchell Community College in North Carolina.

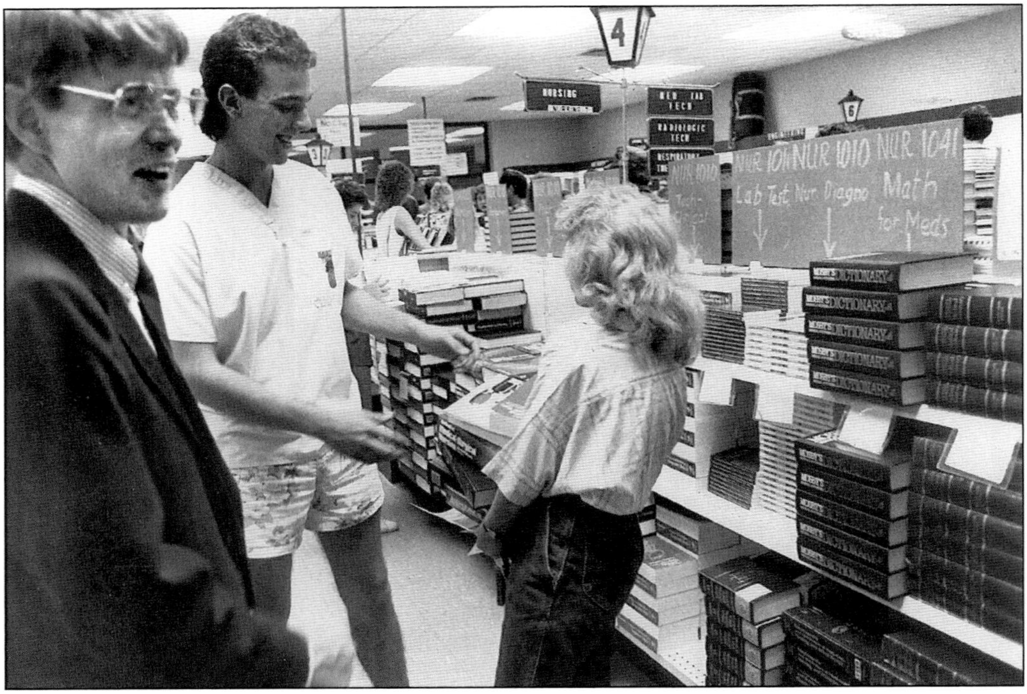

All students dread purchasing their books each semester. They leave the bookstore with less money in their pockets and a heavy load in their arms. Bookstore manager Bill Summar (left) tries to make the experience more enjoyable.

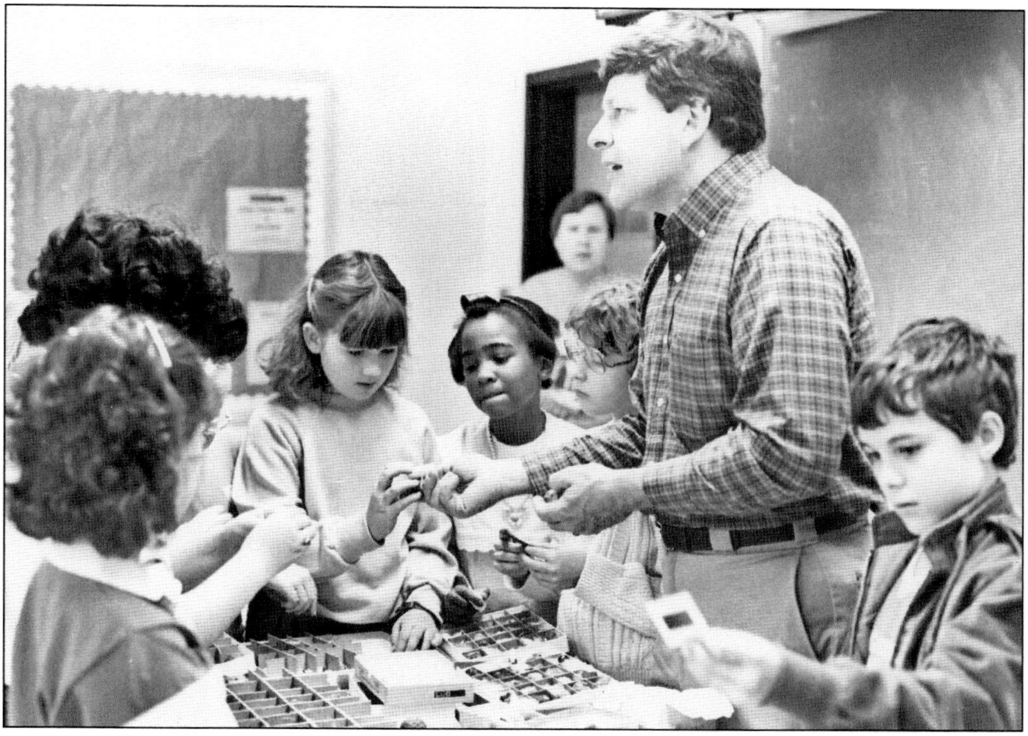

Aubrey Flagg provides hands-on experience for young students in the Saturday Scholar's program. Looking on is program director Barry Gidcomb.

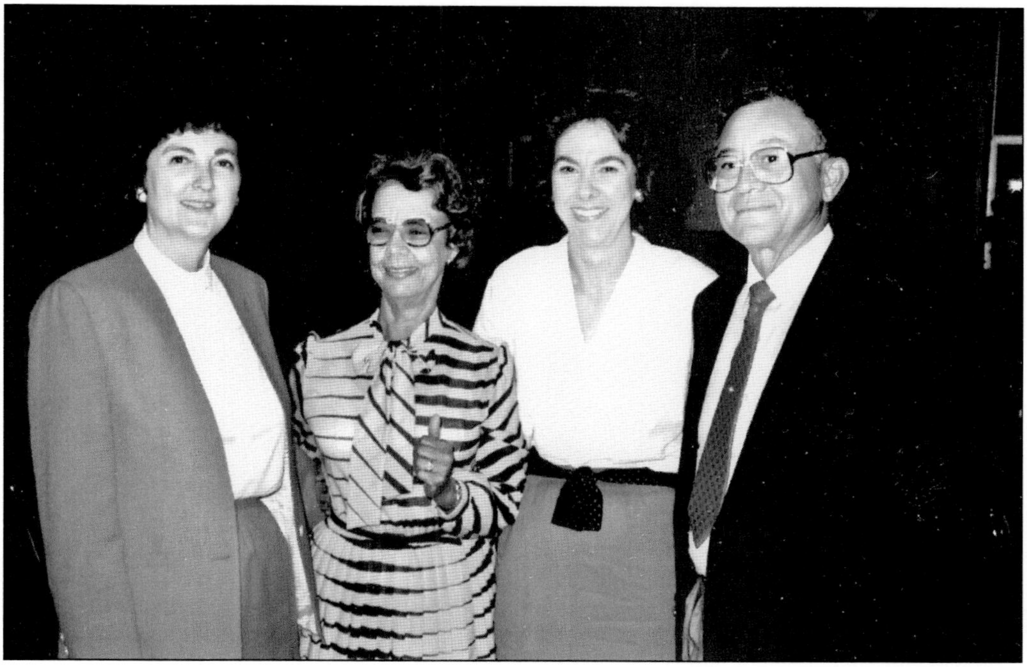

Esther Alexander taught both developmental and speed reading for several years until her retirement in 1987. Pictured at her retirement party are, from left to right, Jean Jones, Esther, Marynelle Criswell, and Esther's husband, Harvey.

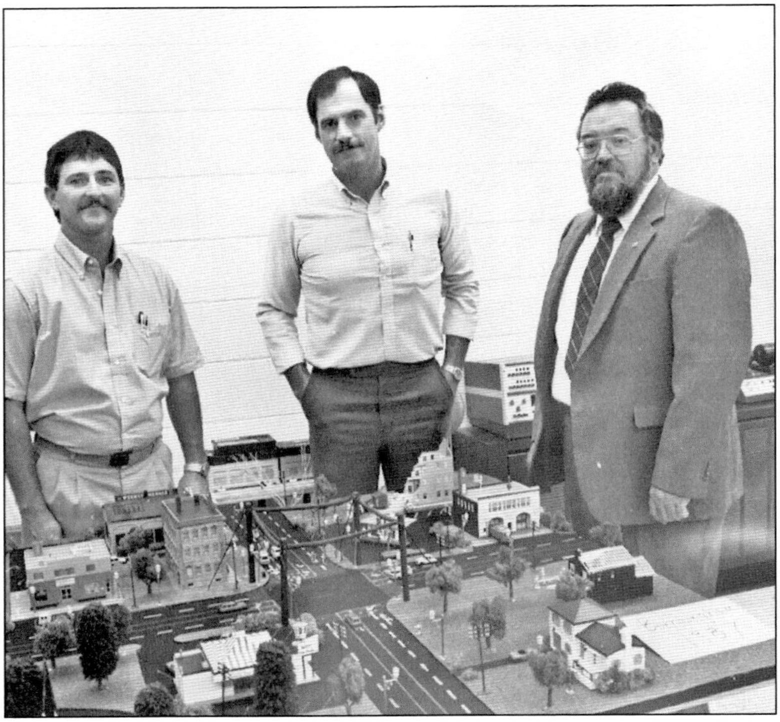

Danny Burns and Frank Cunningham, pictured with electrical engineering instructor Clyde Denton (right), were the top electronic engineering technology students of 1987. They built this computer-operated model city, which they named "Burnsingham." The model city was built for use in a TVA/CoSCC workshop.

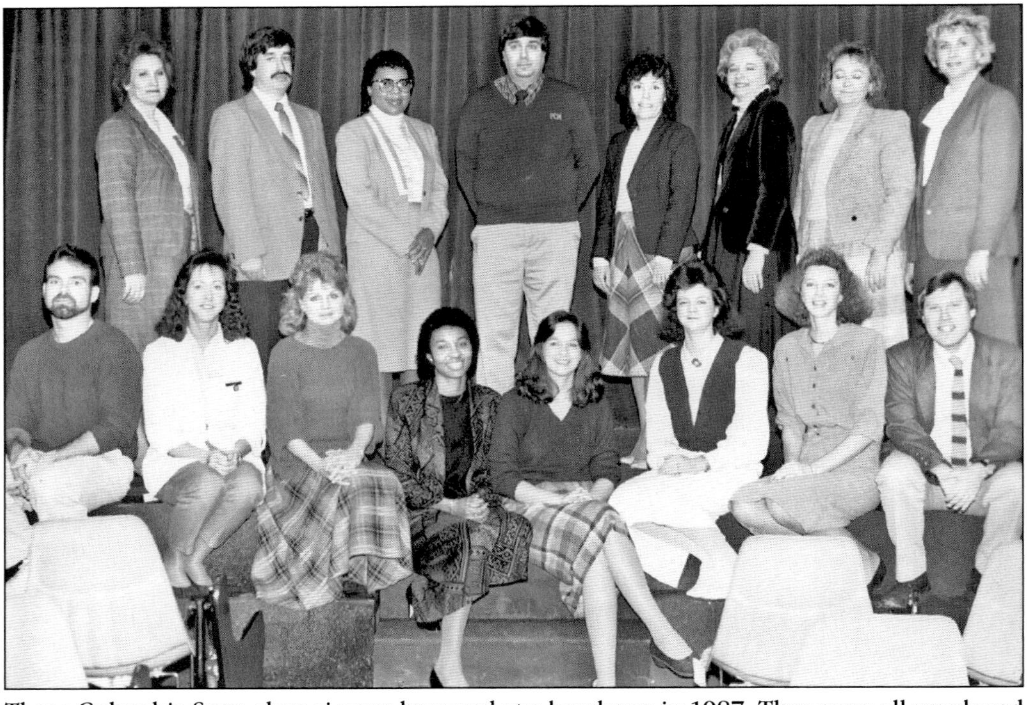

These Columbia State alumni were honored at a luncheon in 1987. They were all employed by the college at that time. From left to right are (front row) Ricky Martin, Brenda Coleman, Mary Kirby, Patricia Harlan, Jerri Grooms, Connie Lehnhart, Alice Pope, and Barry Gidcomb; (back row) Evelyn Brewer, Ken Horner, Sharon Bowen, Phil Matlock, Sara Fralix, Peggy Skillington, Loretta Byrd, and Betty Drumwright.

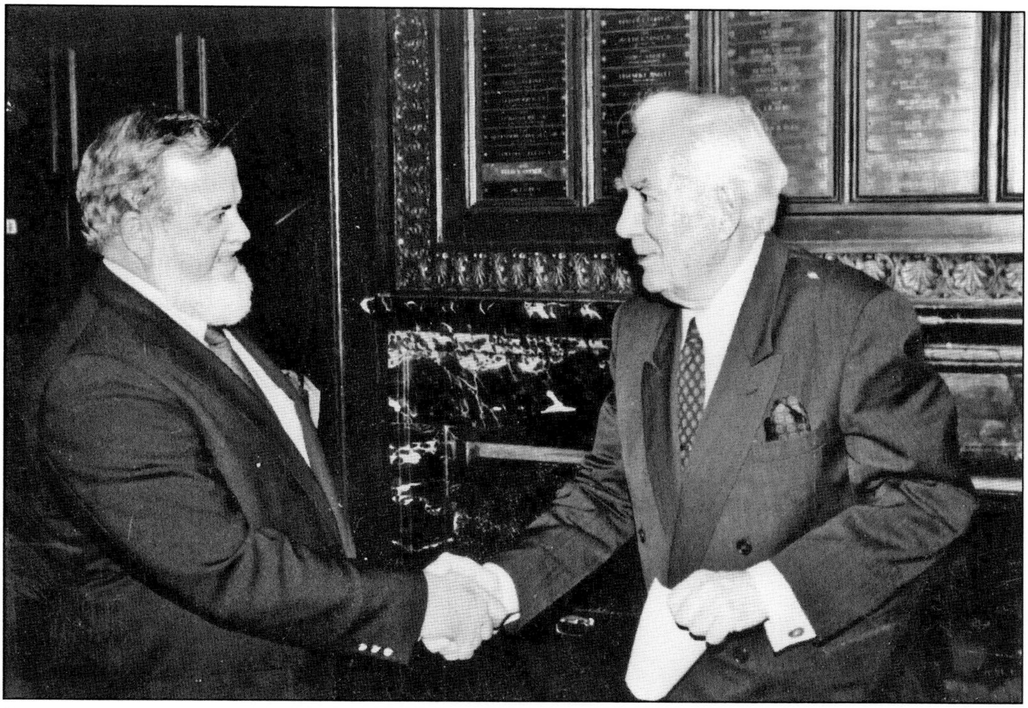

Dr. Lewis Moore is congratulated by Chief Justice Warren Burger upon his receiving the 1988 Benjamin Franklin Award given by the United States Constitution Bicentennial Commission and the National Press Foundation.

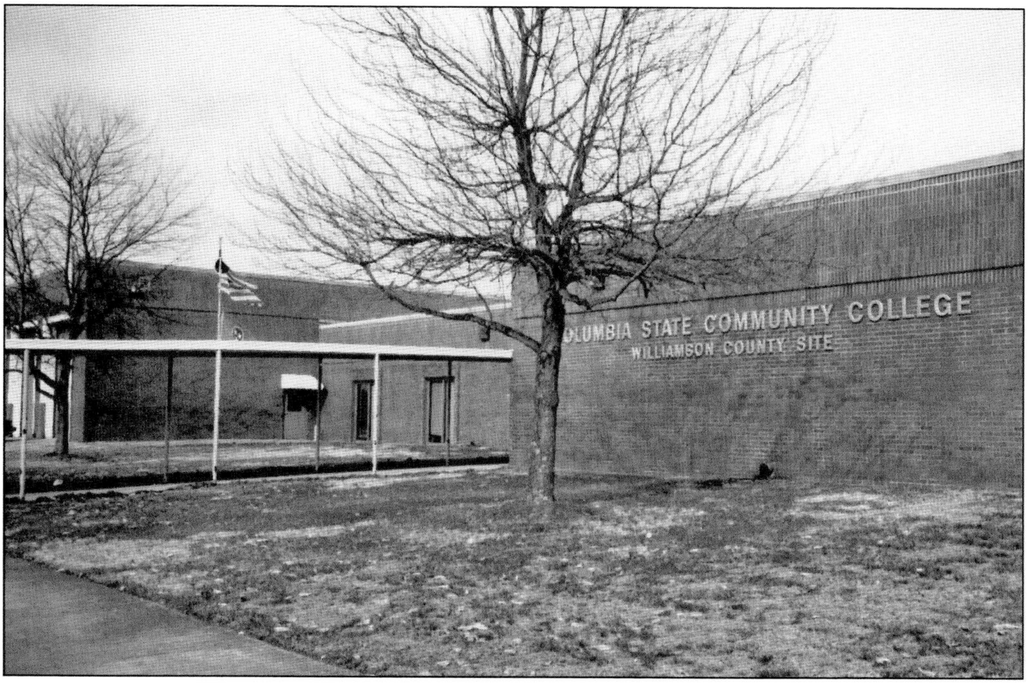

Columbia State began offering courses in the Yates Vocational Center in Franklin in 1988. In 1994, the Yates facility was transferred to the TBR, providing a permanent location for the Williamson County Center.

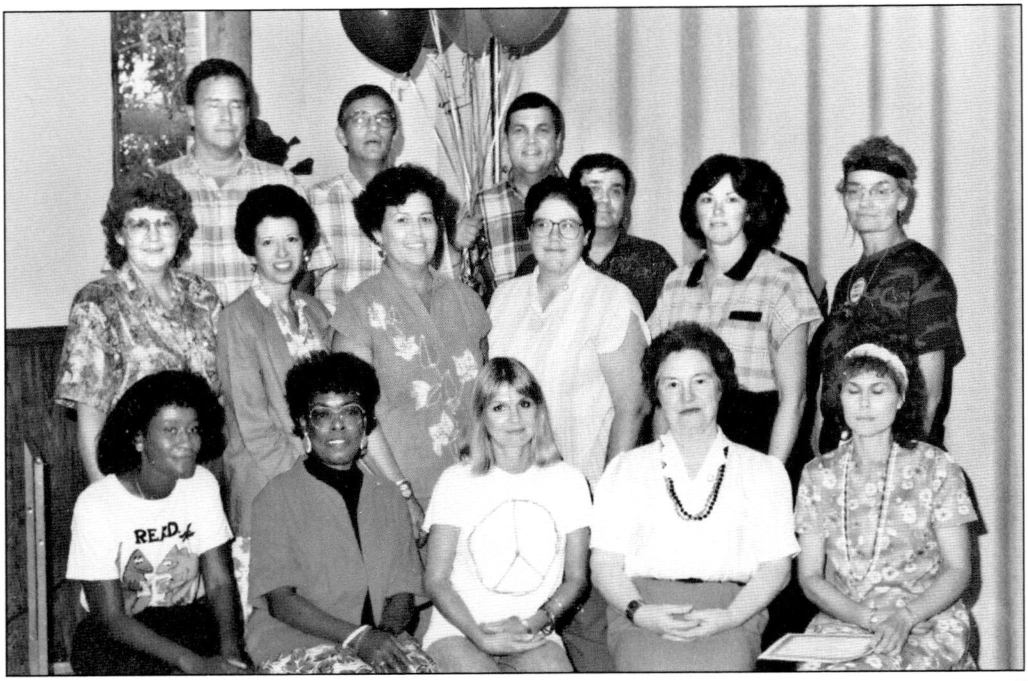

One day of faculty in-service in 1989 was designated as "Hippie Day." Faculty and staff awards were presented to the following, from left to right: (front row) Dorothy Williams, Anna Dooley, Mary Kirby, Frances Logsdon, and Susan Armes; (middle row) Deanna Naddy, Ann Tidwell, Susan Cothran, Livia Derryberry, Lynn Bayless, and Elner Hamner; (back row) Rick Molder, Bill Muehlbauer, Charles Sanders, and Phil Matlock.

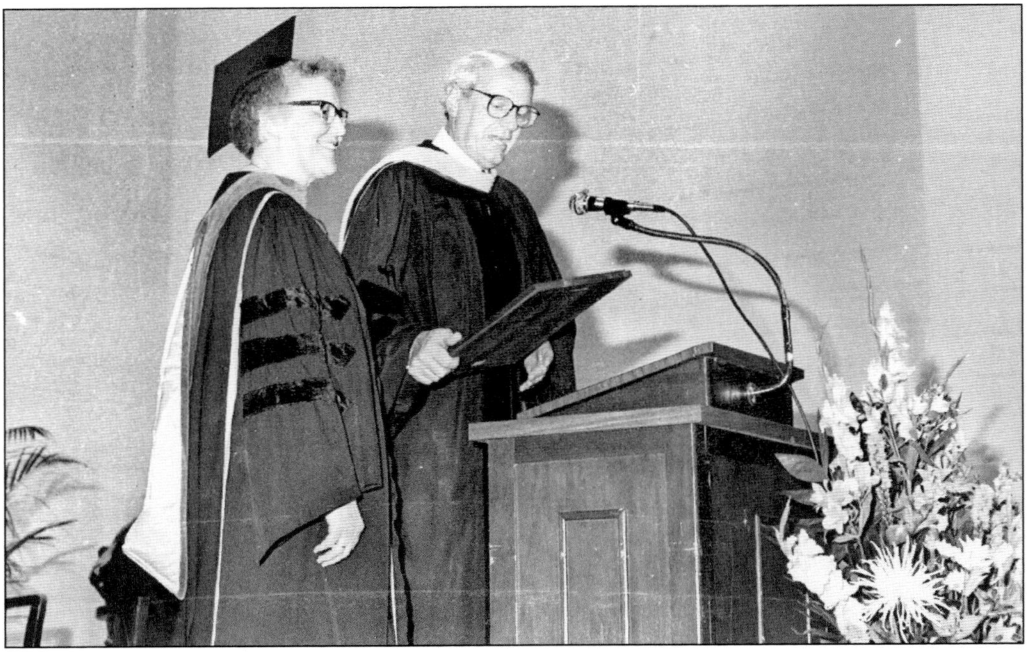

President Sands presents the Distinguished Faculty Award to Dr. (Sister) Gabrielle M. Hubert during the graduation ceremony in 1989. "Gabes," as she was affectionately called by her colleagues, joined the history faculty in 1978 and retired in 1991.

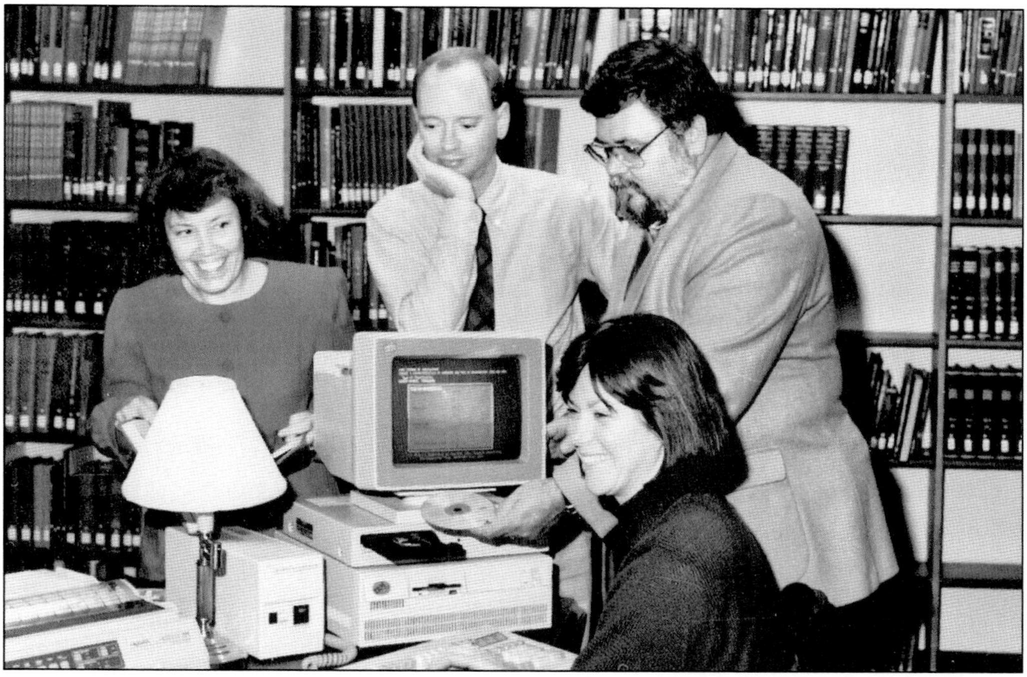

In 1989, a Title III grant was awarded for the retro-conversion of library holdings to a computerized file. Working on this project are, from left to right, Sara Fralix, Richard Harrison, LRC director Marvin Light, and Lynn Bayless (seated). Lynn has served as librarian since 1974. Sara was secretary to the director of the library from 1968 until 1996 and has since served as executive secretary to the president of the college.

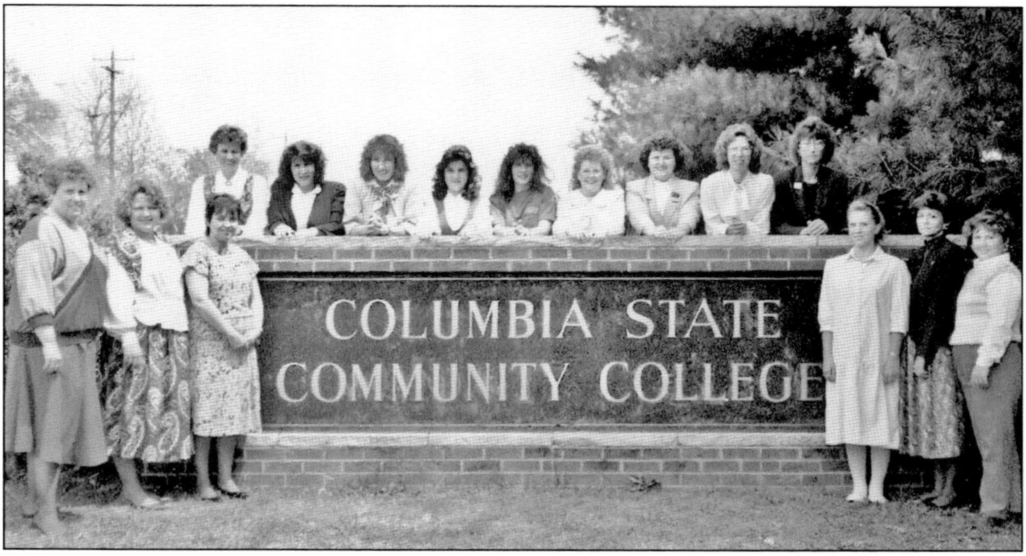

In 1972, the college responded to the demand for upper-division and graduate work. Dr. Uriah "Jack" Clemmer was appointed to work as coordinator for an Upper Division and Graduate Education Center. Now known as the University Center, 2+2 articulation (combining two years of work at Columbia State with two years of work at a university) is available with Middle Tennessee State University, Tennessee State University, and Trevecca. Pictured is the first MTSU 2+2 class in elementary education, which graduated in 1990.

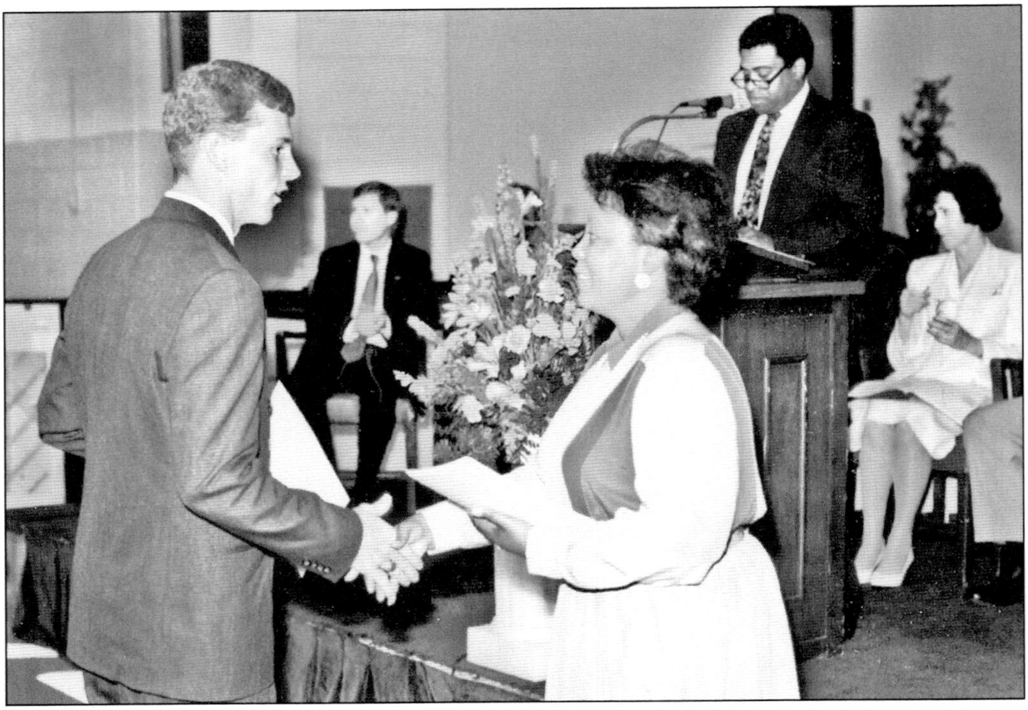

Cecelia Johnson presents a certificate at the annual Awards Day in 1991. In the background are, from left to right, Barry Gidcomb, Johnny Williams, and Betty Kyger.

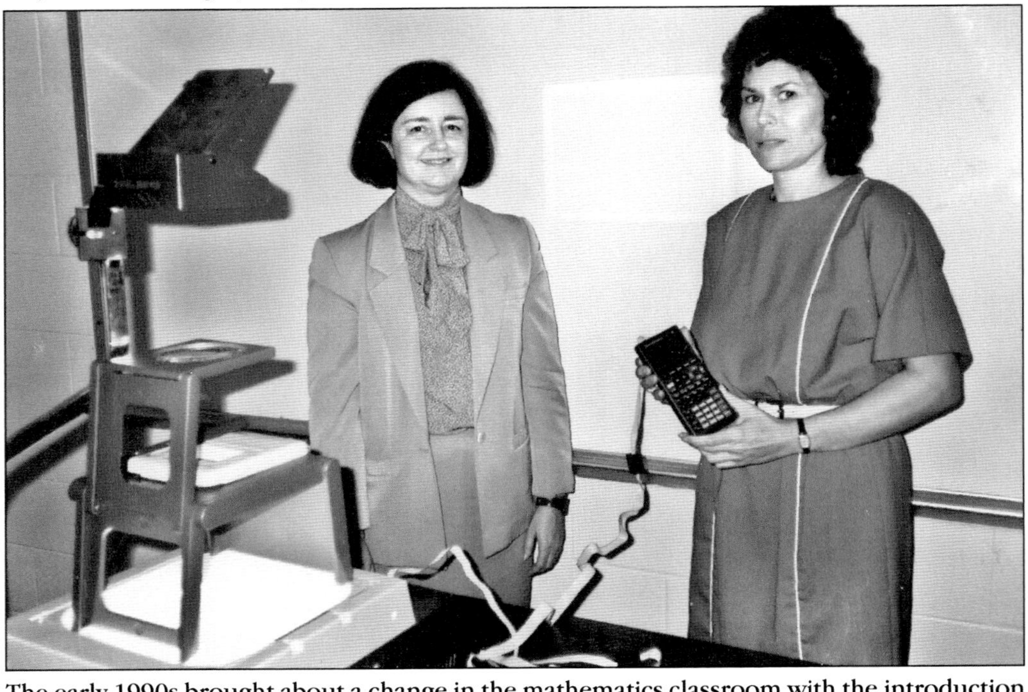

The early 1990s brought about a change in the mathematics classroom with the introduction of the graphics calculator. Ann Petersen (left) and Susan Williford, of the mathematics department, attended many calculator workshops and then conducted workshops for teachers in the college and surrounding locales.

Joni Brooks Lenig attended the Summer Faculty Fellowship Program at the Marshall Space Flight Center in 1992 and 1993. She is pictured with the Certificate of Recognition that she received in 1992. Joni graduated from Columbia State in 1984 and is currently the assistant vice president for faculty and programs.

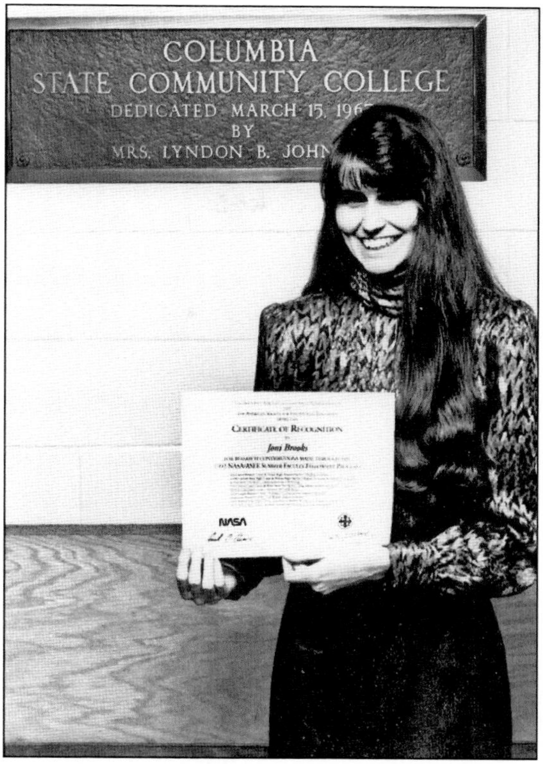

Paul Sands (right) stands with John Dillingham, first social science chair, by the plaque designating room 205 in the Clement Building in John's honor.

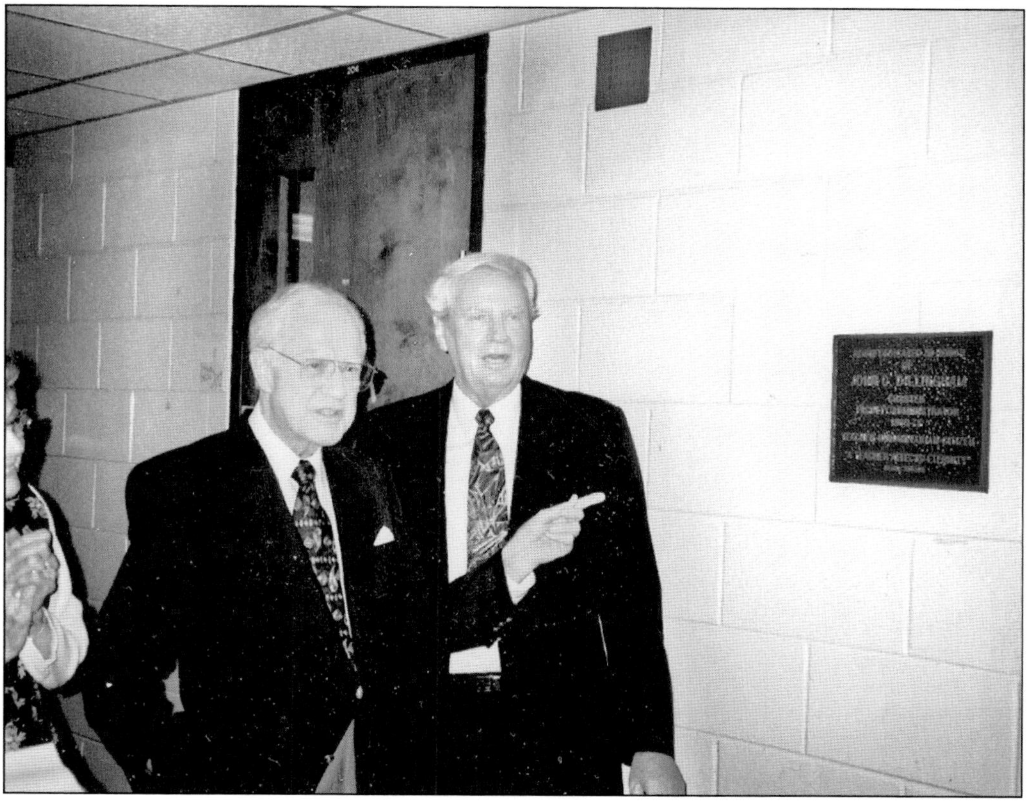

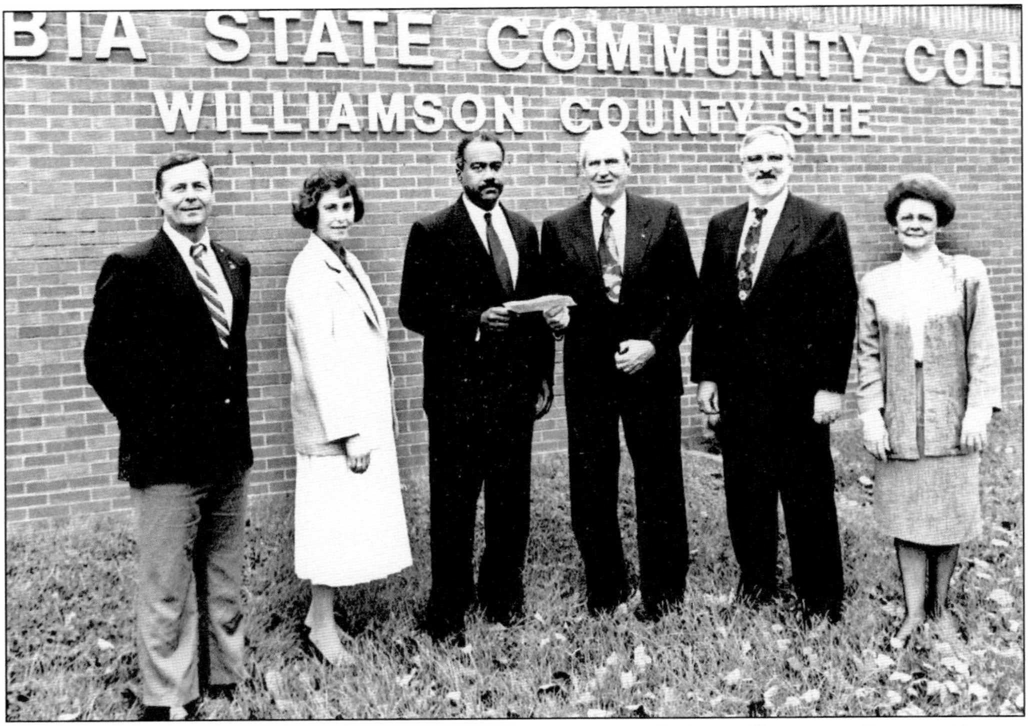

Kenny Blackburn, Bell South vice president and chair of the Williamson County Center Advisory Board, presents a Bell South Education Grant for technology upgrades to President Sands. From left to right are WCC director Ralph Walker, Dean Betty Kyger, Blackburn, Sands, Williamson Medical Center vice president David Ausbrooks, and Nancy Conway of the Williamson County Chamber of Commerce.

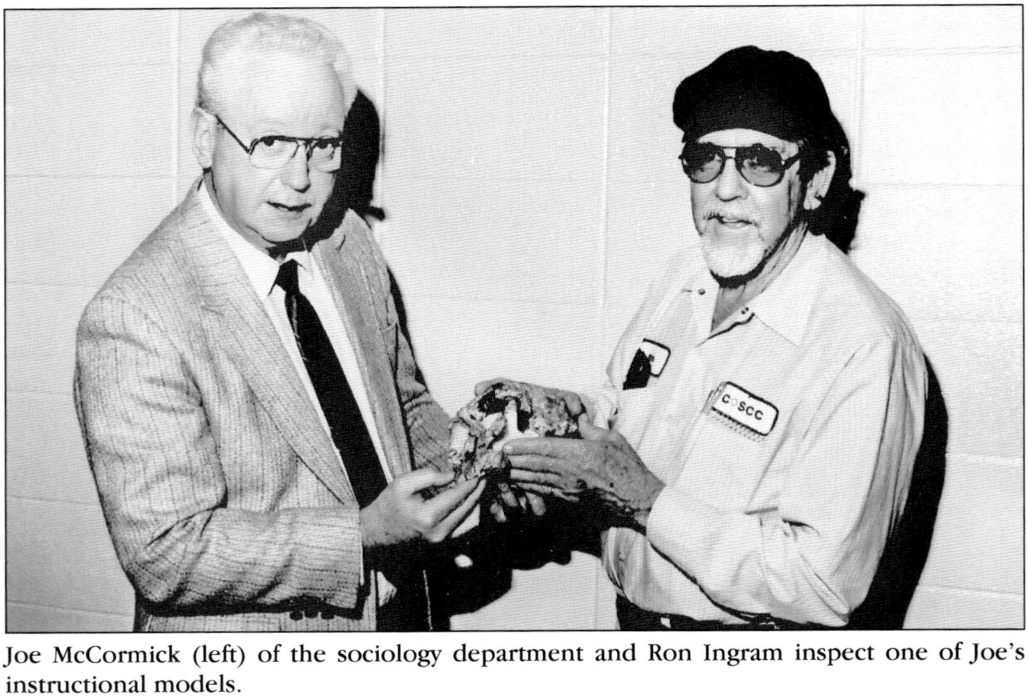

Joe McCormick (left) of the sociology department and Ron Ingram inspect one of Joe's instructional models.

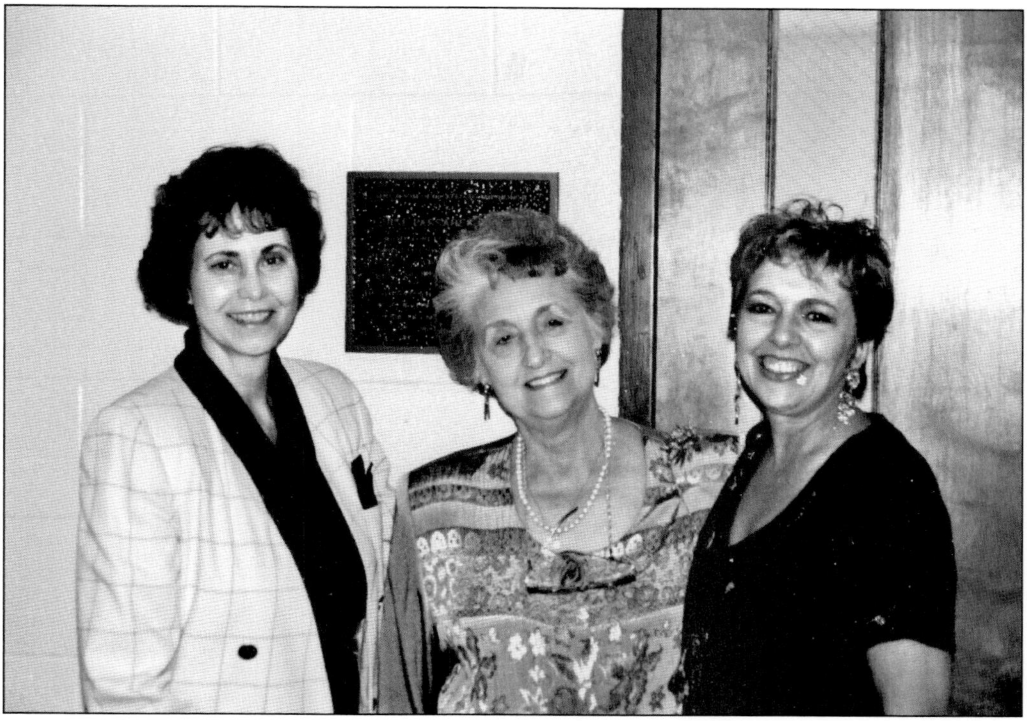

Classroom 112 in the Clement Building was dedicated to Louise Passarella Brown. Standing in front of the plaque are, from left to right, Dean of Instruction Betty Kyger, Brown, and evening coordinator Linda Belew.

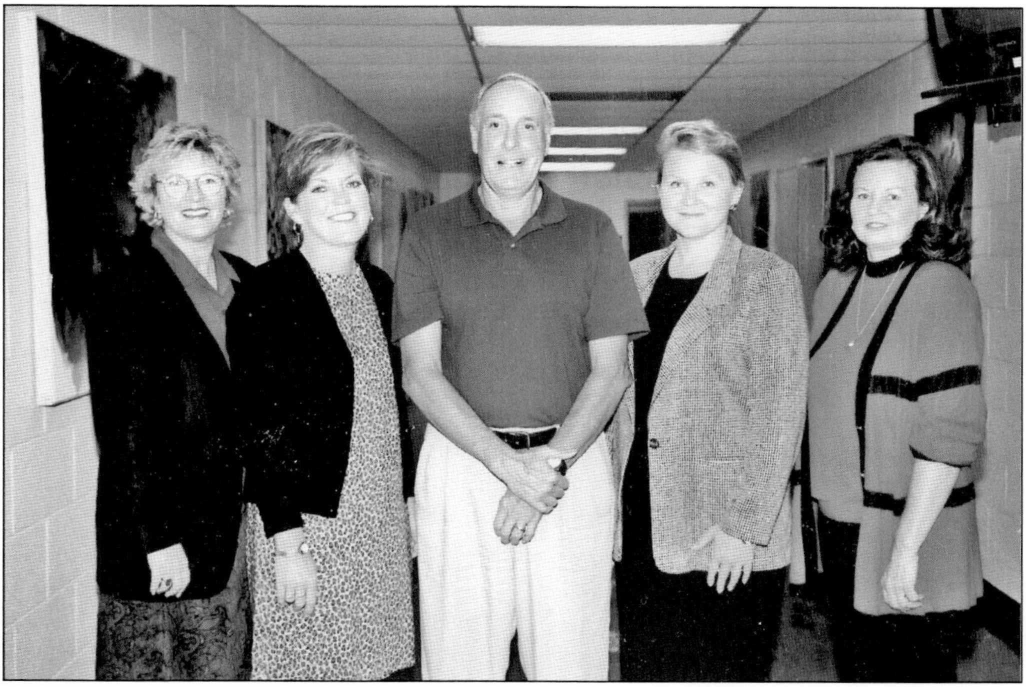

These Covey facilitators have been recognized for their accomplishments. From left to right are Elizabeth McDow, Kae Fleming, Bill McEwen, Bridgette Kelley, and Dr. Paula Petty-Ward.

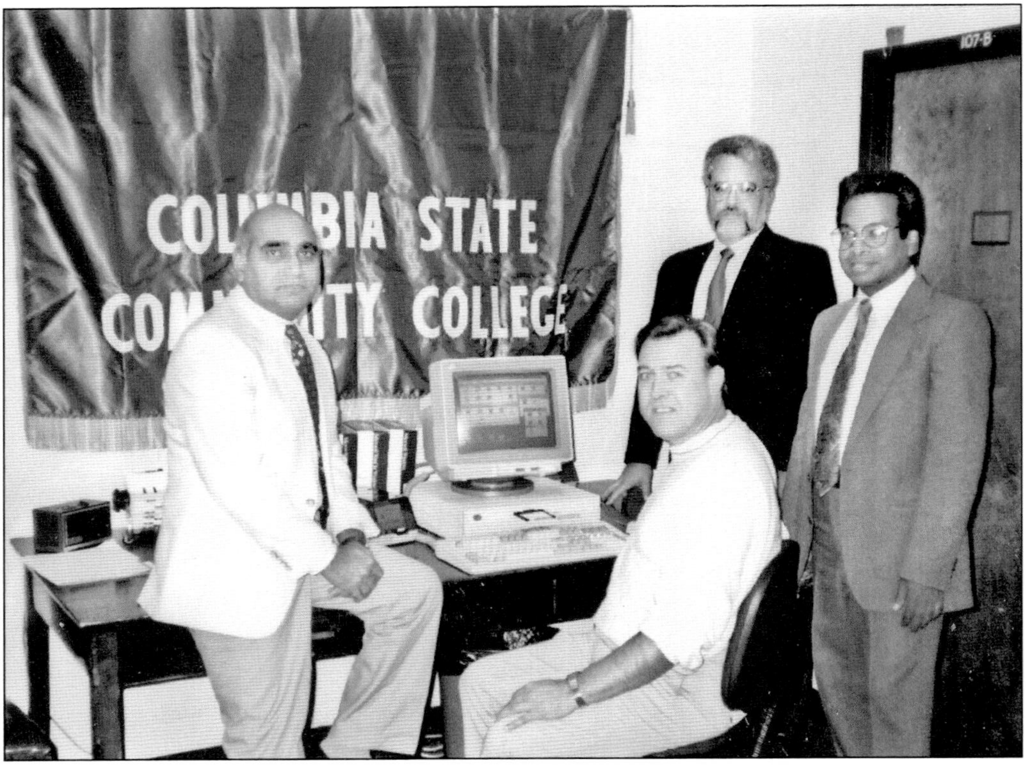

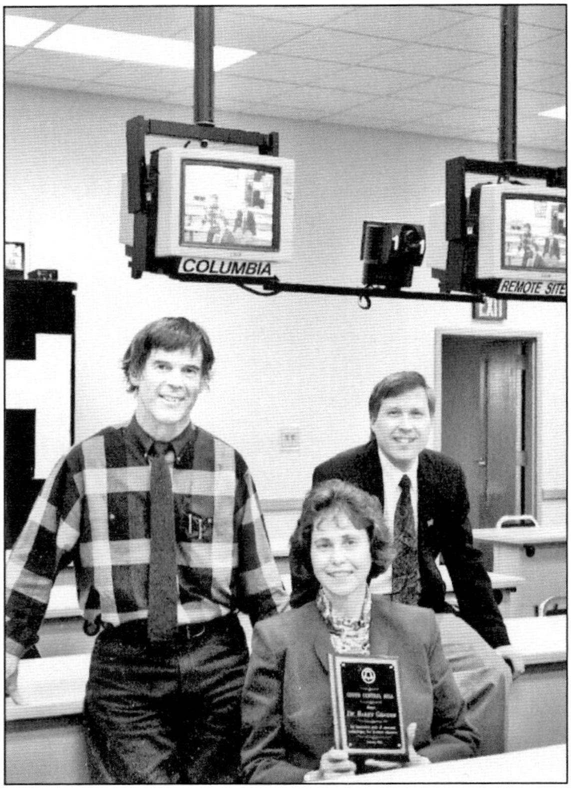

In this picture (from left to right), Chaitram Talele, Jim Murchison, James Maddirala, and Dave Goodpasture (seated) work on the 1993 SACS self-study space utilization committee.

Bill Andrews (left), Betty Kyger, and Barry Gidcomb were honored by South Central Bell for innovative uses of emerging technologies for distance education in 1995. Interactive television has become an increasingly important mode of instruction.

Dr. O. Rebecca Hawkins became Columbia State's third president on December 2, 1996. A native of Tennessee, Dr. Hawkins came to Columbia State from the position of vice president for advancement and planning at Prince George's Community College in Largo, Maryland. She holds a Ph.D. from the University of Maryland.

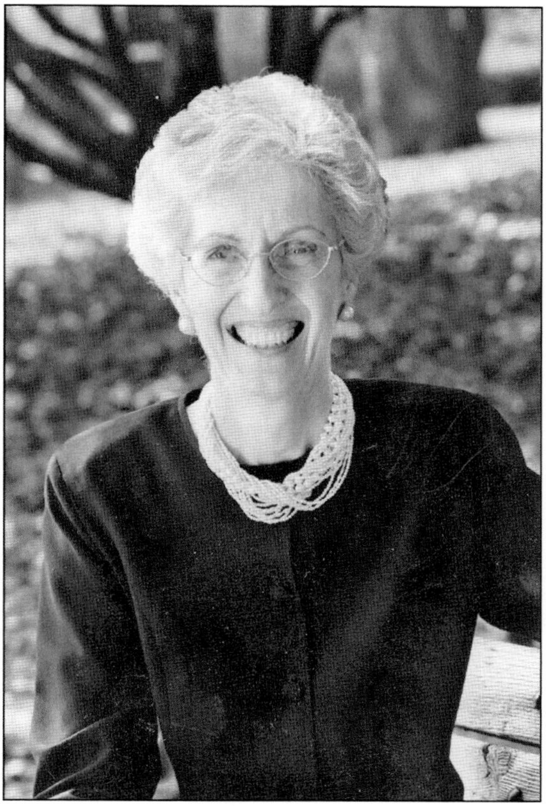

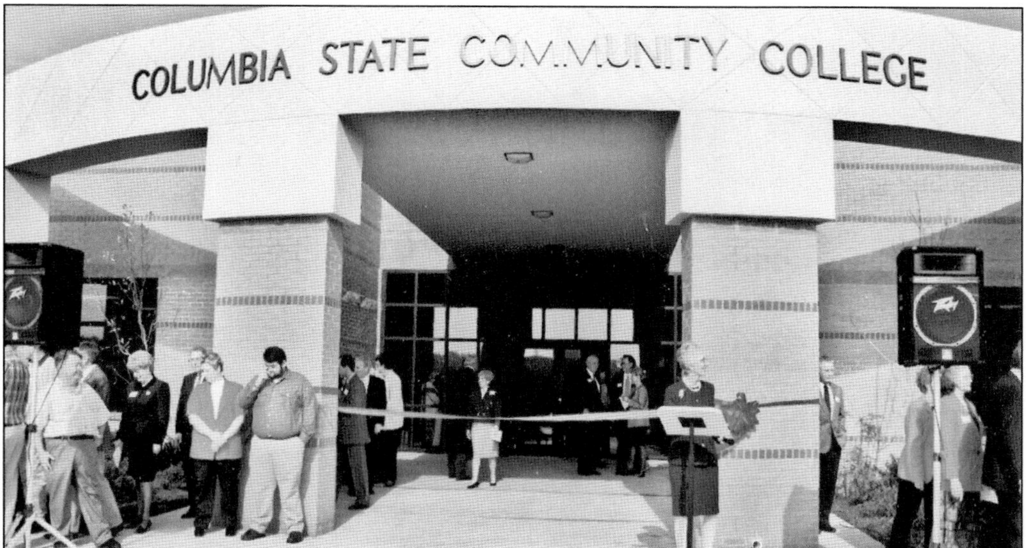

The Clifton Site, which opened in 1997, was established to provide access to post-secondary education to the citizens of Wayne County and surrounding areas. President Hawkins is seen at the podium on the day of the grand opening.

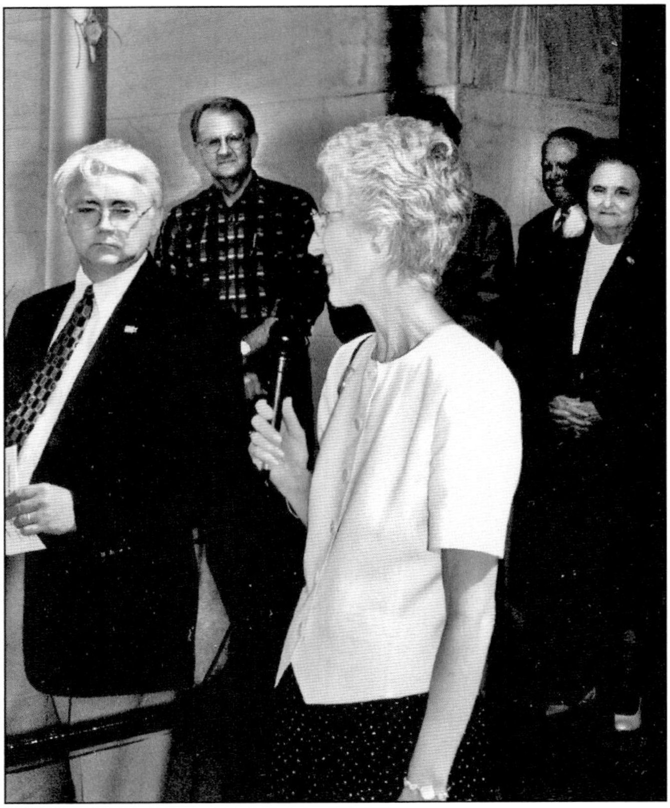

Columbia State was the lead institution for the Humphreys County Learning Center from 1996 until 2002. Pictured at the grand opening of the Center are President Hawkins and Ted Moore (left), a Columbia State alumnus and the executive director of the Humphreys County Economic Development Council.

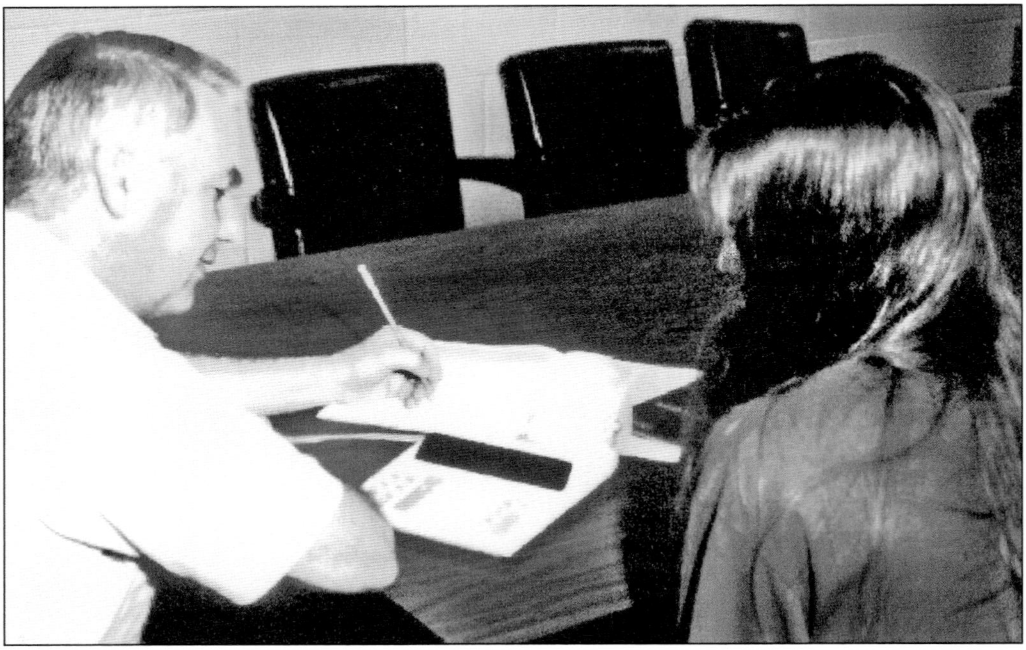

David Ogden, director of financial aid, counsels a student about scholarships and other financial aid information.

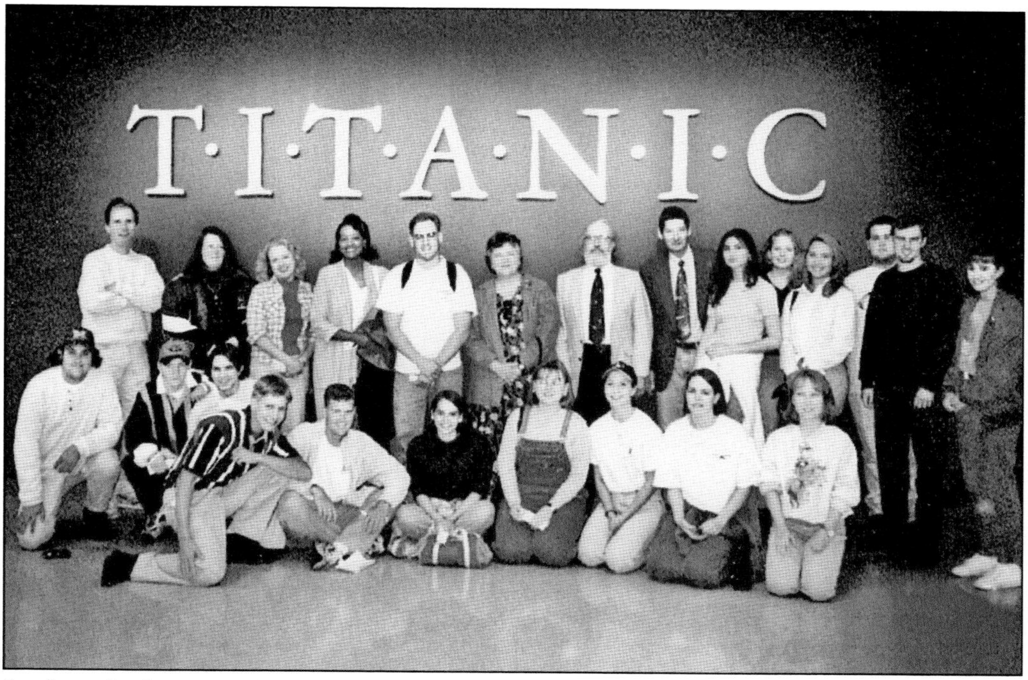

Students in the Honor's Program attended the *Titanic* exhibit in Memphis in 1997. Faculty members who accompanied the students were Stu Lenig, Beverly Mitchell, Jim Senefeld, and Mart Austin.

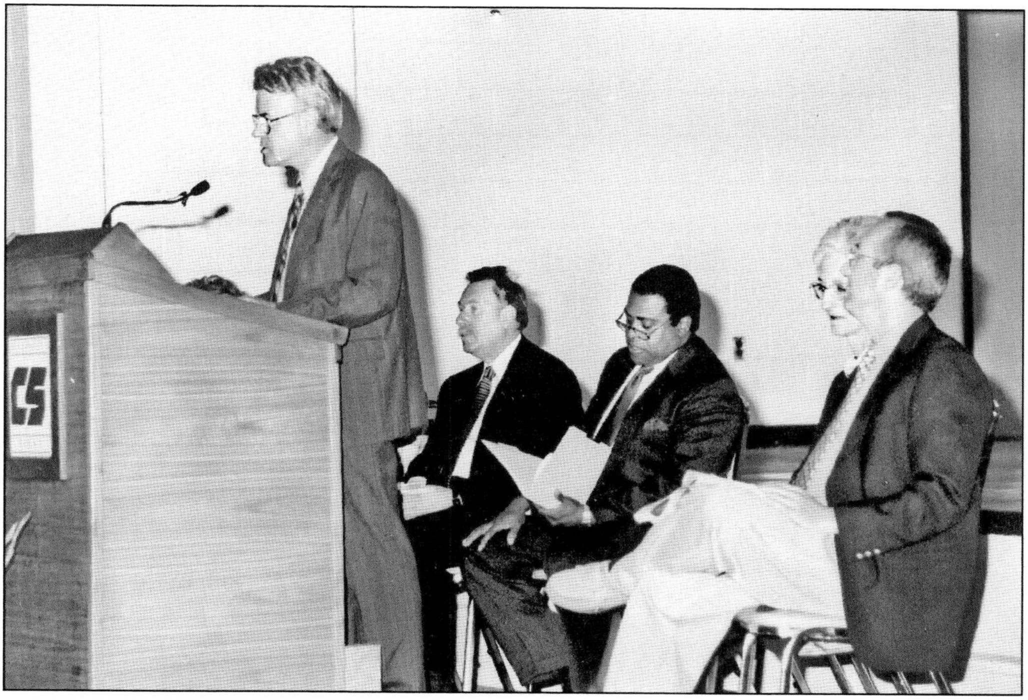

Steve Stropes delivers the address at the 1997 Student Awards Convocation. Seated, from left to right, are Abe Pallas, Johnny Williams, President Hawkins, and Bryan Long.

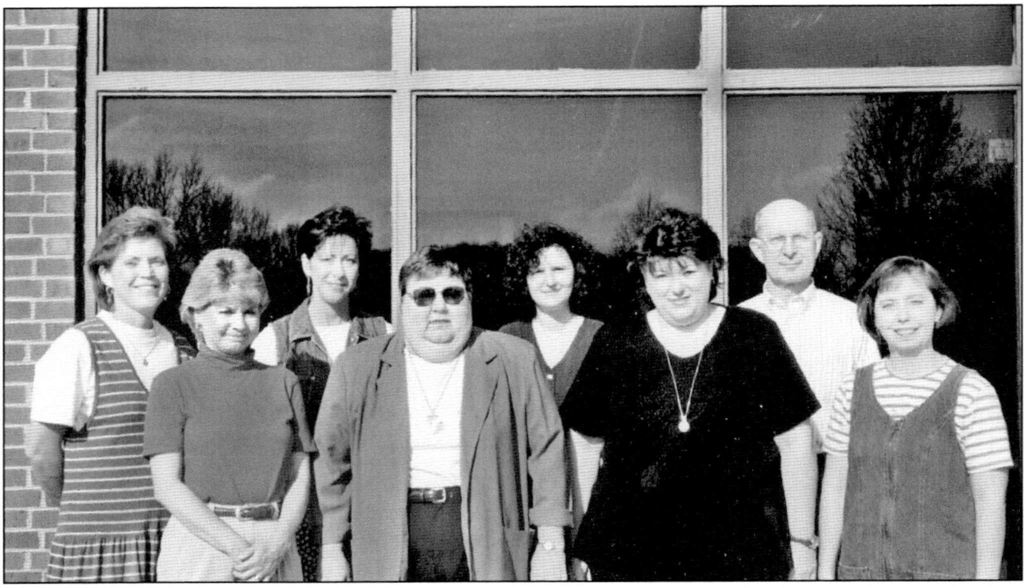

Allied health advisors were recognized with the Outstanding Advising Program Award in 1999. Members of the winning team include, from left to right, Kae Fleming, Mary Kirby, Brenda Coleman, Nancy Wells, Renee Tew, Lisa Trimble, Bill Gandy, and Nancy Hopper.

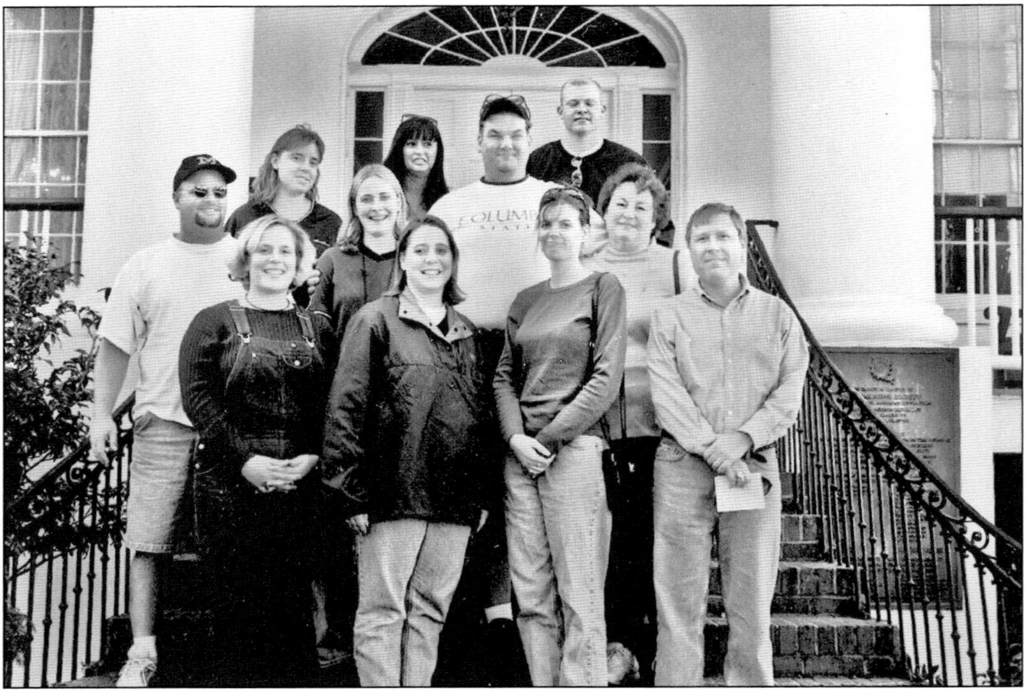

Each year the students enrolled in the Humanities Seminar make a trip to Natchez, Mississippi. The first group to visit Historic Rosalie in Natchez in October 1999 are shown with instructor Barry Gidcomb. Pictured from left to right are (front row) Stacia Chapman, Raquel Waters, Michelle Miller, and Gidcomb; (middle row) Fred DeMint, Amy Spears, Willard Rouse, and Linda Rudy; (back row) Melanie Baron, Sheila Stima, and Ehrin Ehlert.

The first two recipients of the President's Medal were both members of the original Columbia State faculty. The 2000 recipient was Lewis E. Moore Jr. The 2001 recipient was Carolyn Allred-Winnett.

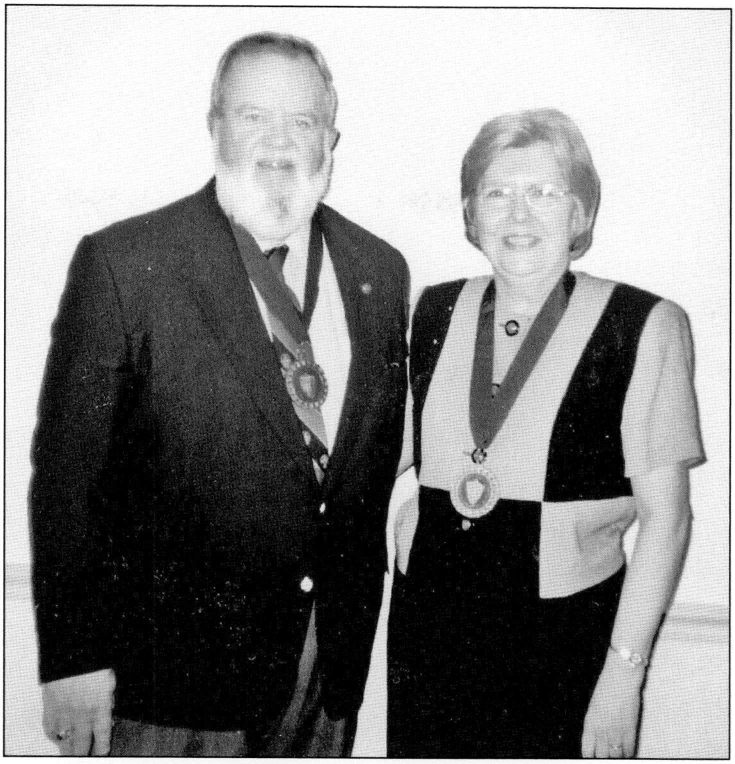

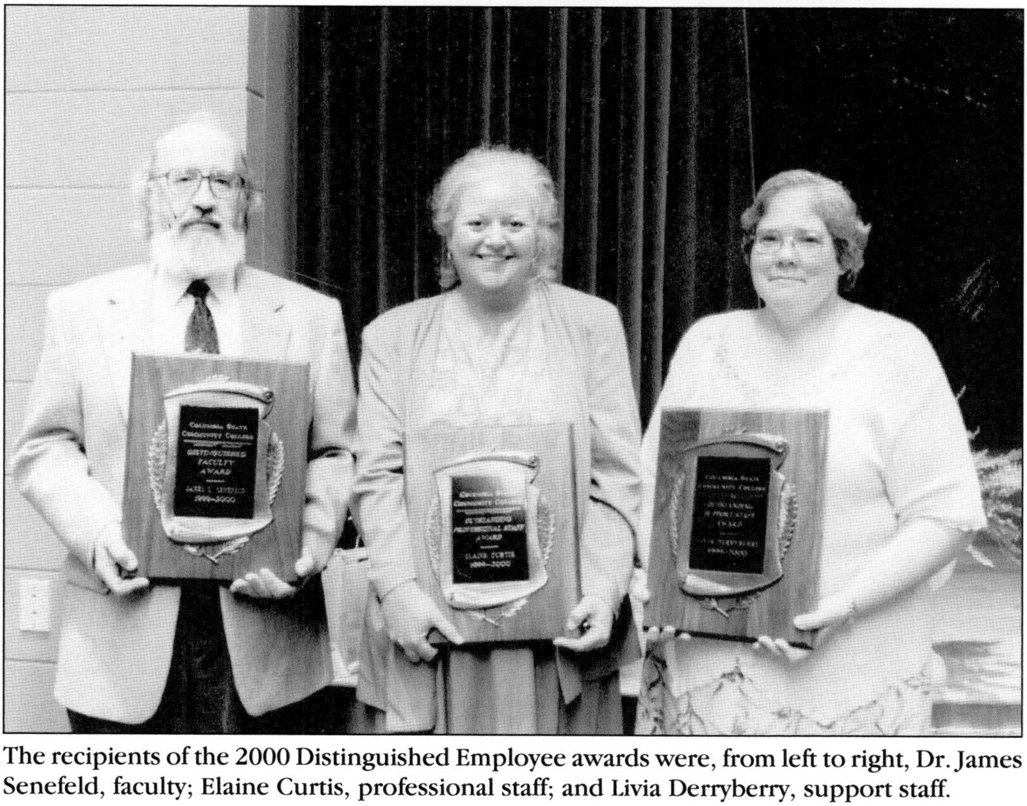

The recipients of the 2000 Distinguished Employee awards were, from left to right, Dr. James Senefeld, faculty; Elaine Curtis, professional staff; and Livia Derryberry, support staff.

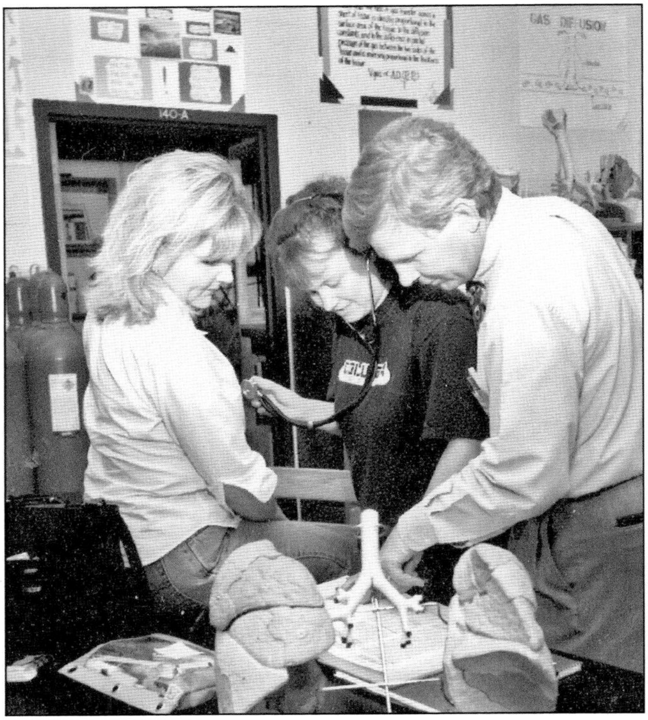

The Respiratory Care program is accredited by the Committee for Accreditation for Respiratory Care. David Johnson, program director, discusses lung function with students Carol Scott (left) and Ronda Clark.

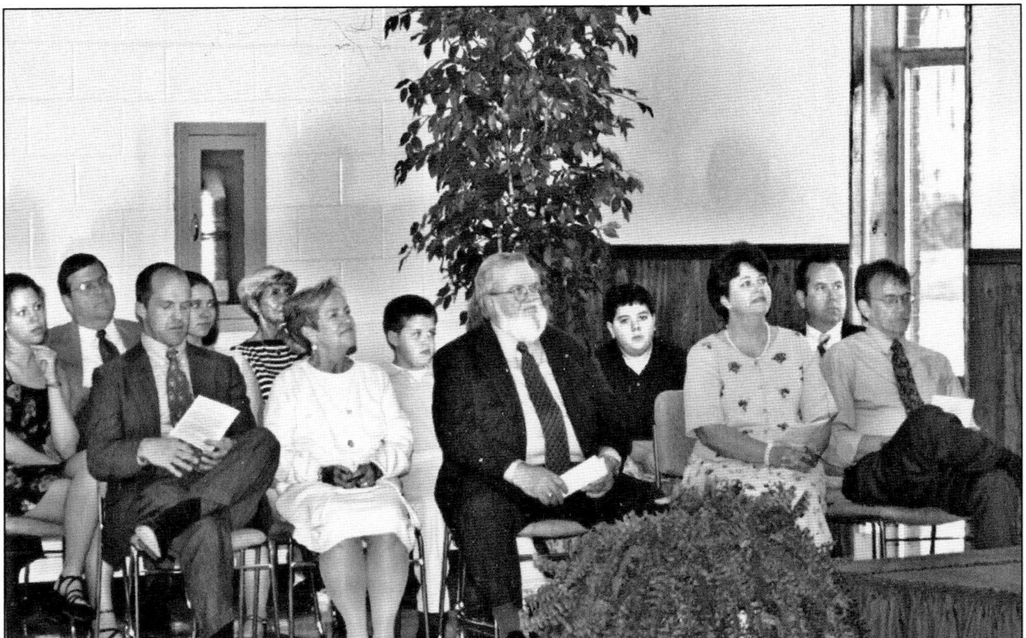

Tennessee and Columbia State's first community college faculty member, Lewis Moore, sits with family and friends at his retirement reception in April 2000. From left to right are Lucy Fleming, Charles Sanders, Chip Moore, Becca Rodgers, Barbara McIntyre, Lil Moore, Lucas Fleming, Lewis Moore, Mica Fleming, Bonnie Rodgers, John Fleming, and Jim Rodgers. The Moore children, Chip, Bonnie, and Melinda (not pictured), are all graduates of Columbia State.

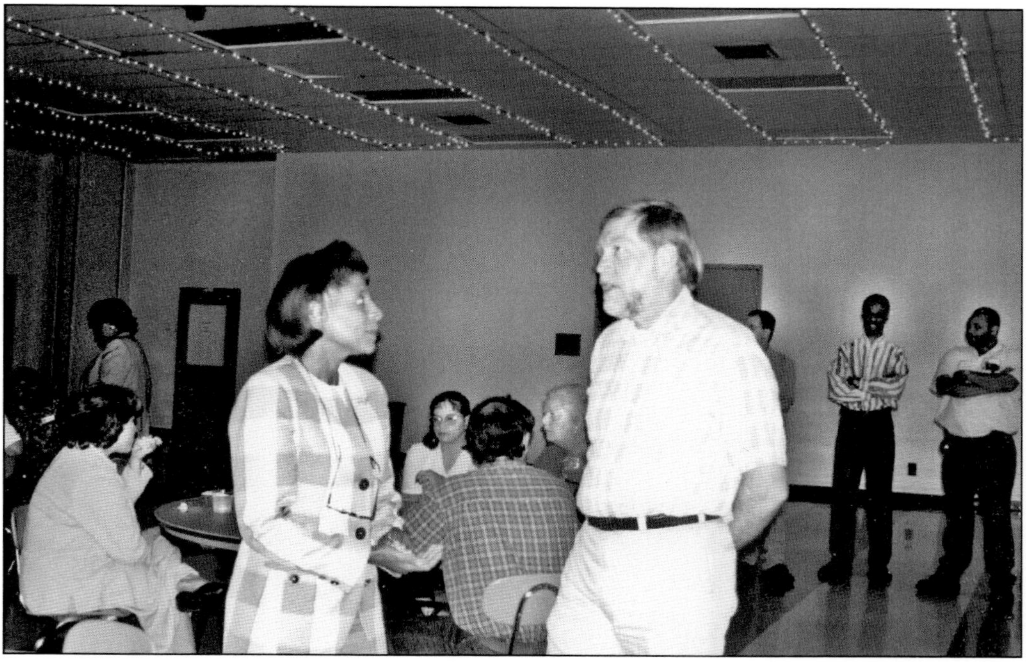

Dr. Larita Alford and Mike Shuler are shown at Larita's going-away party. Larita is now at Bermuda College.

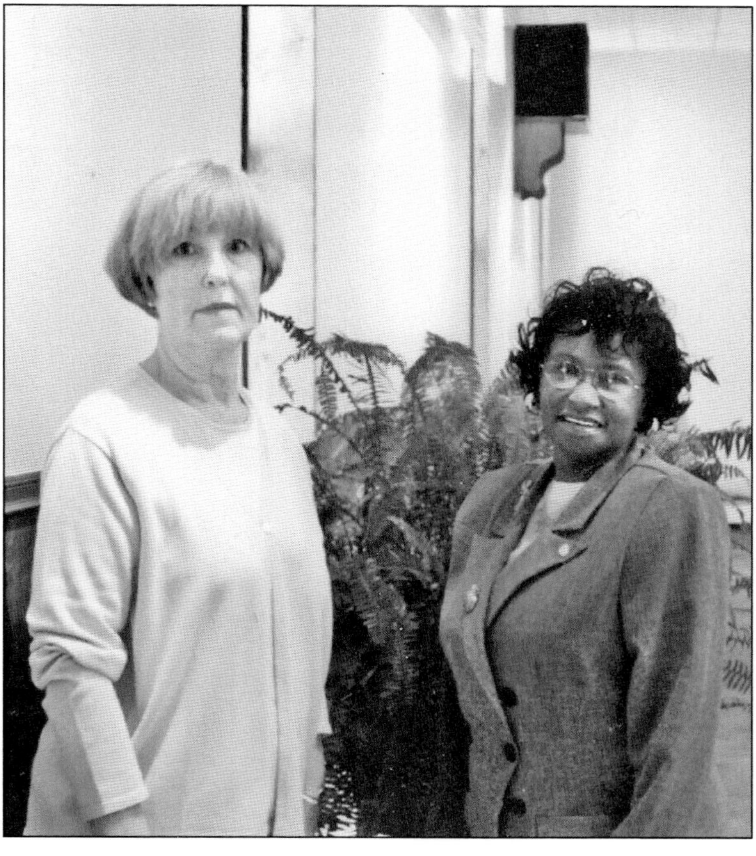

Billie Watts (left) and Pat Bowman, shown at the 2003 Employee Awards Convocation, are two long-time college employees. Billie is a secretary in the business and technology division. Pat is a secretary in the health sciences division.

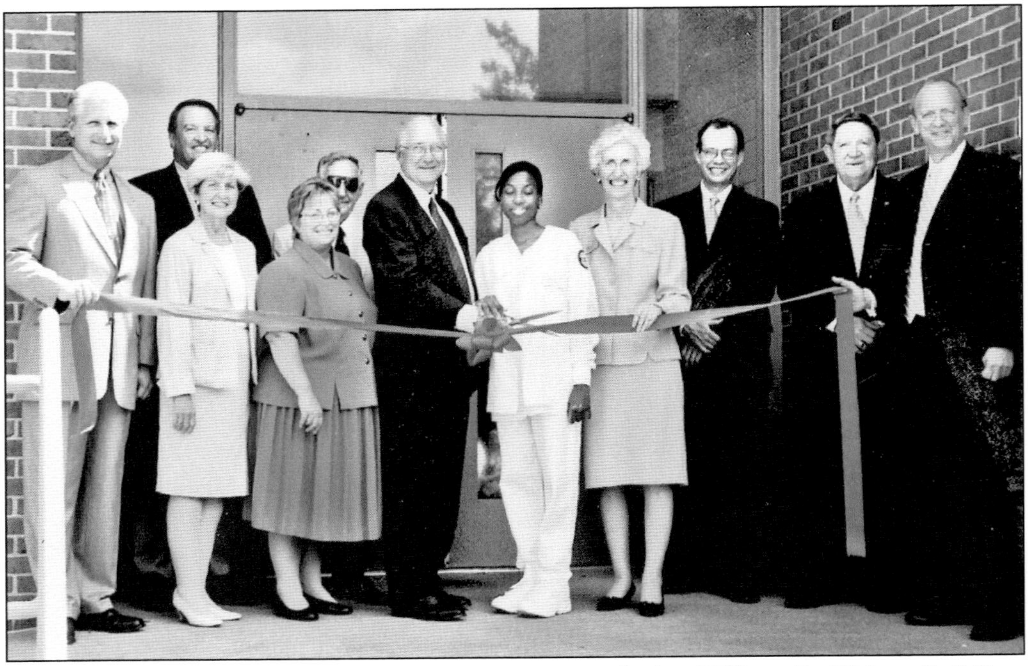

The original Finney Memorial Library was renamed the William R. Walter Building. Participating in the ribbon cutting are, from left to right, State Sen. Bill Ketron, County Executive James Bailey, Mayor Barbara McIntyre, Health Sciences Division chair Lois Ewen, Dr. Harold Pryor, Walter, student Dana Williams, President Hawkins, Dr. Charles Ball, Waymon Hickman, and TBR chancellor Charles Manning.

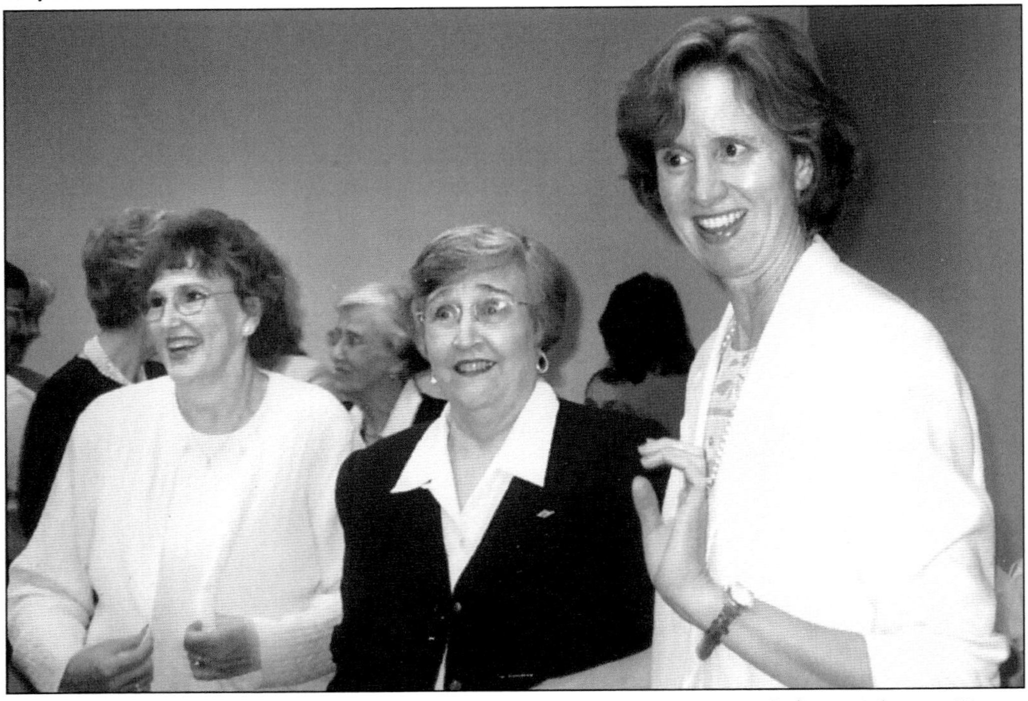

Sue Greenfield enjoys her retirement party with colleagues. From left to right are Nancy Bass, Sue, and Mary Susan Kennedy.

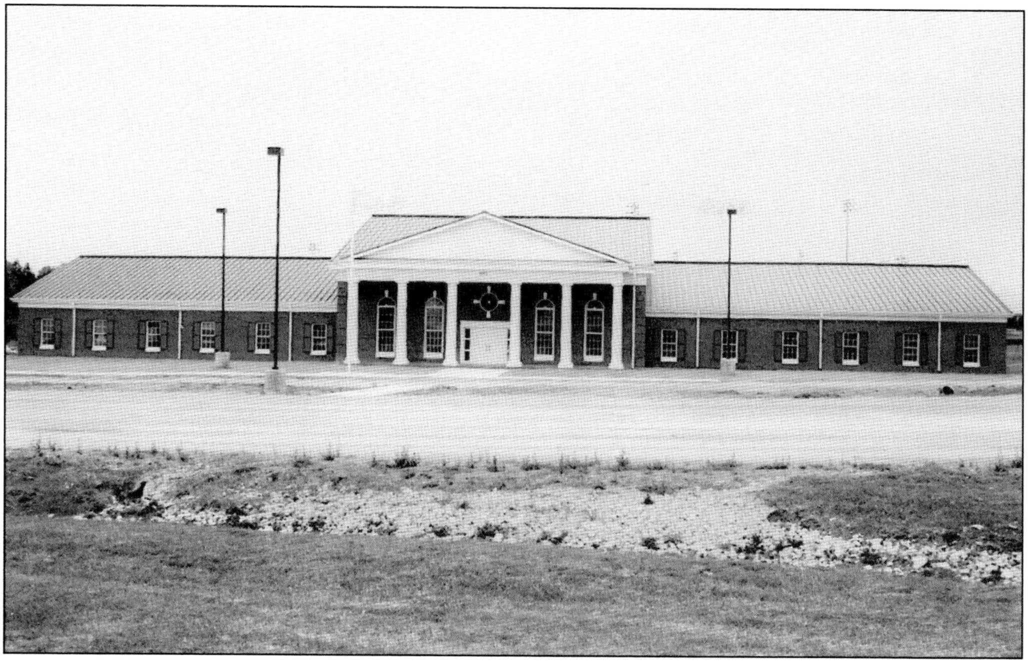

The Lewisburg Site opened in 1996 and offers college classes for students in Marshall and surrounding counties. Additional non-credit training programs, both general interest and employment-related, are conducted throughout the year. A new addition, dedicated in September 2001, contains classrooms, a science lab, career center, library, and community meeting facilities.

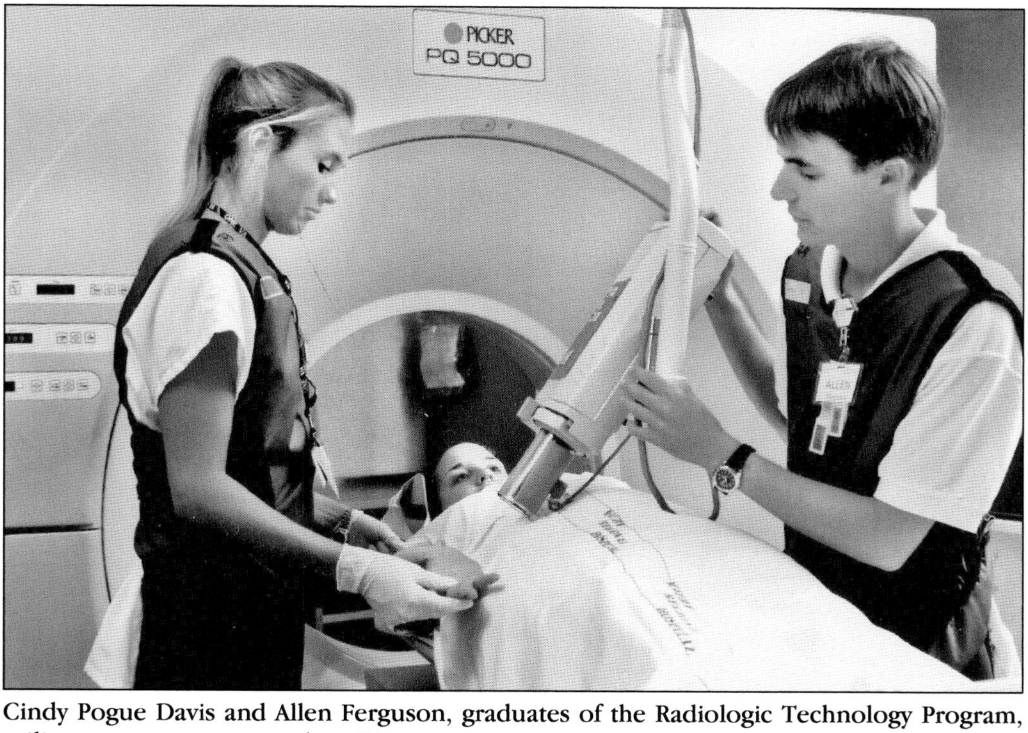

Cindy Pogue Davis and Allen Ferguson, graduates of the Radiologic Technology Program, utilize computer tomography (CT) equipment at Maury Regional Hospital.

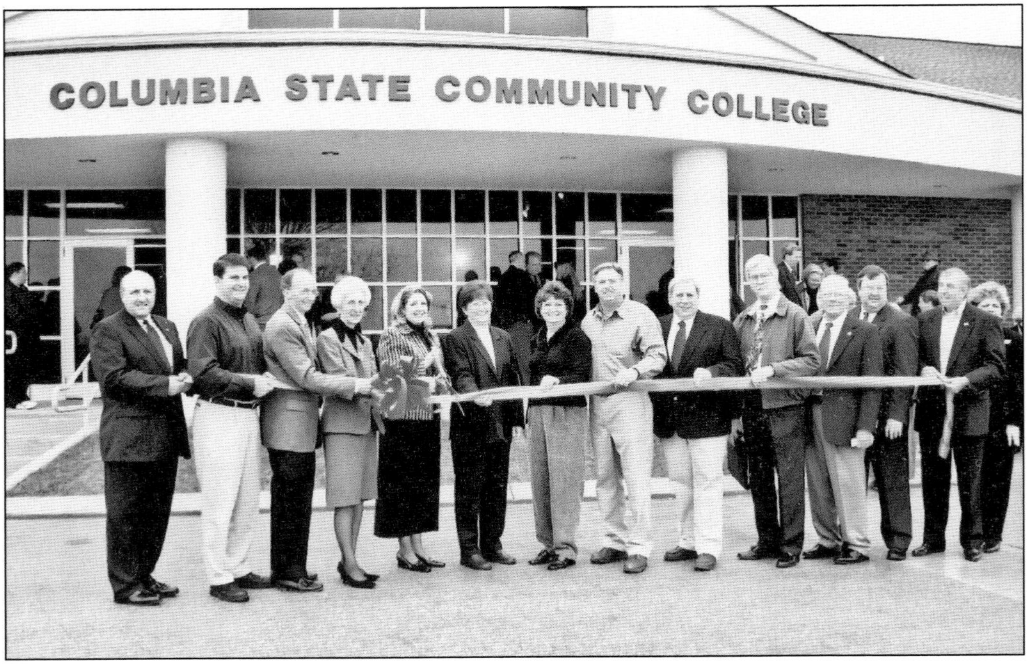

The Lawrence County Center (LCC) opened in 1988 and was dedicated as the Chuck Brewer Memorial Center. In 2001, Lawrence County began plans to expand the center—a $1.4 million project. The USDA Rural Development Agency provided a $150,000 grant. A new addition was completed and dedicated in 2002. From left to right are Tim Pettus, Blake Lay, Darrin McKamey, President Hawkins, LCC site director Ruth Ann Holt, Ametra Bailey, Sarah and Don Sweeton, Steve Hill, Larry Reynolds, Randy Brewer, Robert Pulley, and Daphene Cope.

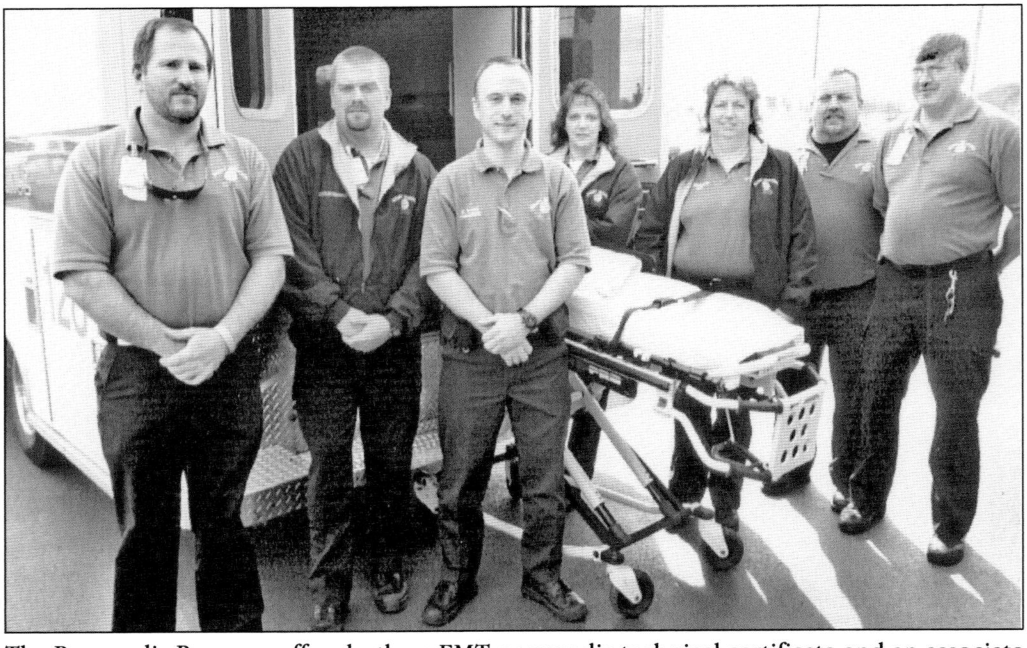

The Paramedic Program offers both an EMT-paramedic technical certificate and an associate of science in general technology degree.

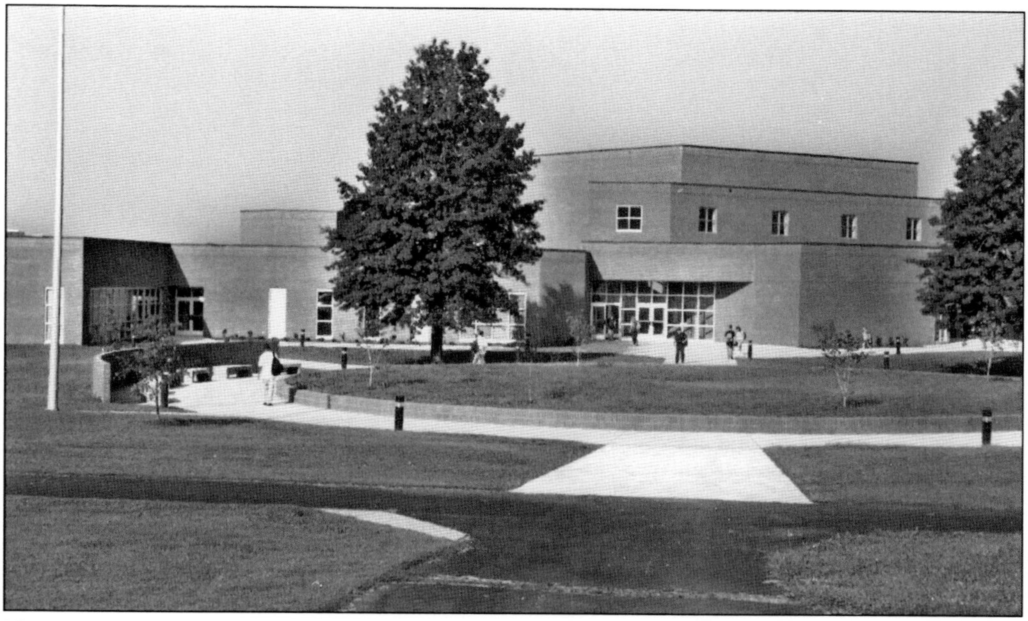

The Waymon L. Hickman Building opened in 2001. It houses general-purpose and music classrooms and labs, an ITV classroom, the Pryor Art Gallery, the Cherry Theater, a computer lab, a darkroom, a MIDI lab, community meeting rooms, and a television-video production studio.

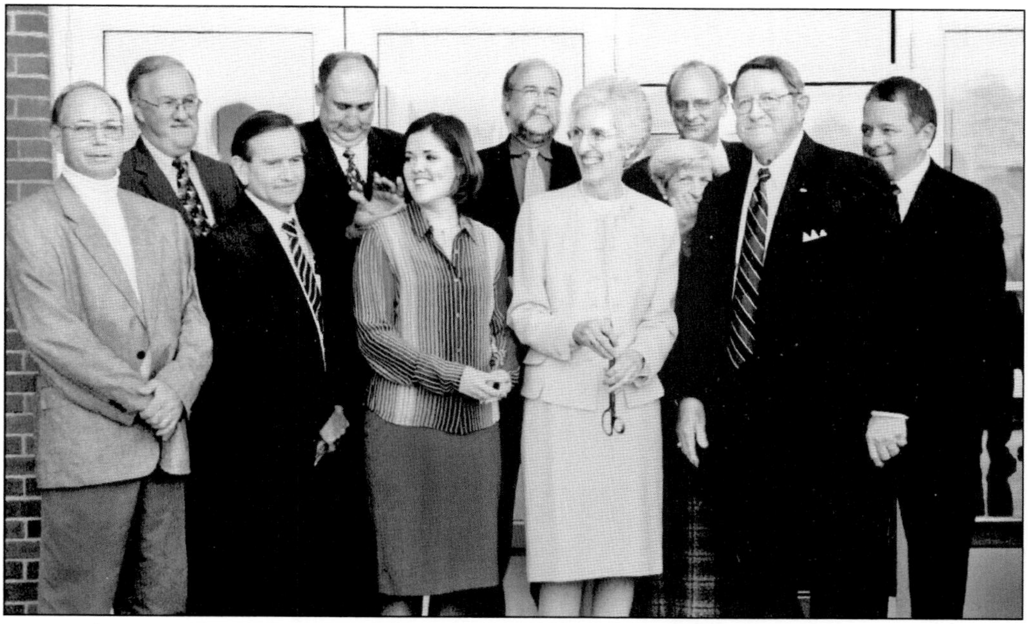

Pictured at the ribbon cutting and open house for the Hickman Building are, from left to right, (front row) Garry Sensing and Charles Fortner (both of RCR Building Corporation), SGA vice president Megan Brophy, President Hawkins, and Waymon Hickman; (back row) Richard Williams (architect), Maury County Executive Ed Harlan, Jim Thompson (architect), Mayor Barbara McIntyre, TBR chancellor Charles Manning, and former chancellor Charles Smith.

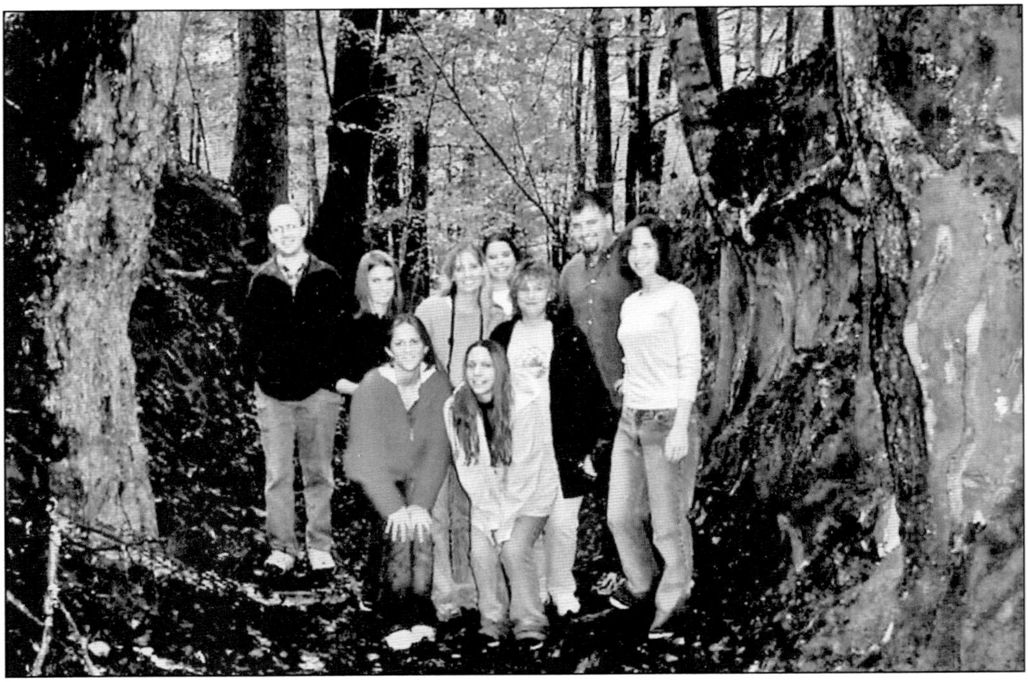

Humanities Seminar students stand in a portion of the sunken trace on the Natchez Trace Parkway in October 2003.

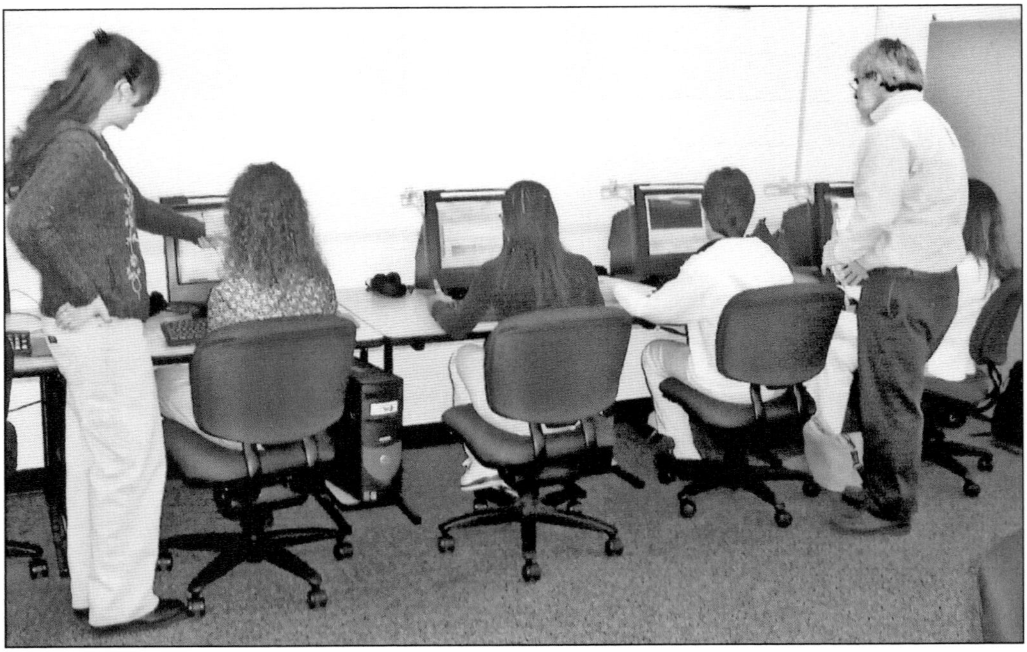

The Teaching and Learning Center (TLC) is a place where students can go for tutoring and computer-assisted instruction. Glenna Winters and Michael Goode (both standing) check on student work in the TLC. The TLC currently houses the Center of Emphasis.

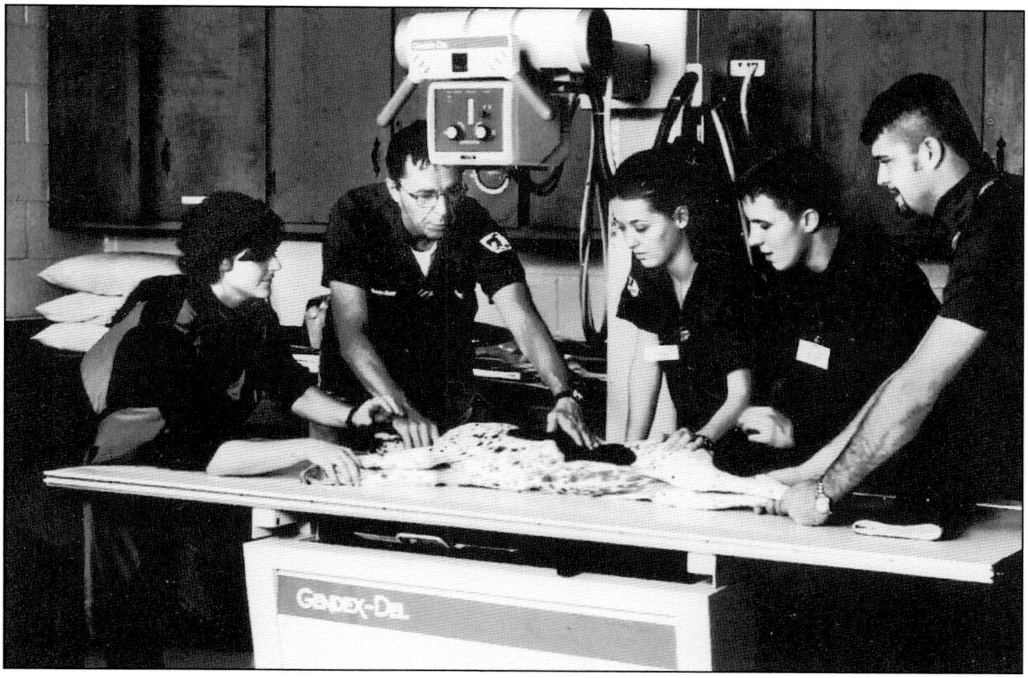

The Veterinary Technology Program began in the early 1970s and received full accreditation in 1980. It is accredited by the Committee on Veterinary Technical Education and Activities of the American Veterinary Medical Association. Dr. Boyce Wanamaker, program director, and students check the condition of Annie after surgery. Pictured from left to right are Jessica Spain, Wanamaker, Emy Heithcock, Heather Scott, and Ben Heithcock.

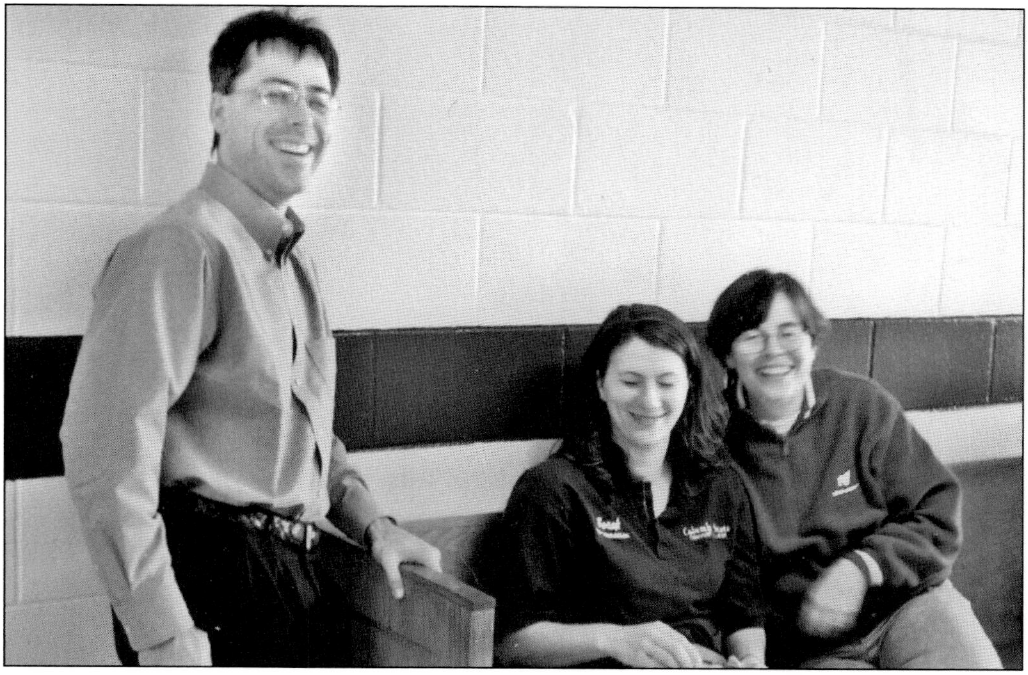

Columbia State "Poet Laureate" Jeff Hardin jokes with some of his students outside his classroom in the Clement Building.

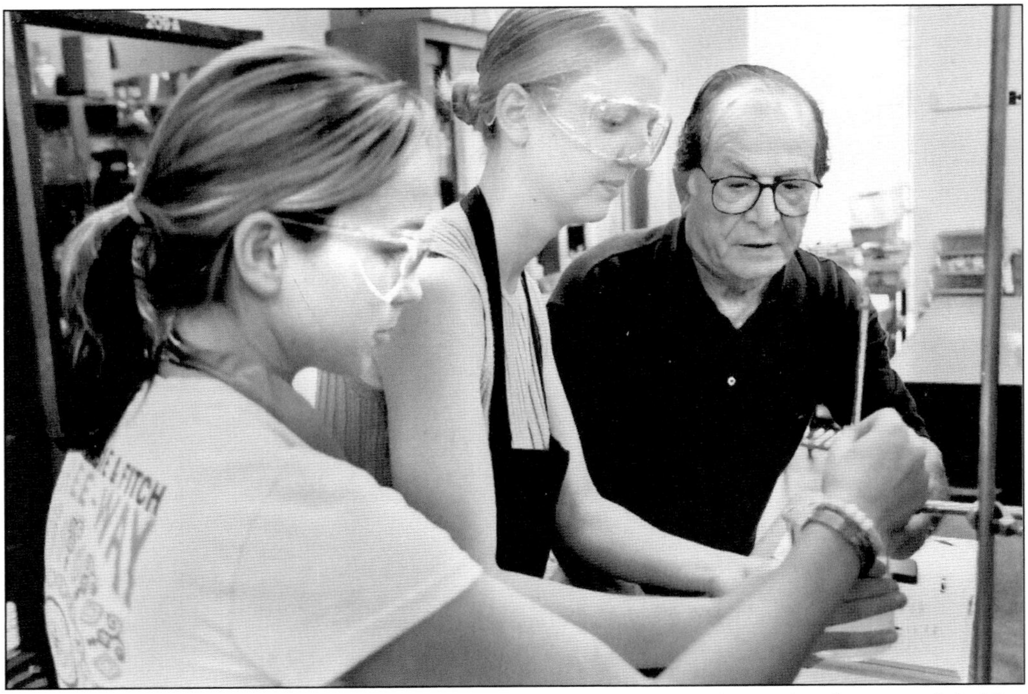

B.I. Naddy works with students Stacy Story (left) and Brianne Sides in the chemistry lab. The lab, housed in the Warf Science Building, was renovated during the summer of 2004 and named for Dr. Naddy.

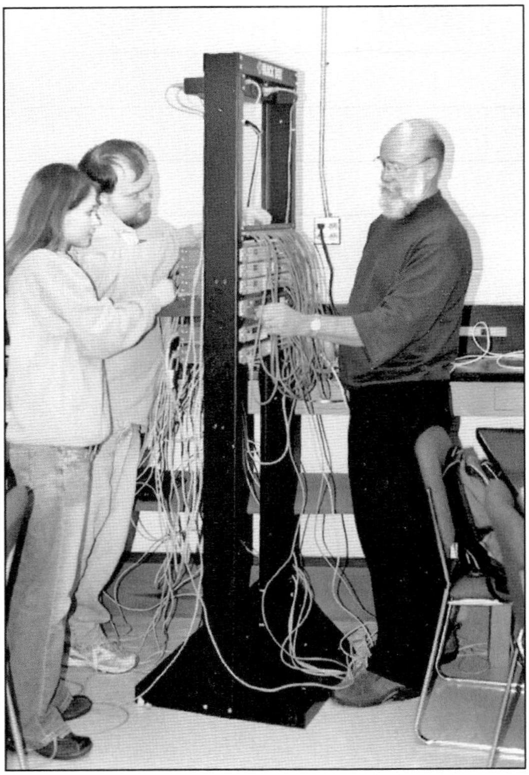

Ed Wilson (right) and students Kelly Boshers and Tony Hunter connect network hubs to PCs in the "Introduction to Networking" class.

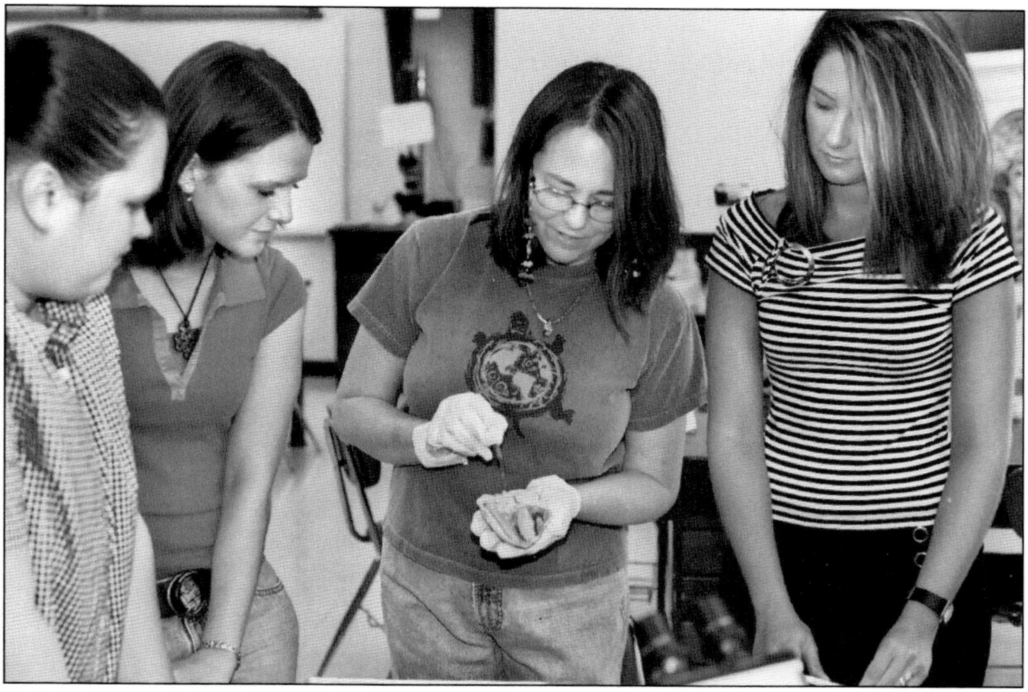

Karen Kendall-Fite points out the sections of a sheep heart to students in anatomy and physiology. From left to right are Denise Brashears, Arlene Abels, Kendall-Fite, and Dana Roberts.

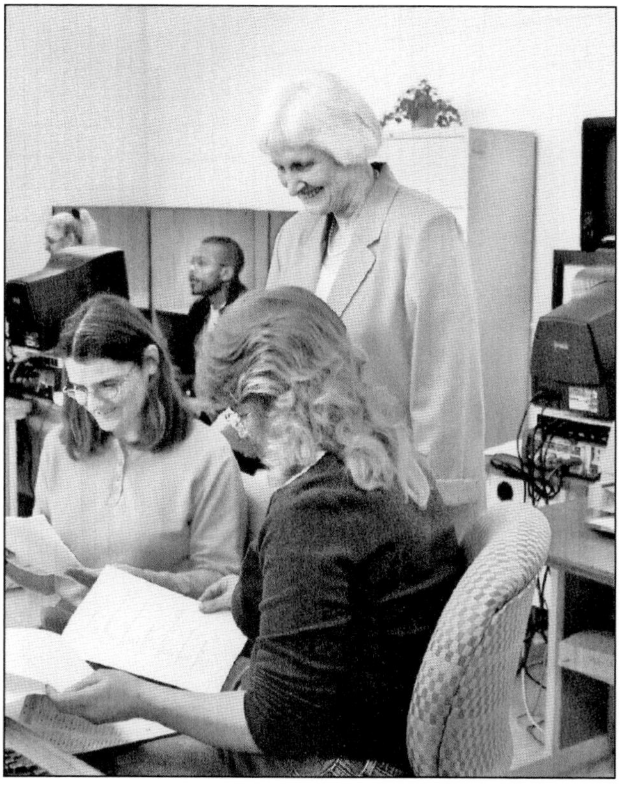

The World of Work is a self-paced, non-traditional lab environment that allows students flexibility in their scheduling of classes. Margaret Pickel (standing), of the office administration department, helps Teresa Haislip (left) and July Davidson.

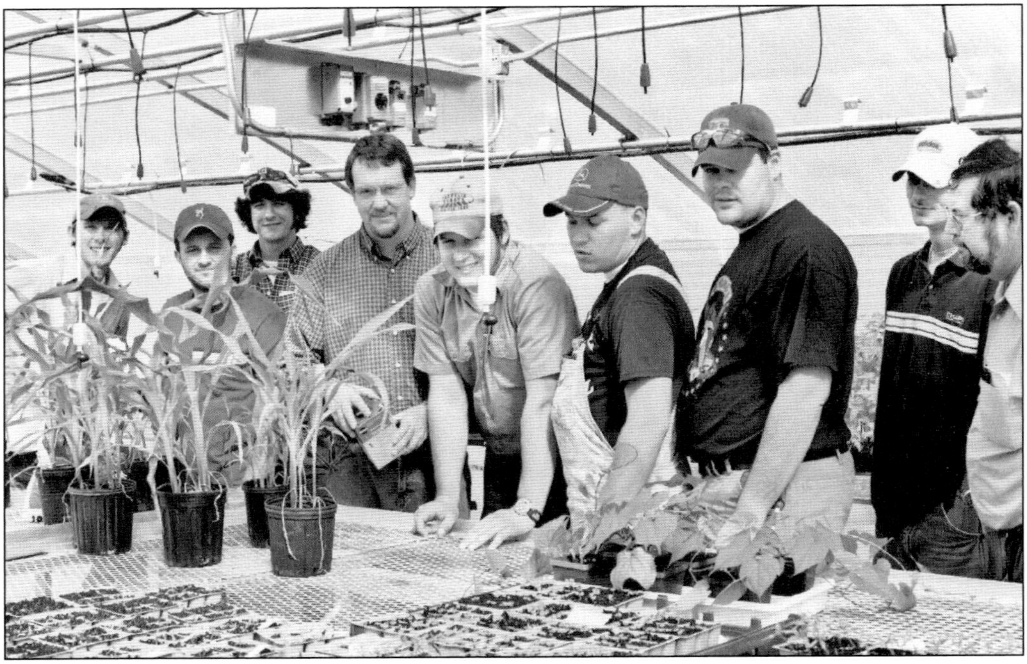

Columbia State built its first greenhouse in the 1970s. A new major in horticultural technology, with emphases in landscape management and turf grass management, was begun in 2003. Dearl Lampley works with students in the new greenhouse, completed in 2004. From left to right are Tyler Brewer, Nick Eledge, Brian Tucker, Lampley, Seth Hall, Matthew Griffith, Kyle Bratton, Dustin Williams, and adjunct Wayne Jackson.

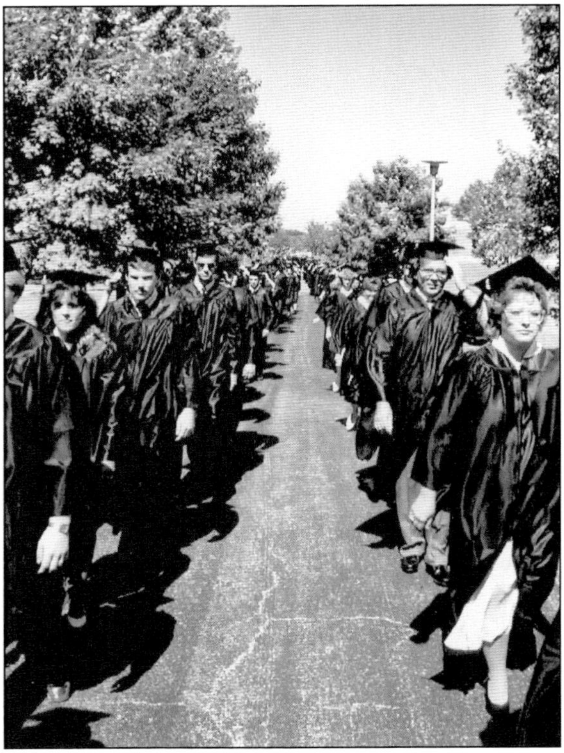

Each year, sophomores make the welcome trek to the gymnasium for graduation.

Three

College Activities

A myriad of activities have enhanced the lives of Columbia State students and the population of the area that the college serves. These activities bring students and community together in fun and fellowship with the result of increased learning and understanding.

Student government, career-oriented, faith-based, and alumni relations are the types of the most active organizations. Eating, singing, and dancing events are particularly enjoyable. Other activities have included subject-matter contests for students in the college's service area, involvement in state and national celebrations, public service projects, fund-raising activities, and student newspapers.

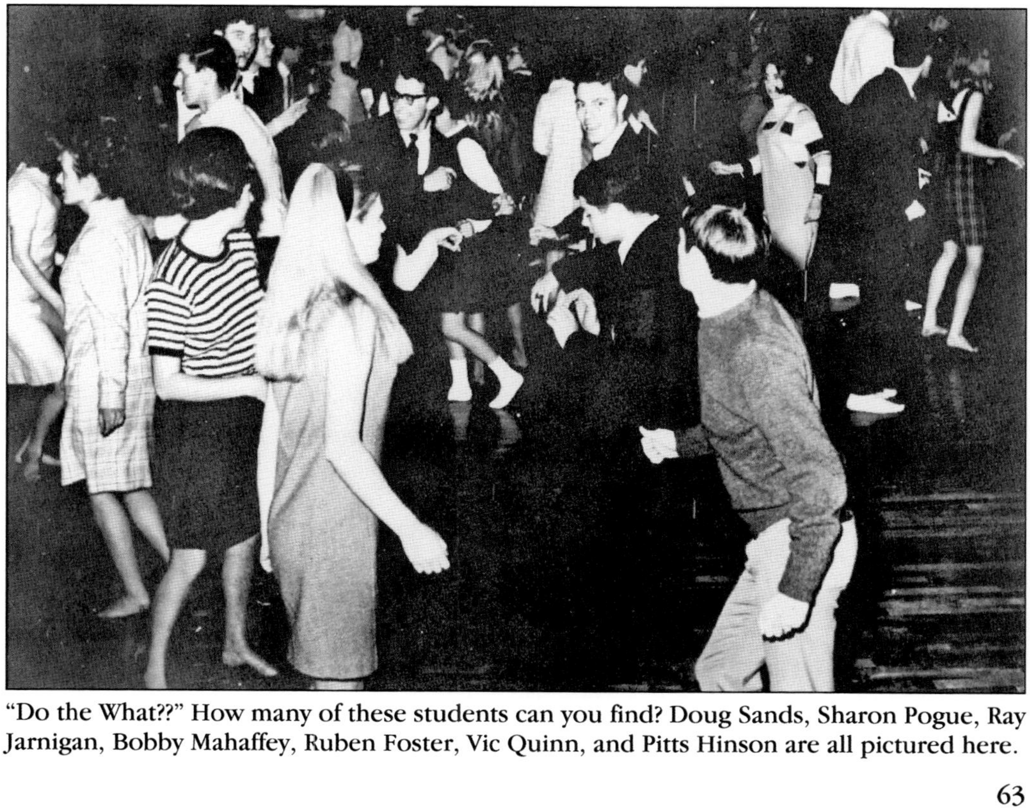

"Do the What??" How many of these students can you find? Doug Sands, Sharon Pogue, Ray Jarnigan, Bobby Mahaffey, Ruben Foster, Vic Quinn, and Pitts Hinson are all pictured here.

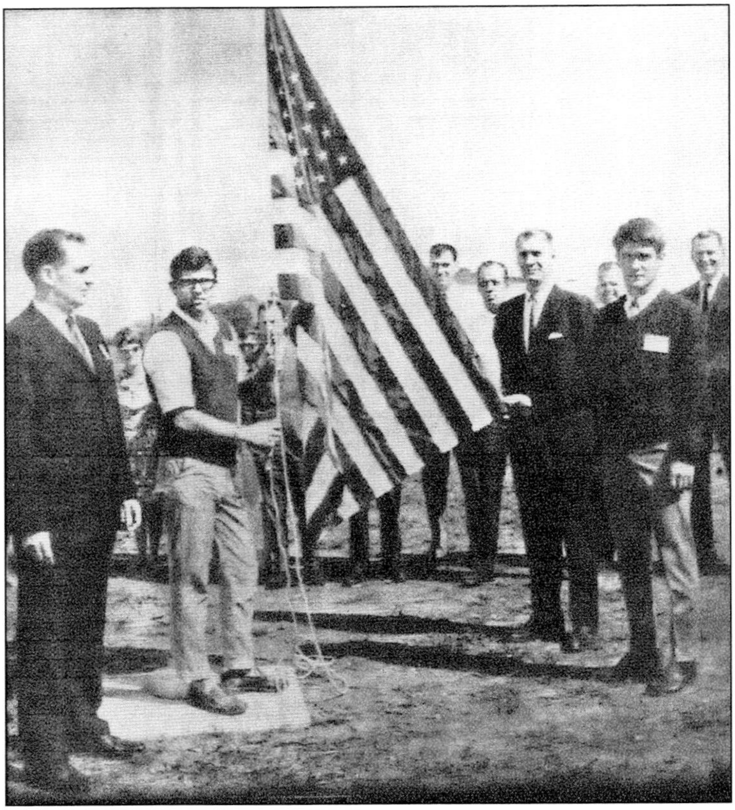

The college's first flag was presented in a ceremony in September 1967 by Sam Kennedy on behalf of Roscoe Curtiss and Herbert Griffin Post 19 of the American Legion. From left to right in the foreground are Dr. James Clark, who accepted the flag; Roger Demastus, president of the Ambassador Club; Kennedy; and Ray Jernigan, president of the student body.

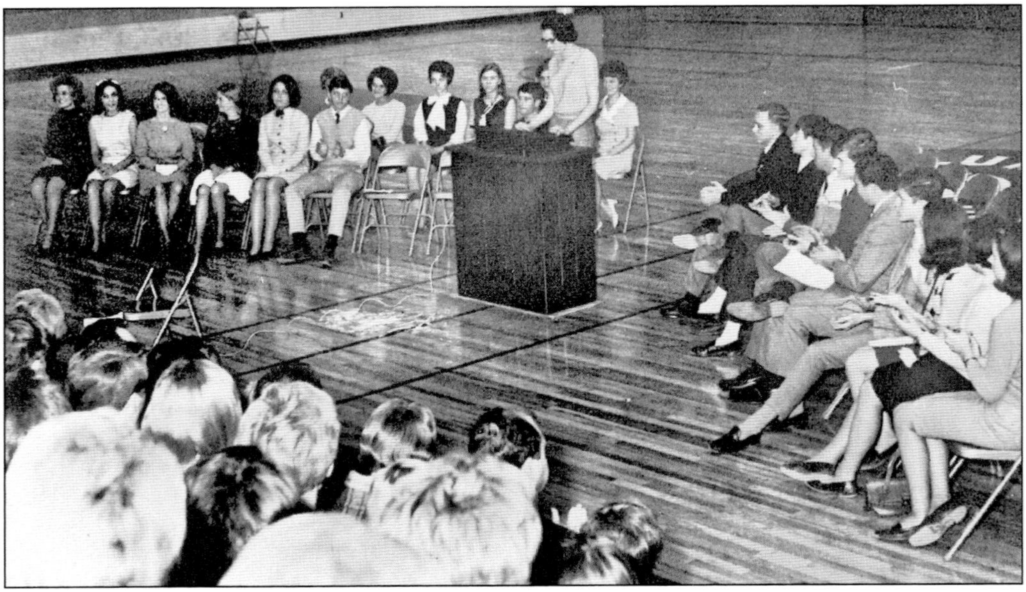

The first official assembly on the new campus was held at 11 a.m. on January 25, 1968. Martha Woody introduced the homecoming candidates and senate nominees to the student body.

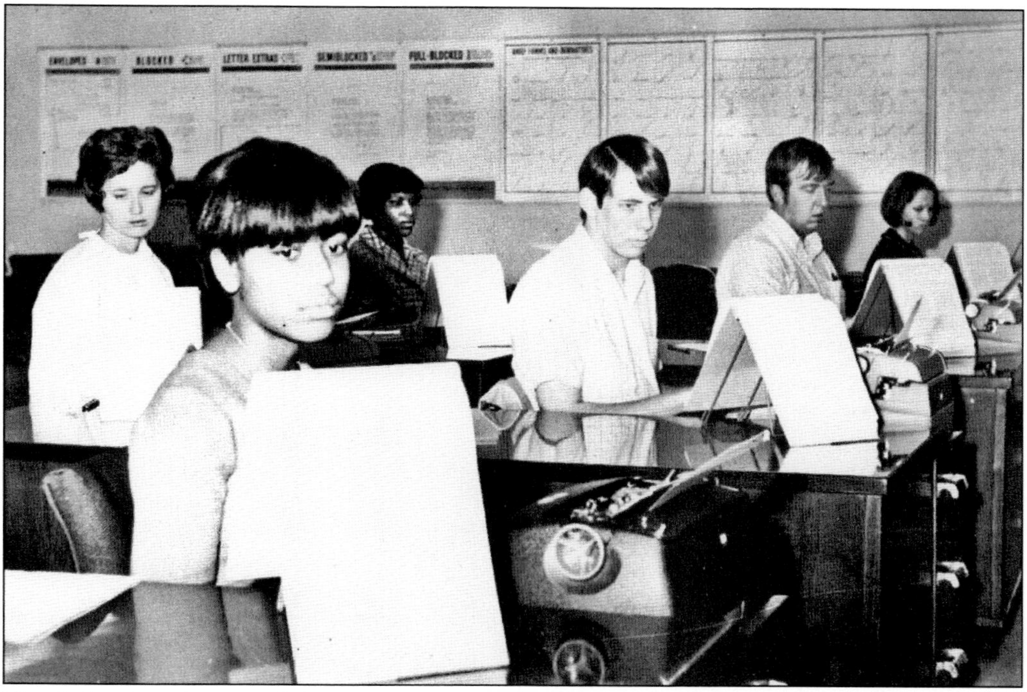

The Columbia chapter of the Future Secretaries of America was initiated in 1966 under the leadership of Ava Eaton. Its purpose was to acquaint members with the challenges that they would face in future careers. Pictured is a typing class from 1968–1969.

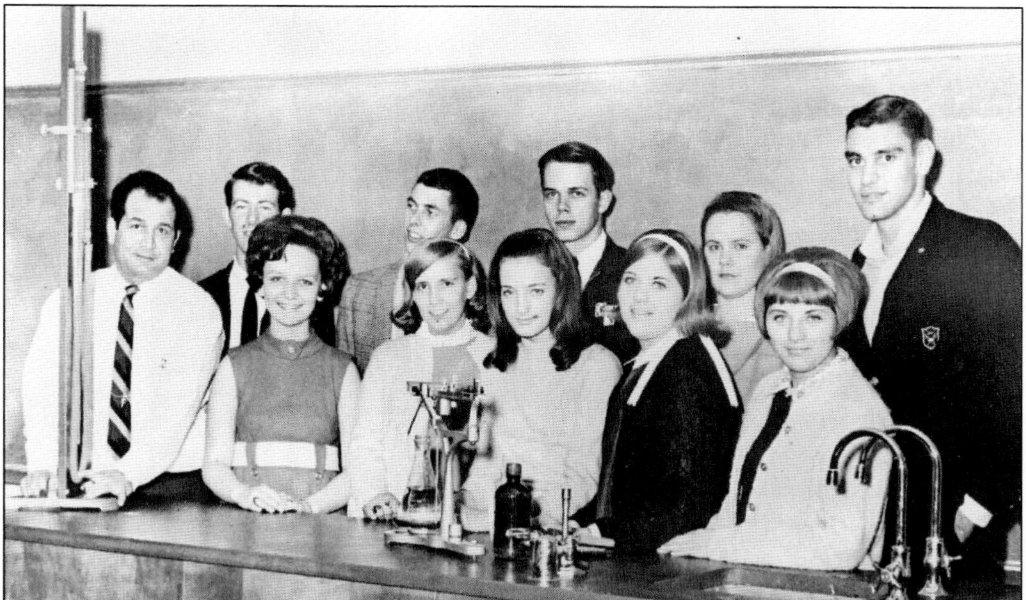

The science club was one of the earliest clubs organized on campus. The club sponsor was B.I. Naddy (far left). Club officers were Billy Chappell, president; Sarah Henry, vice president; Gail Norman, secretary; and James Gardner, treasurer.

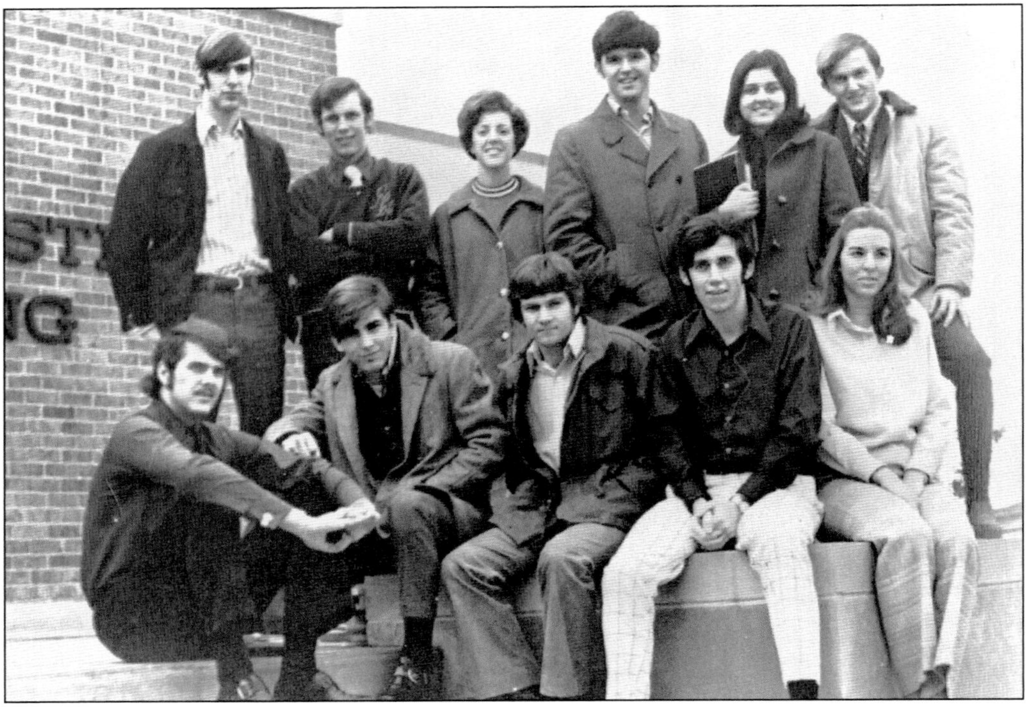

Student Government Association members are pictured here in 1971. The SGA works to coordinate activities of the student body and conduct campus elections. From left to right are (front row) Bob Willoughby, Bob Richards, Dwight McGee, Fred Rhodes, and Lynn Daimwood; (back row) Mike Dillingham, David Burgess, Vicki Crunk, Bill Sharp, Brenda Collie, and Jerry Willis.

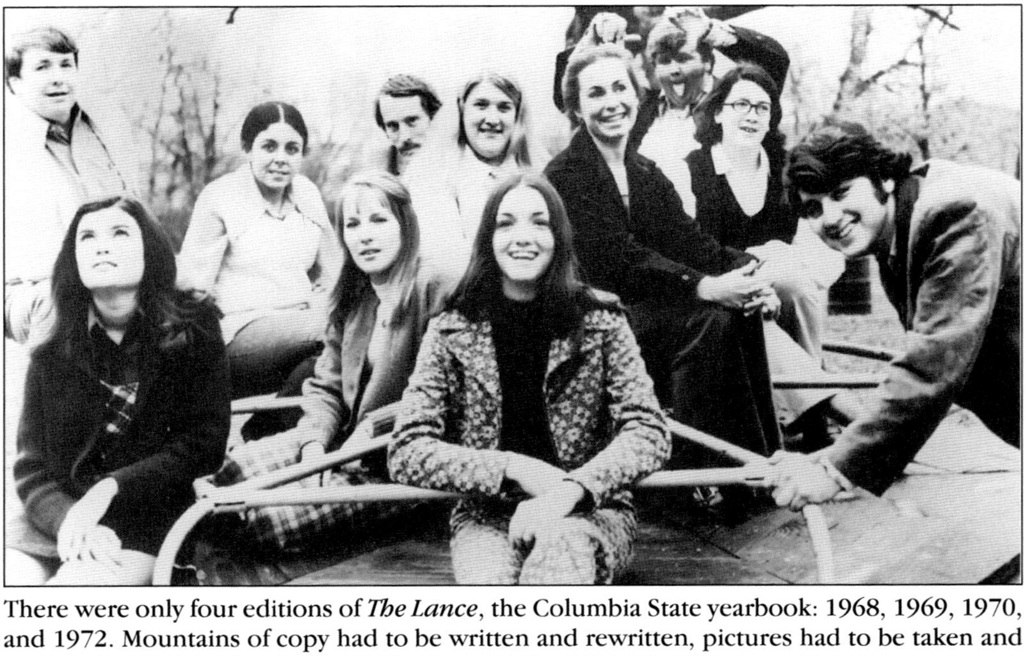

There were only four editions of *The Lance*, the Columbia State yearbook: 1968, 1969, 1970, and 1972. Mountains of copy had to be written and rewritten, pictures had to be taken and retaken, and ads had to be sold. Members of the 1971–1972 *Lance* staff enjoy some much deserved recreation.

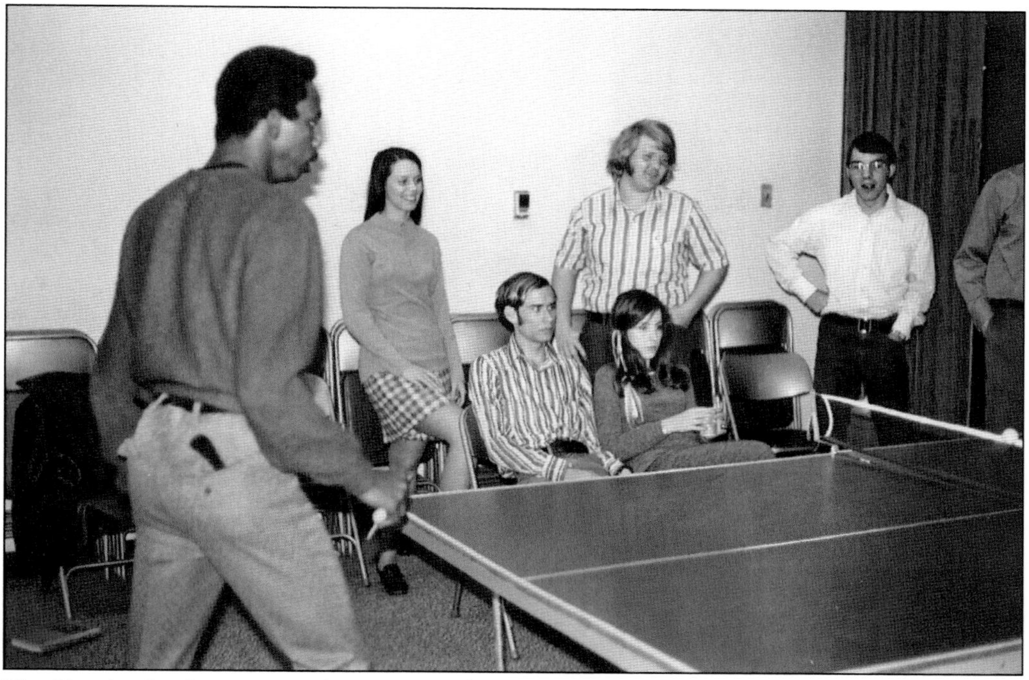

The Baptist Student Union began in 1968 as an organization to serve as a link between local Baptist churches and students. A BSU building was built across the highway from the campus. Ladies from various Baptist churches in the area provided lunches for students and staff. The BSU was open for devotional periods, study, television, and various games.

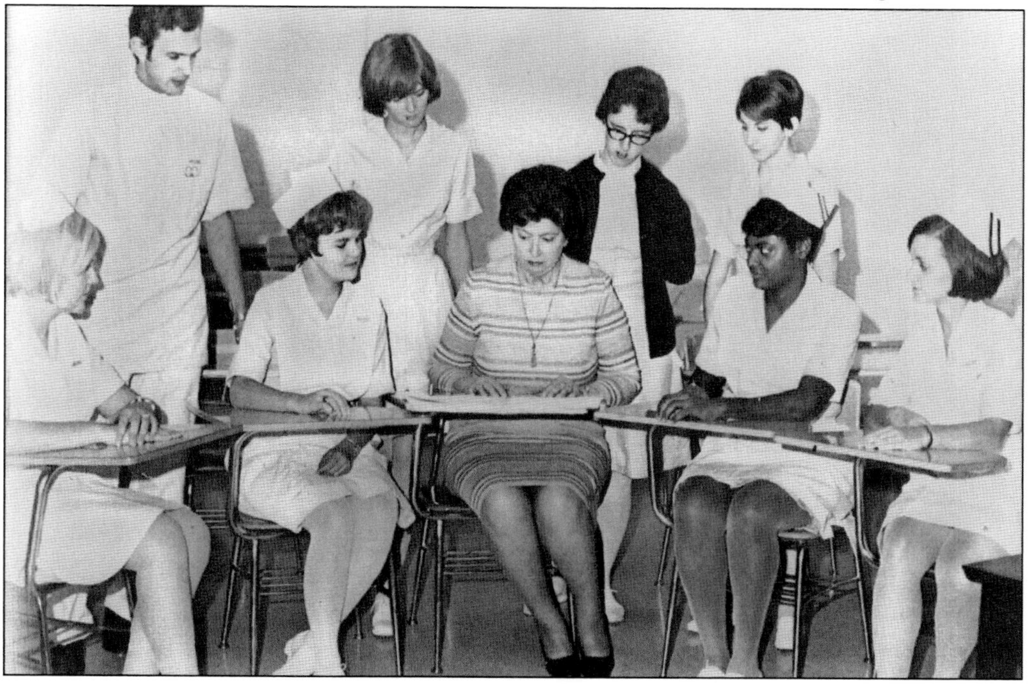

Pictured here are members of the Student Nurses Association in 1971. Seated in the center is Dorothy Powell, sponsor and director of nursing. During the year, delegates from Columbia State attended the national and state SNA conventions.

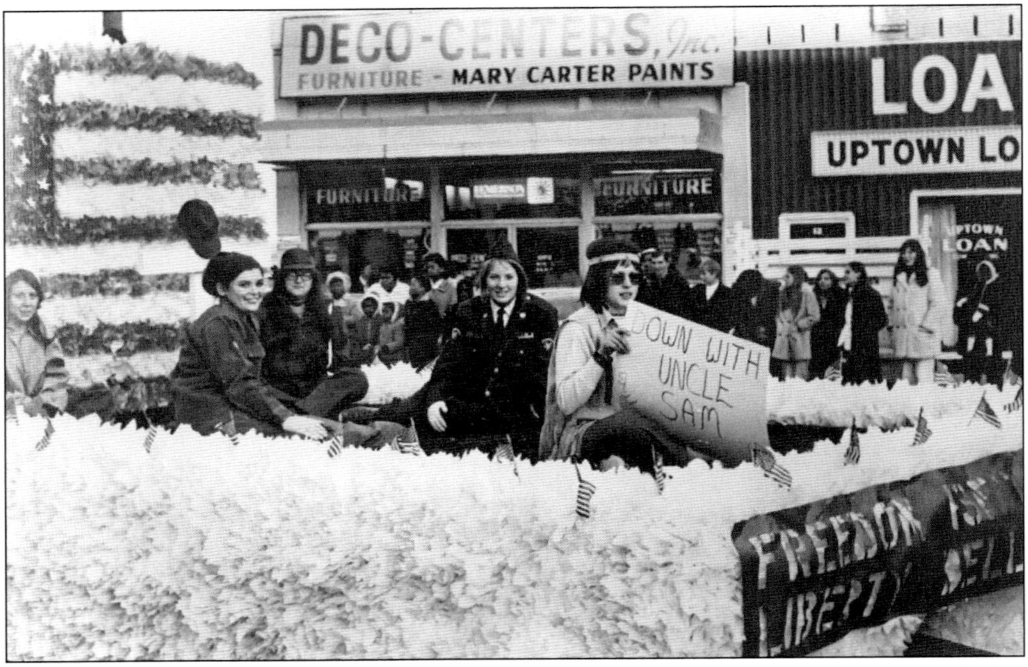

Columbia State's first sorority was started during 1970. The Liberty Belles' projects included the March of Dimes, UNICEF, and cerebral palsy. The Liberty Belles' float in the 1970 Columbia Christmas parade depicted the various sentiments of the time.

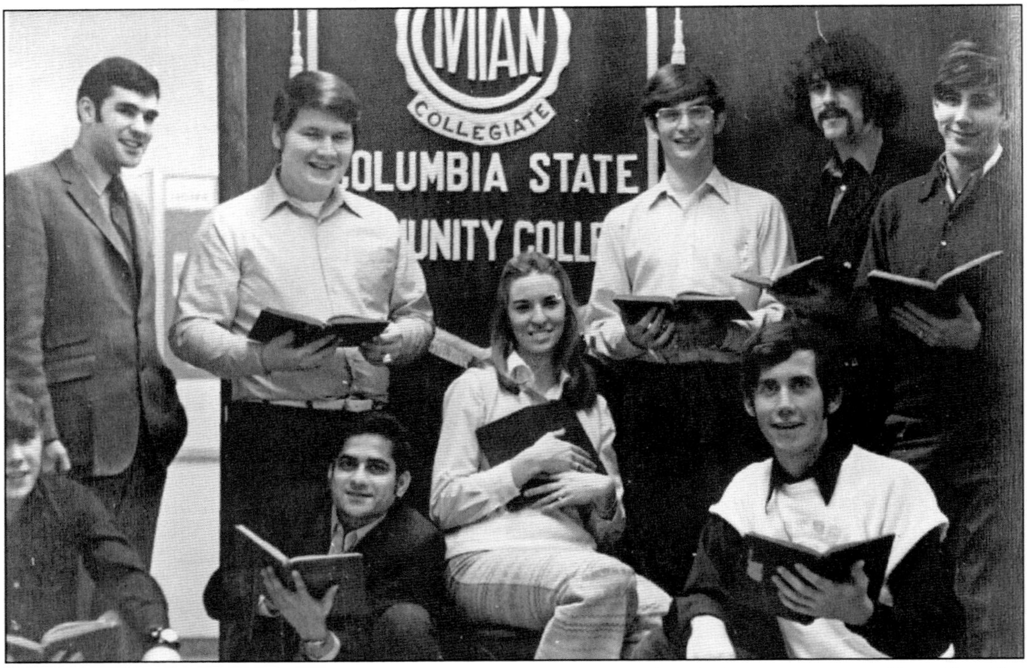

The Collegiate Civitan Club was organized during 1970. The club's motto was "Sacrifice for Civitan." Activities were scheduled with concern for ecology and patriotism. Pictured from left to right are Joe Wiley, Mike Kesler (faculty sponsor), David Boehms, Ram Gadre, Lynn Daimwood (sweetheart), Pat Moredock, Fred Rhodes (president), David Lovett, and Steve Richards (vice president).

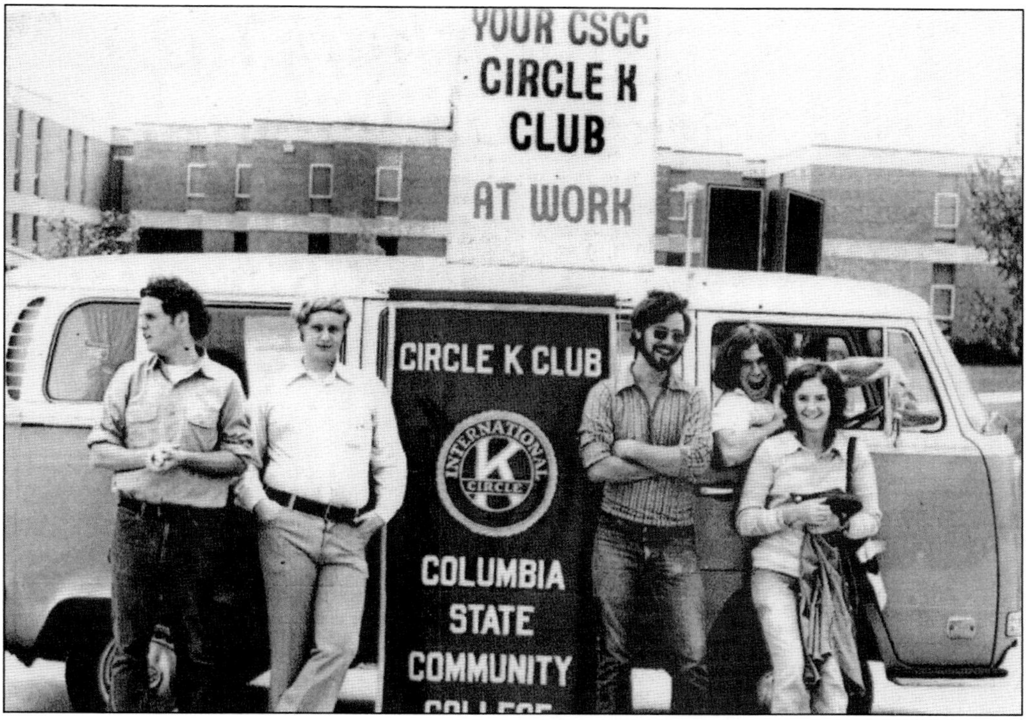

The Columbia State Circle K Club was organized in 1970. The club participated in UNICEF drives, organized Americanism Week, and donated blood to the Red Cross. Students often recruited for their clubs on registration day.

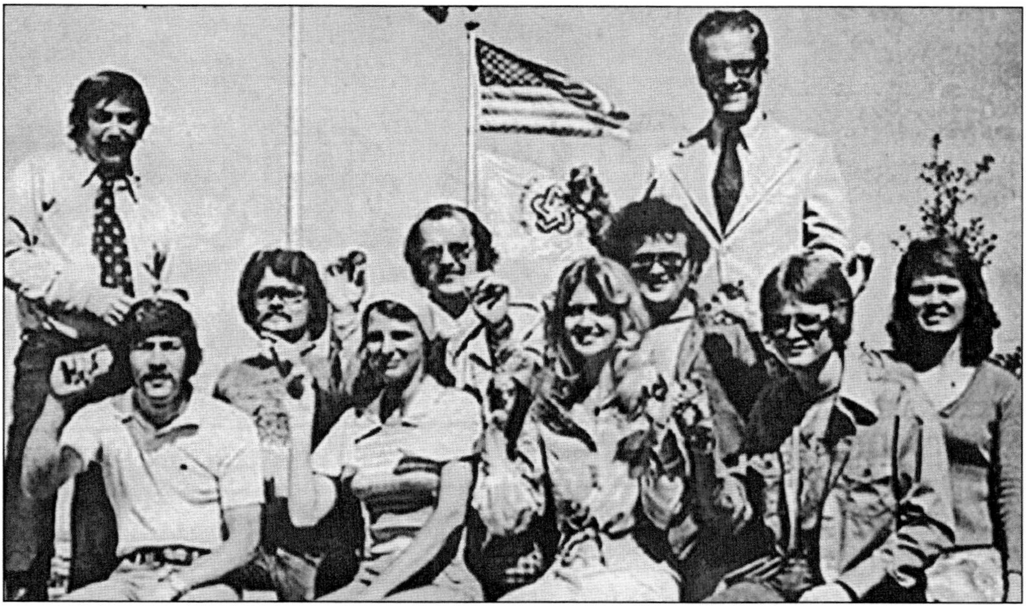

Phi Beta Lambda was organized in 1971 as a service organization. In 1976, Phi Beta Lambda minted a coin to commemorate the nation's bicentennial and the 10th anniversary of the college. Pictured from left to right are (front row) Tommy Burgess, Teresa Brewer, Karen Jenkins, and Joe Sparkman; (back row) Danny Sisk, Walter Crick, Pat Smith, and Carol Roberts. Standing are club sponsors Tom Friedlob (left) and W.B. Williams.

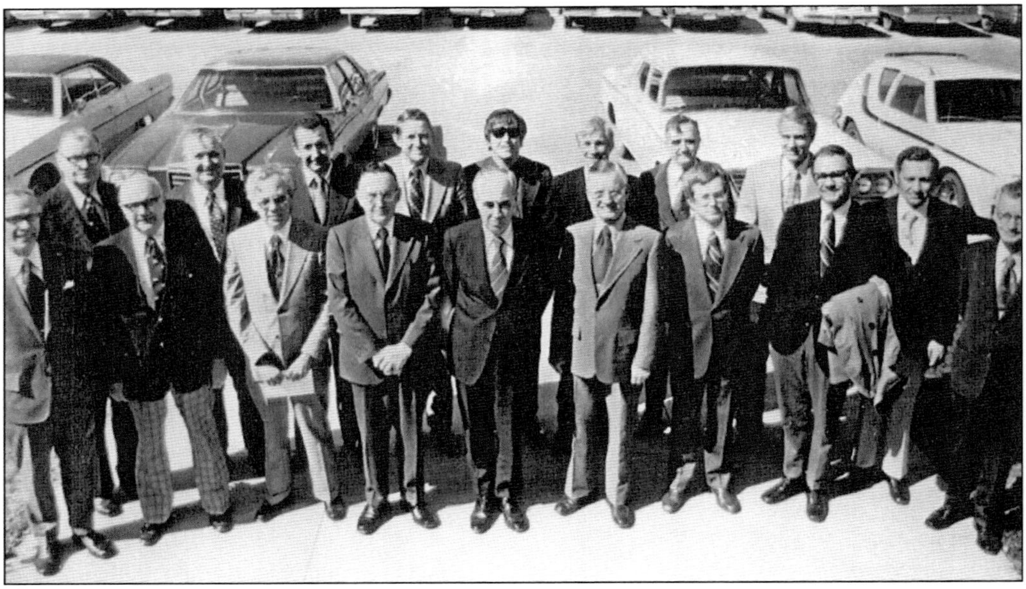

The first Columbia State Foundation Board of Trustees was organized in 1971. The 1974–1975 board is pictured here. From left to right are (front row) J.B. Walker, Wally Beasley, Robin Courtney, President Pryor, Lon McFarland, Edward M. Lindsey, Judge Jerry Scott, James H. Jones Jr., and Burke Holman; (back row) Tom Hitch, Dr. M.H. Weathers, Harlan Bowsher, Waymon Hickman, Terrence Cooksey, Sam Kennedy, Dr. U.M. Clemmer, and Dean Paul Sands. Emma Porter Armstrong, Randolph Howell, J. Howard Warf, and George Martin are not pictured.

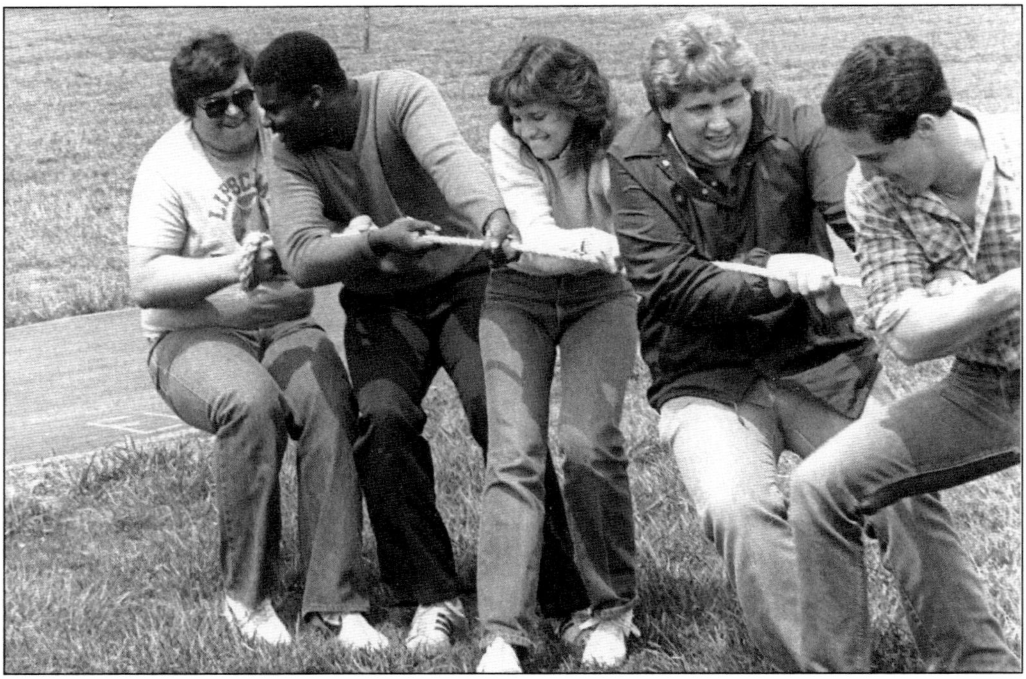

During the 1970s and 1980s, Octoberfest was a popular student activity. Car-bashing, egg-tossing, good food, bonfires, and dancing were all part of the 1985 Octoberfest. Participating in a tug-of-war are Amy Holcomb (center) and friends.

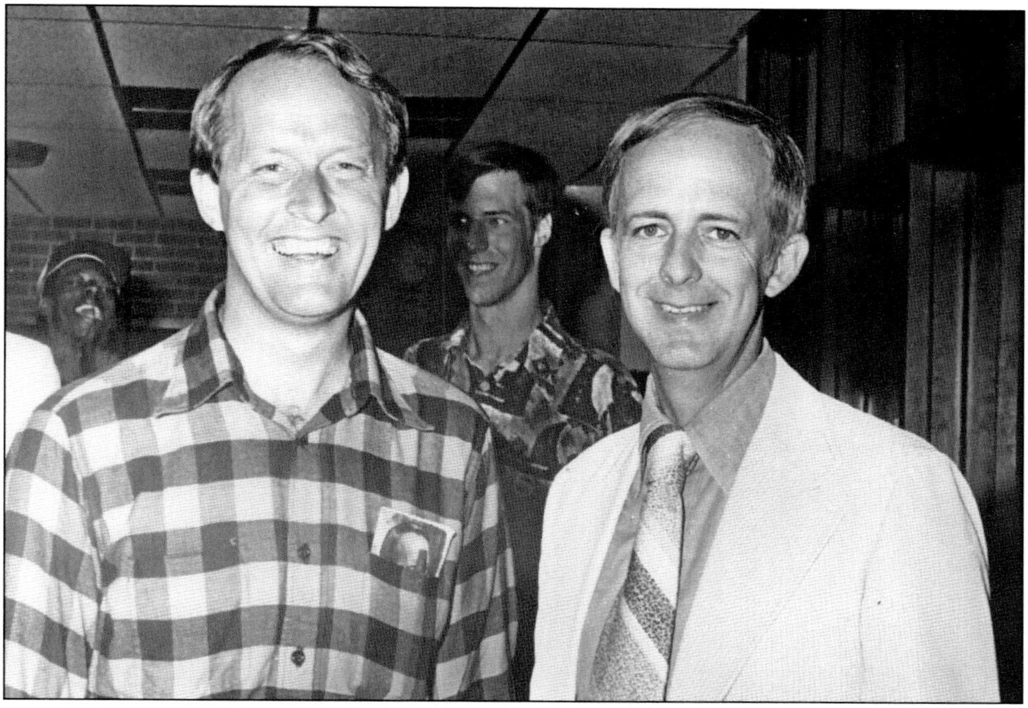

Lamar Alexander, candidate for governor, dropped by the campus one Friday afternoon while walking across Tennessee. He is pictured here with Dean of Students Jerry Battles. The student in the center is Tom Jones, who was later an Alumnus of the Year selection.

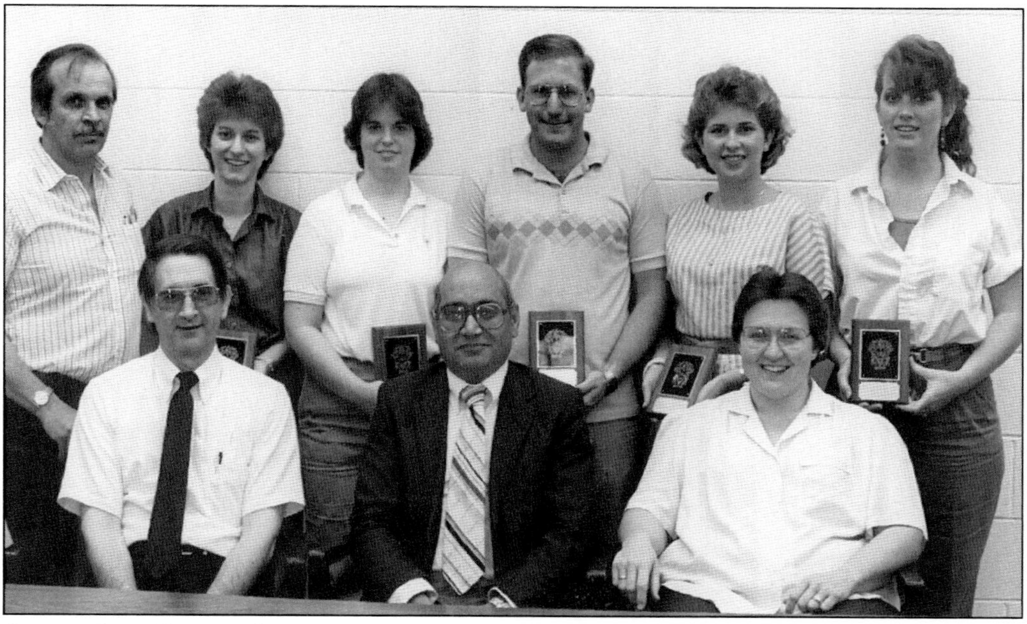

Gamma Beta Phi president Larry Lawson presents the Peer Counselors with an appreciation plaque in 1985. From left to right are (front row) director of counseling Jack Forsythe, Gamma Beta Phi advisor Chaitram Talele, and peer counselor coordinator Karen Siska; (back row) Larry Lawson, Amy Rochelle, Tricia Holt, Ron Whitman, Lisa Stooksberry, and Rhonda Bryant.

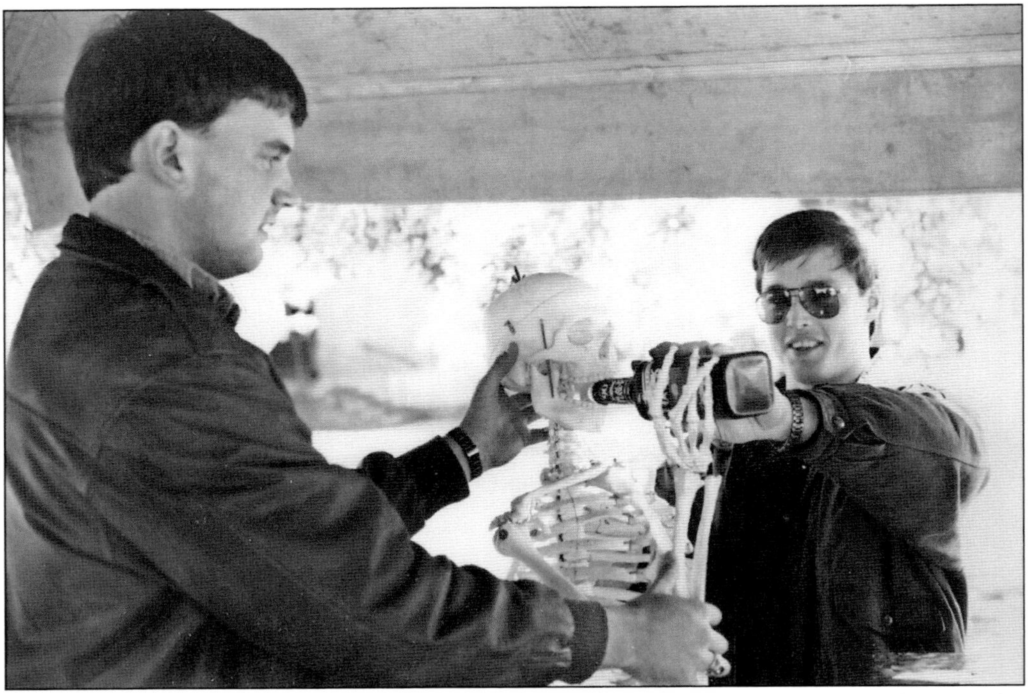

Activities on campus during Alcohol Awareness Week were aimed at alerting students to the dangers of drinking and driving. The "person" in the middle is "Fred."

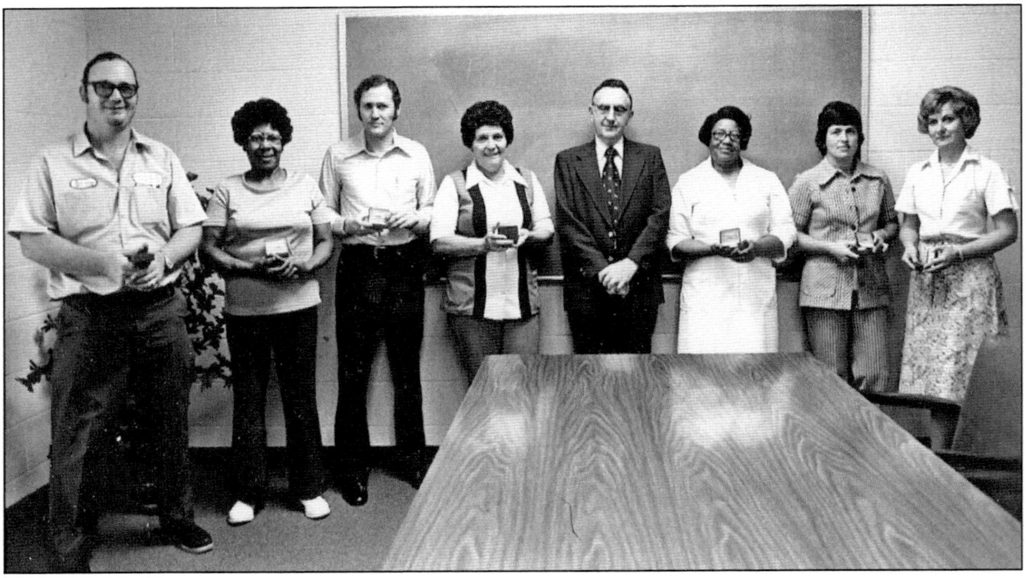

Staff Award recipients, pictured from left to right with Dr. Pryor, are Jimmy Shouse, Johnnie Thompson, Larry Johnson, Dot Sanders, Pryor, Annie Jordan, Barbara Rummage, and Naomi Harris. It has become a tradition to present awards to the outstanding support and professional staff person each year.

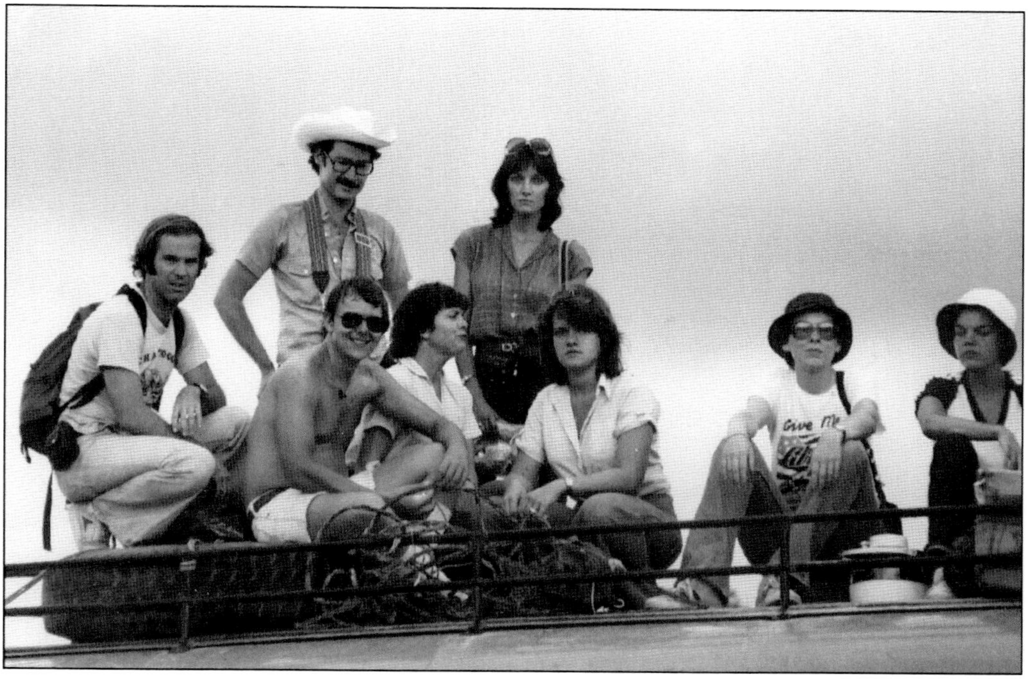

Bill Andrews, of the history department, and students are atop a bus in Guatemala on the road to Tikal in 1979.

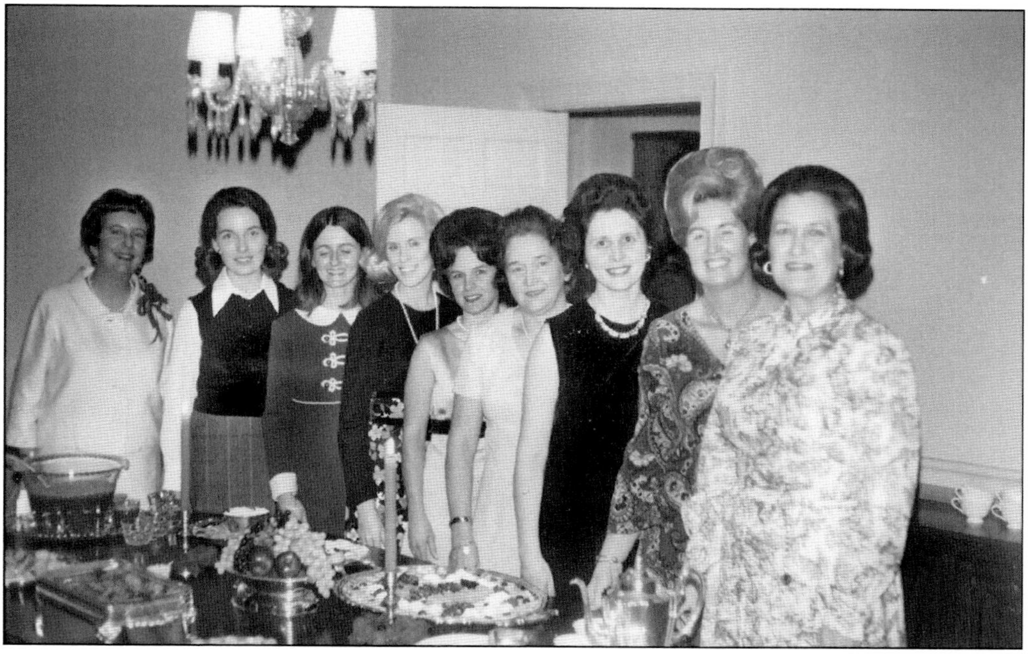

The Columbia State Women's Club was first organized as the Columbia State Wives' Club soon after the college opened. The club awarded an annual scholarship to a female student. The organization hosted the annual Christmas Party at the president's home. Pictured from left to right at one those parties are Pat Hampton, Julie Bragg, Judy Flagg, unidentified, Laurel Dugger, Virginia Clemmer, Ginny Watson, Ava Eaton, and LaRue Pryor.

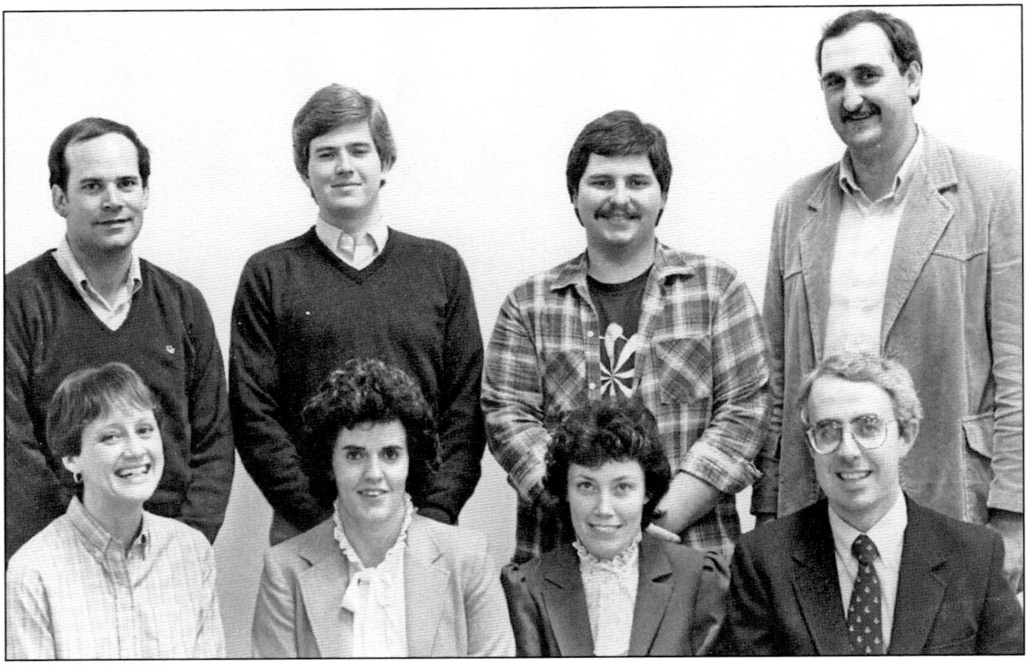

The first meeting of the Columbia State Alumni Association was in 1982. From left to right are (front row) Charlotte Henson, Linda Moore, Sara Fralix, and Pitts Hinson; (back row) Mike Ketchum, Mike Flynt, Bryant Williams, and Ed Harlan. Not pictured were Phil Comstock, Christa Martin, Mike Kenny, and Bonnie Moore.

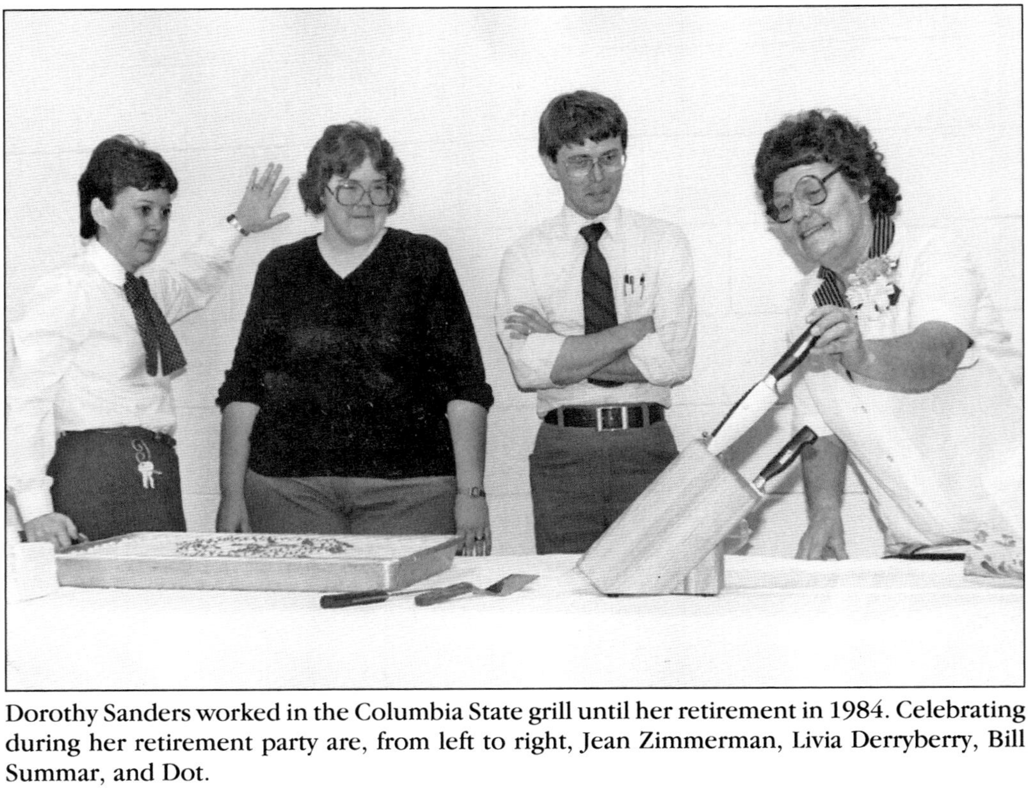

Dorothy Sanders worked in the Columbia State grill until her retirement in 1984. Celebrating during her retirement party are, from left to right, Jean Zimmerman, Livia Derryberry, Bill Summar, and Dot.

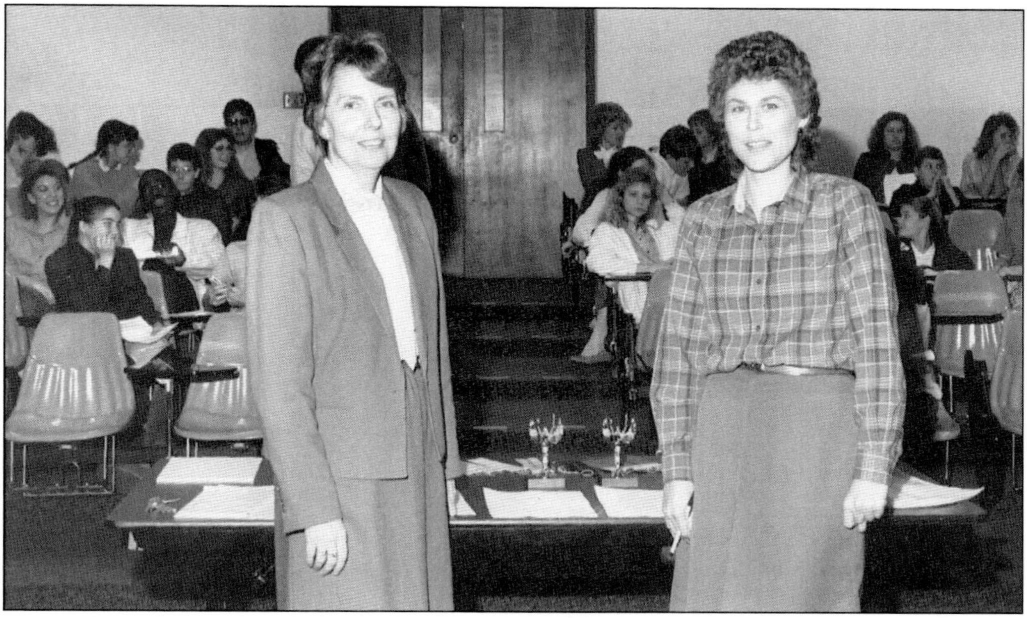

Each year since 1985, the mathematics department has hosted a math contest. This contest began as the Maury County Single A Schools Math Contest and later became the Maury County Small Schools Math Contest. Carolyn Allred-Winnett (left) and Susan Williford were the coordinators of the contest. Columbia State also hosts annual high school competitions in humanities and social sciences.

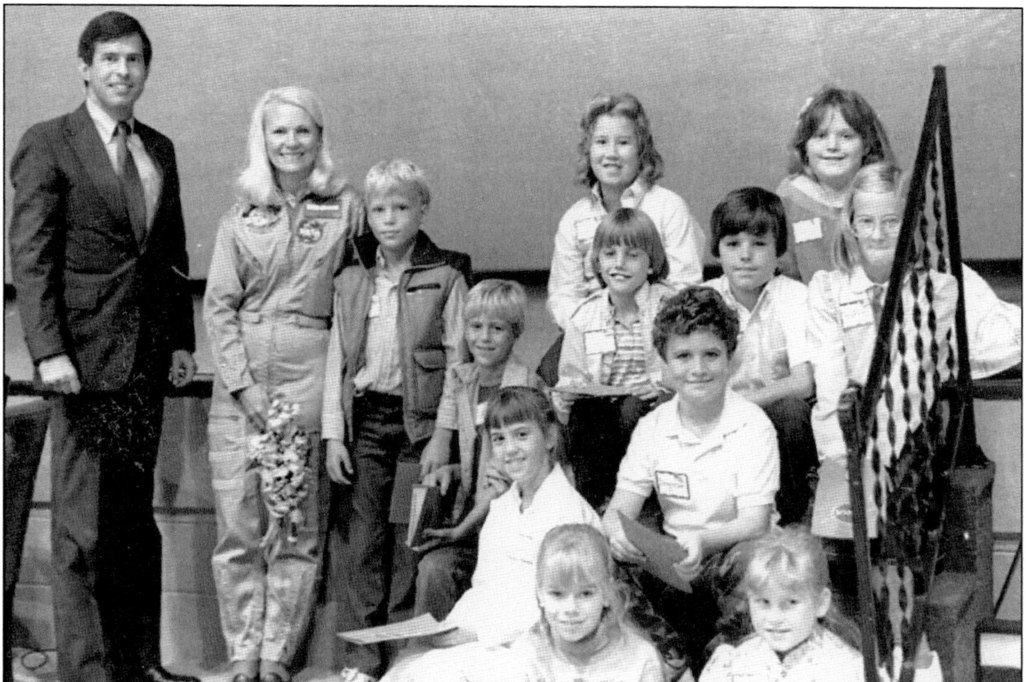

Astronaut Rhea Sedden, a native Tennessean, spoke to the Columbia State student body at an assembly in 1985. Sedden is pictured here with Congressman Bart Gordon and a group of elementary students who also attended.

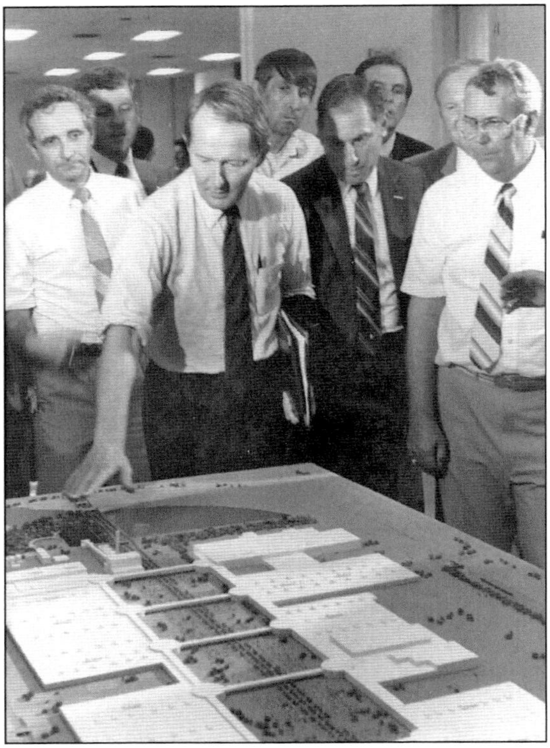

Gov. Lamar Alexander looks over a model of the Saturn complex in 1985 while community leaders look on.

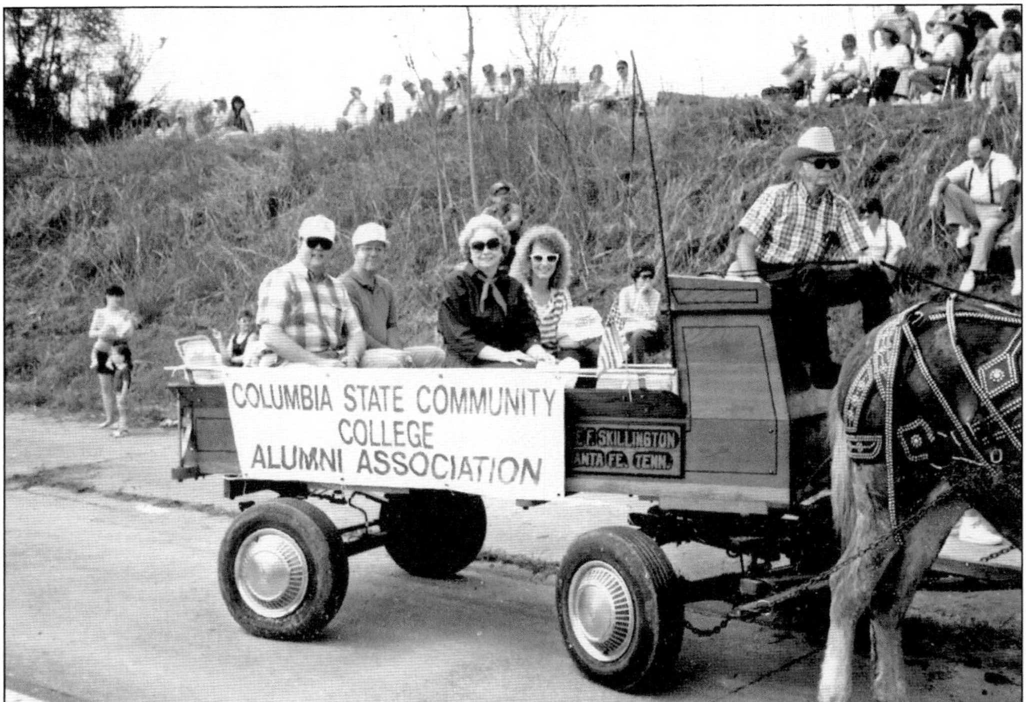

Each year, the Mule Day Parade is enjoyed by persons traveling to Columbia from "all over." Charles Sanders, Jimmy Gardner, Peggy Skillington, Charlotte Martin, and Joe Frank Skillington enjoy a great Mule Day Parade with Joe Frank's wagon and team.

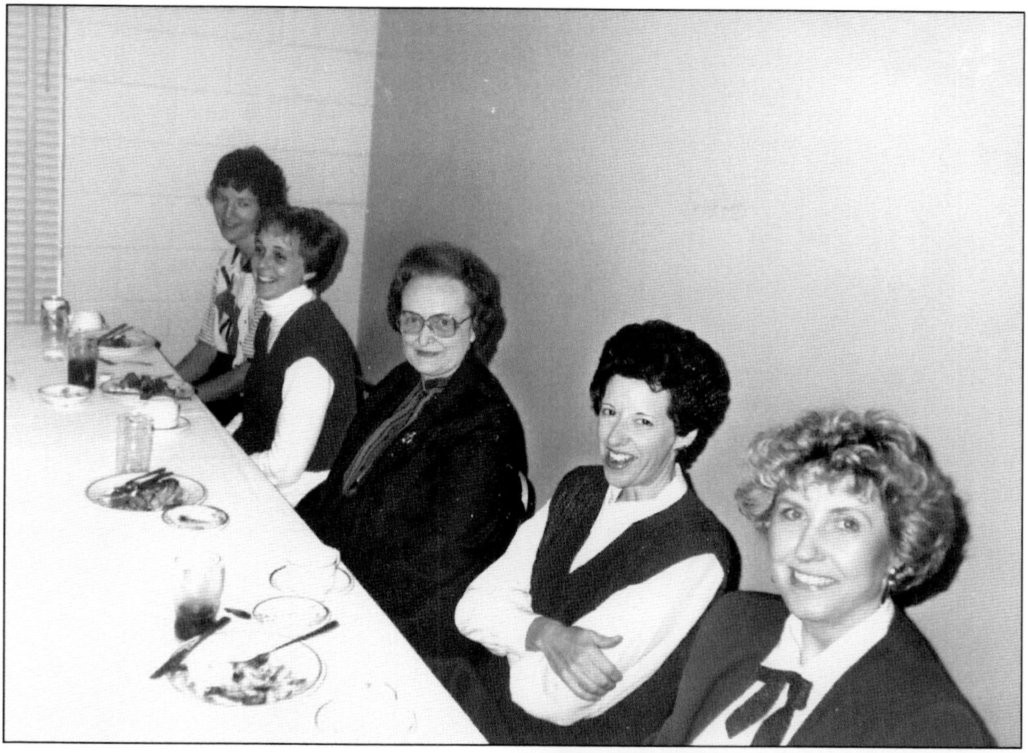

Gamma Beta Phi has hosted many annual staff appreciation luncheons. Enjoying one of these "special treats" are, from left to right, Ellen Meade, Judy Redden-King, Margaret Bain, Ann Tidwell, and Betty Drumwright.

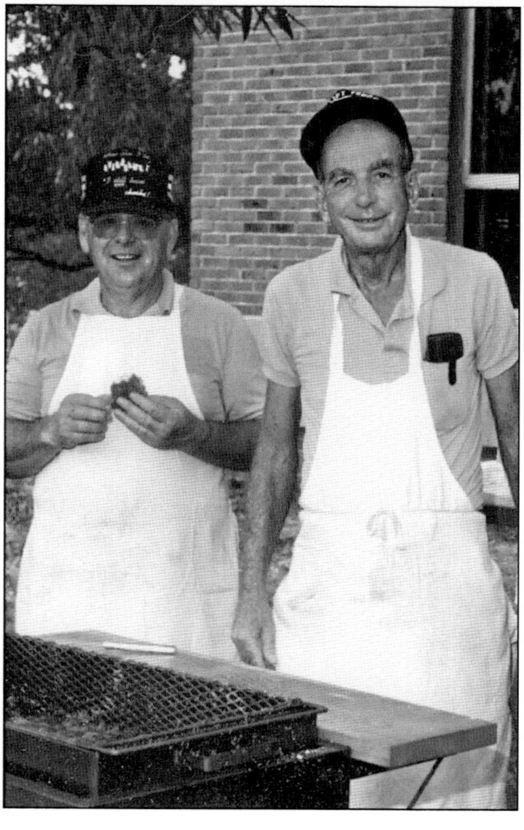

For many years, the campus fish fry was a much anticipated event that occurred during faculty in-service in the fall. Faculty and staff awards were given after the luncheon. Two of the chefs, also buildings and grounds personnel, who prepared the delicious food were Austin Floyd (left) and Charlie Norman.

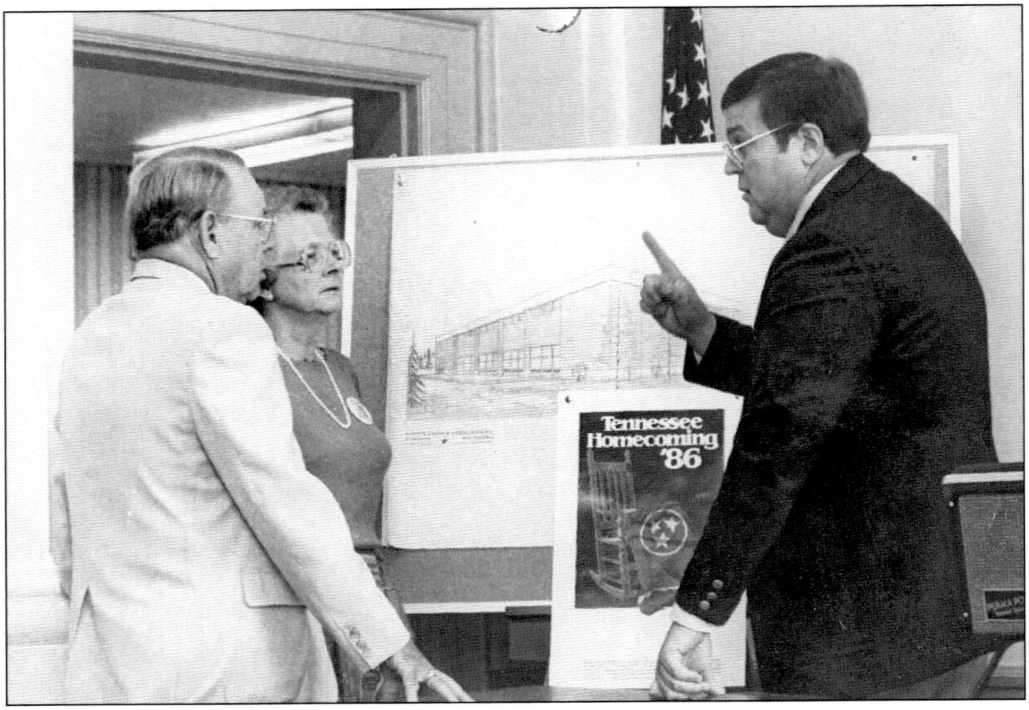

Charles Sanders (right) discusses plans for Tennessee Homecoming '86 with county co-chairs Frank and Dot Sowell. Columbia State was designated an "official Tennessee Homecoming '86 campus."

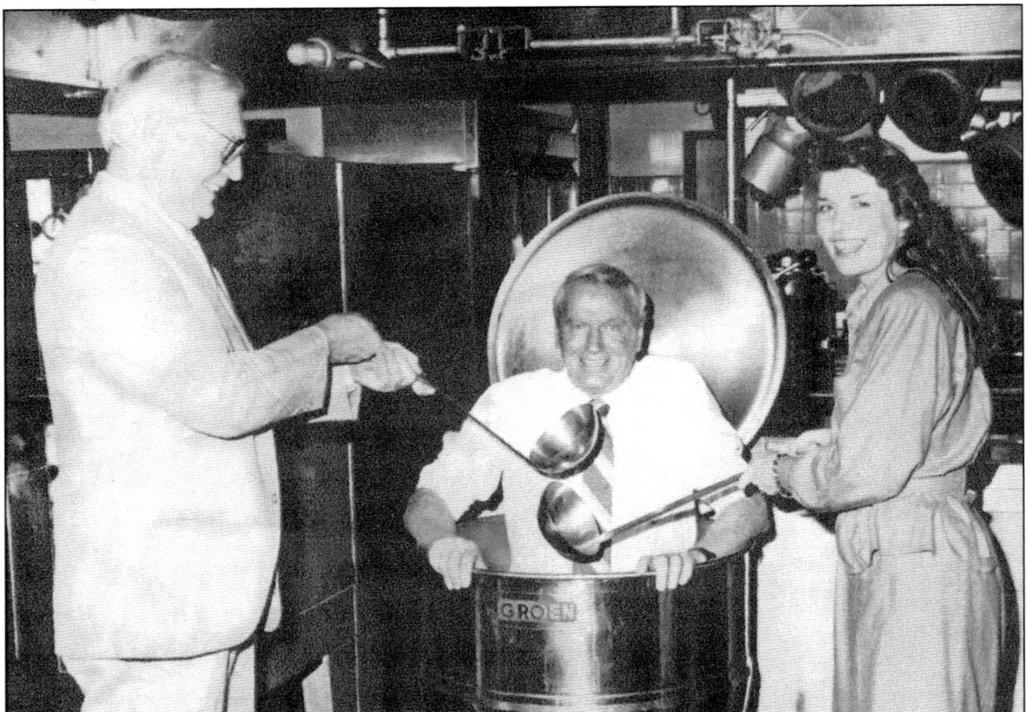

Sam Kennedy (left) and Robin Perry "roast" Paul Sands at a March of Dimes fund-raiser.

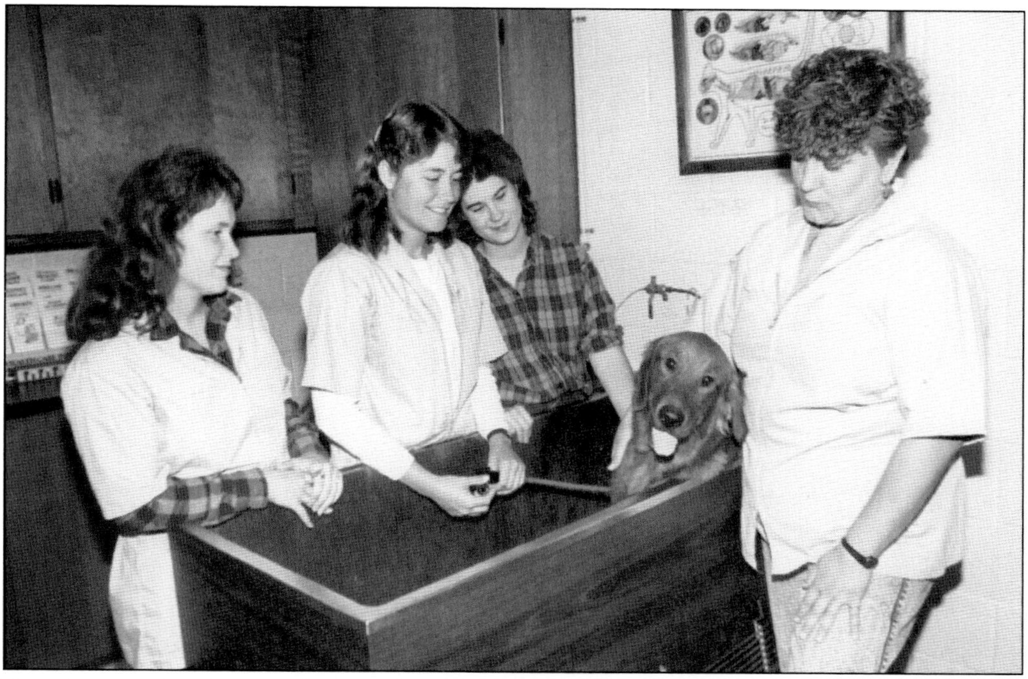

Veterinary technology students practice washing techniques on Rusty. From left to right, Anissa Jones, Liz Otten, Debbie Floyd, and Carol Thompson are preparing for a pet wash as a community-service project. The vet tech students belong to a student chapter of the National Association of Veterinary Technicians in America.

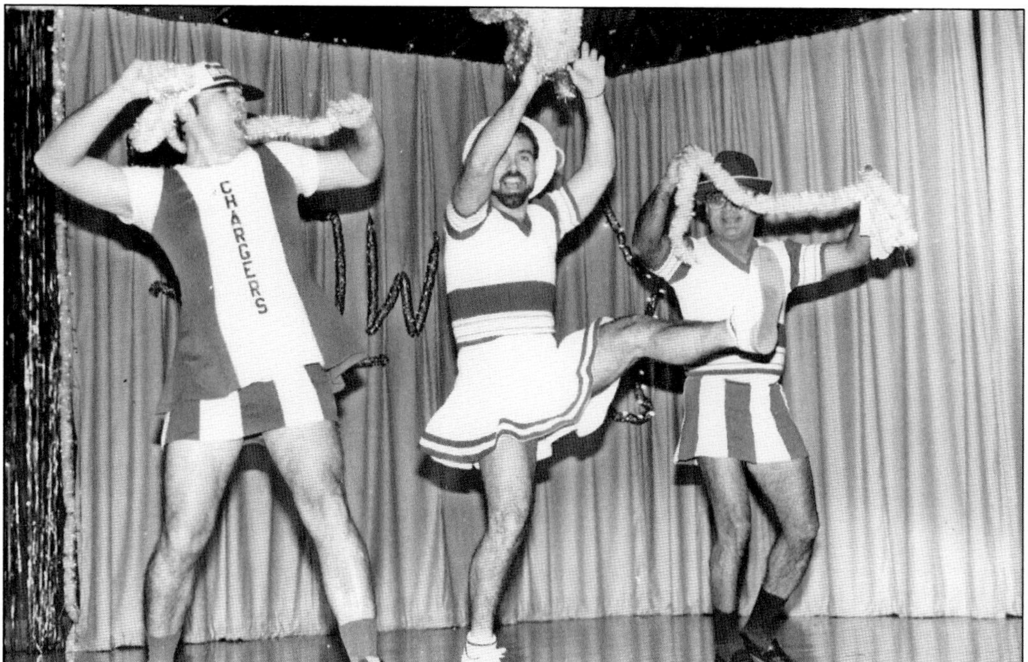

Faculty in-service has never been so much fun. From left to right, Dave Goodpasture, Ricky Martin, and Chaitram Talele perform in a fund-raising event. Charles Sanders (not pictured) played the drums.

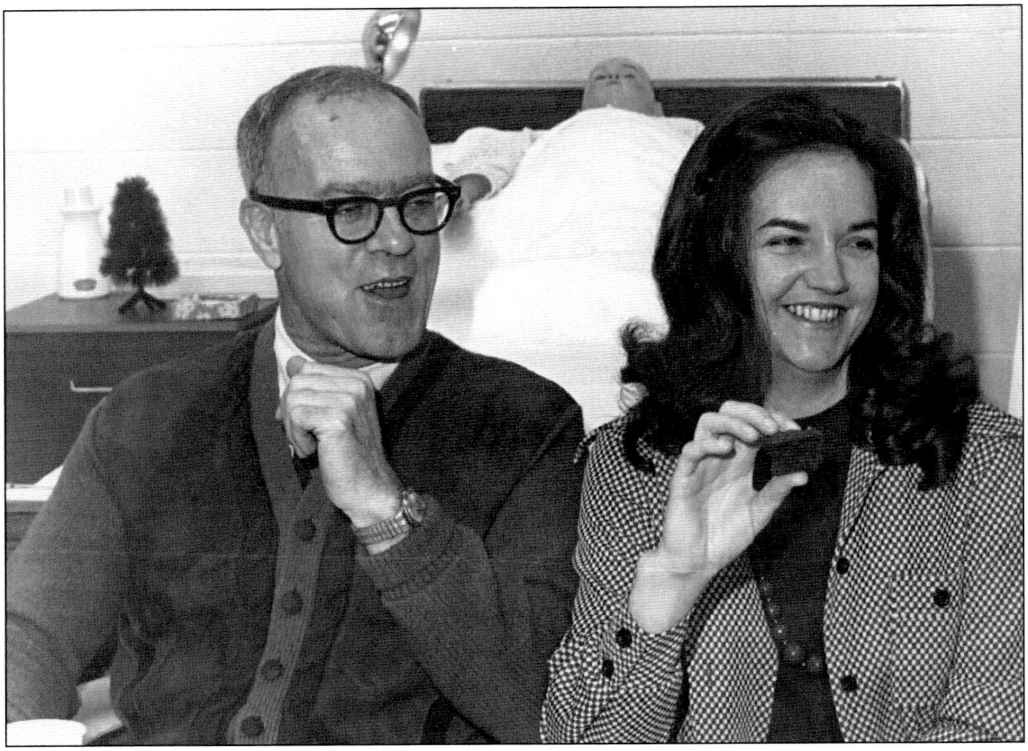

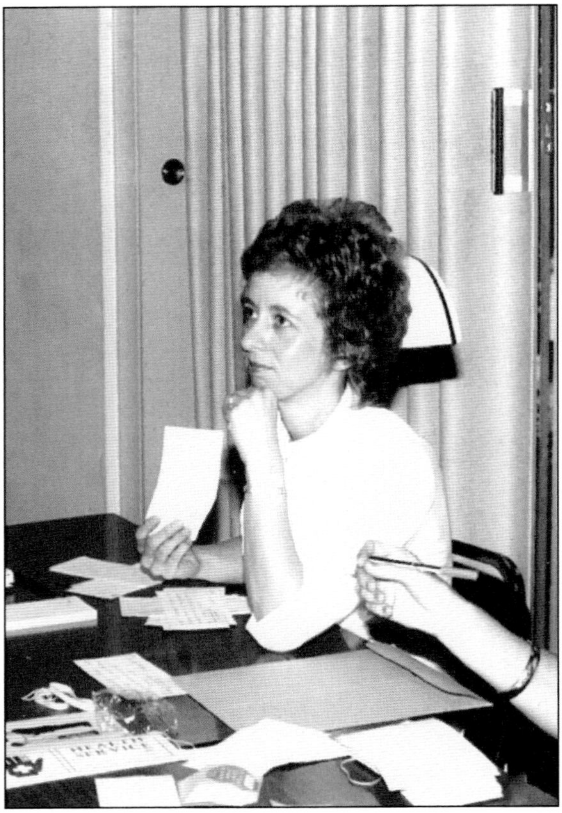

Jean Garmon and Dick Cooper (dean of Administrative Services) enjoy refreshments at a retirement party that was held in one of the labs used by the nursing department. Jean was secretary to the dean of instruction at the time and later became an instructor of developmental studies mathematics.

Patricia Rochelle, college nurse since 1972, provides health-related information to students, faculty, and staff. Whether in the clinic in the Warf Building in Columbia or traveling to other sites, Nurse Rochelle counsels students and staff, gives injections, and handles emergency situations that arise.

Political science students participate in mock presidential campaigns. Rhonda Hooks (center) is now a Columbia State alumnus who delivered the 2004 commencement address.

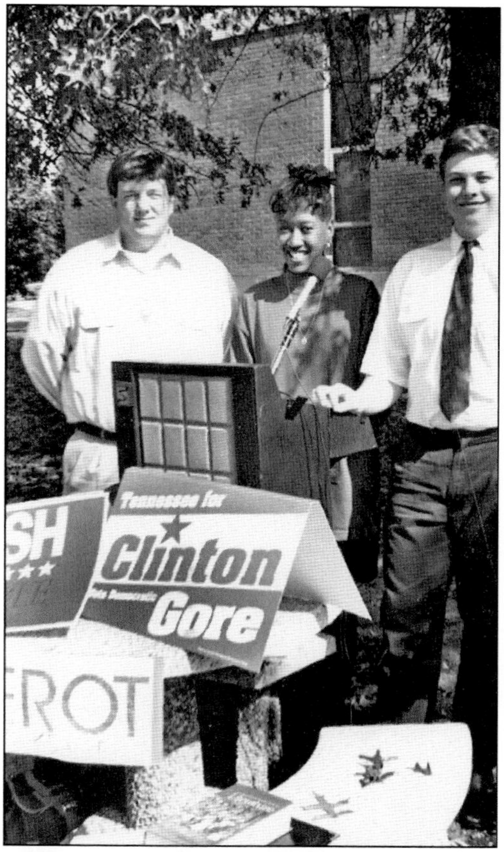

The graduation luau was a tradition that was enjoyed by everyone. It has unfortunately been discontinued. Pictured at the 1983 luau are, from left to right, Ricky Martin, coordinator of student activities; student John Fly, SGA president; and Todd King.

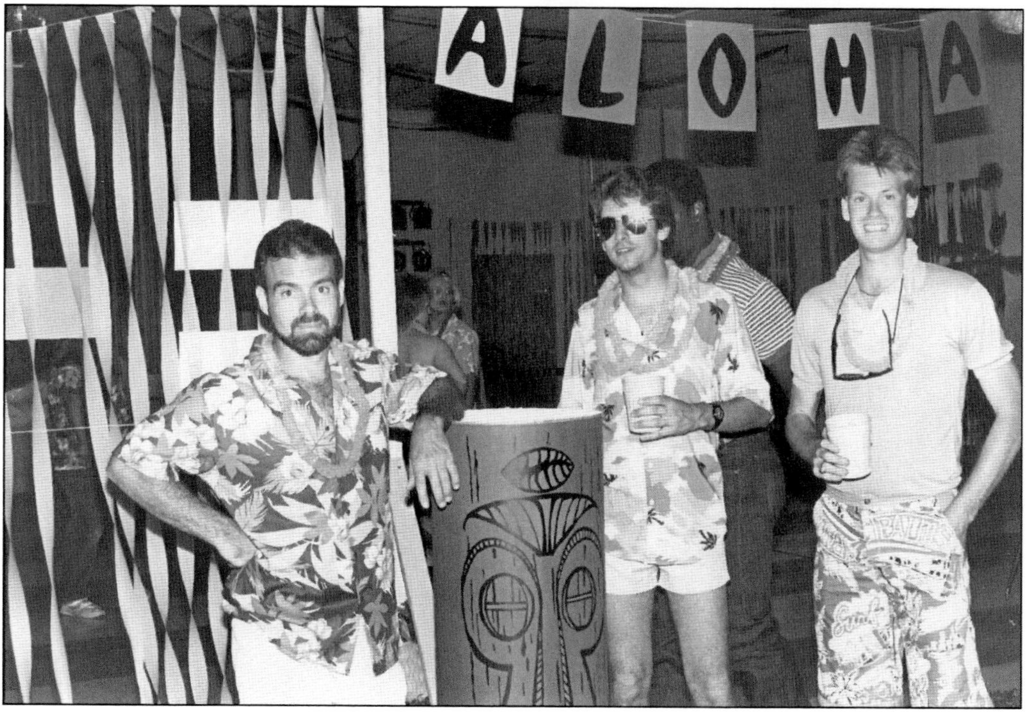

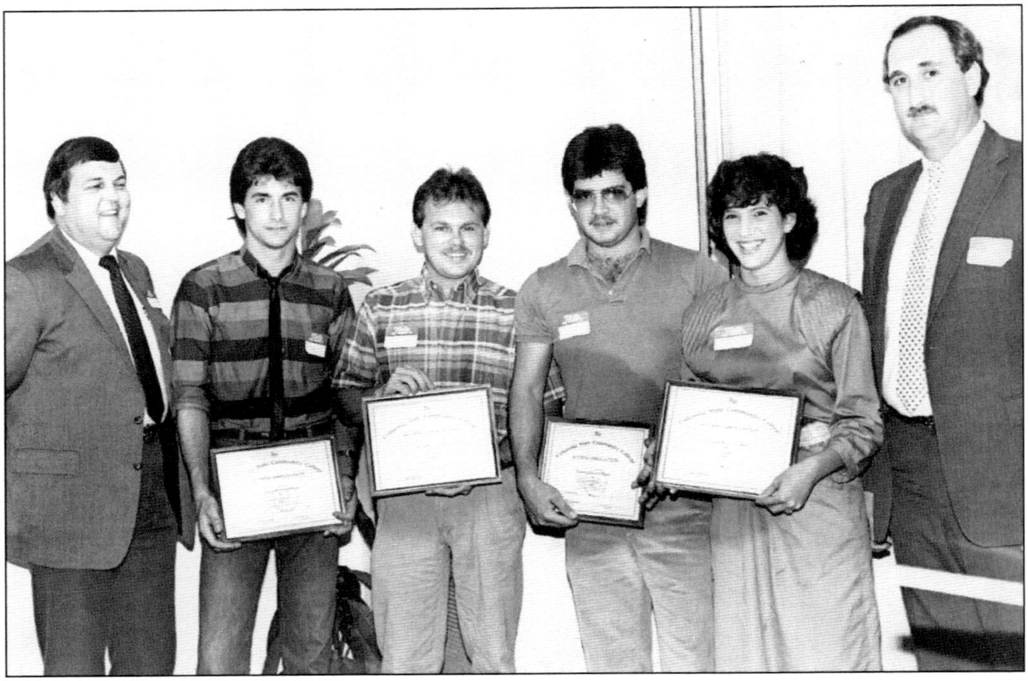

Columbia State alumni receive Alumni Association Certificates. Pictured here are, from left to right, director of development Charles Sanders, John Fly, Barry Spears, Sami Naddy, Gina Bastone, and Ed Harlan, alumnus and county executive.

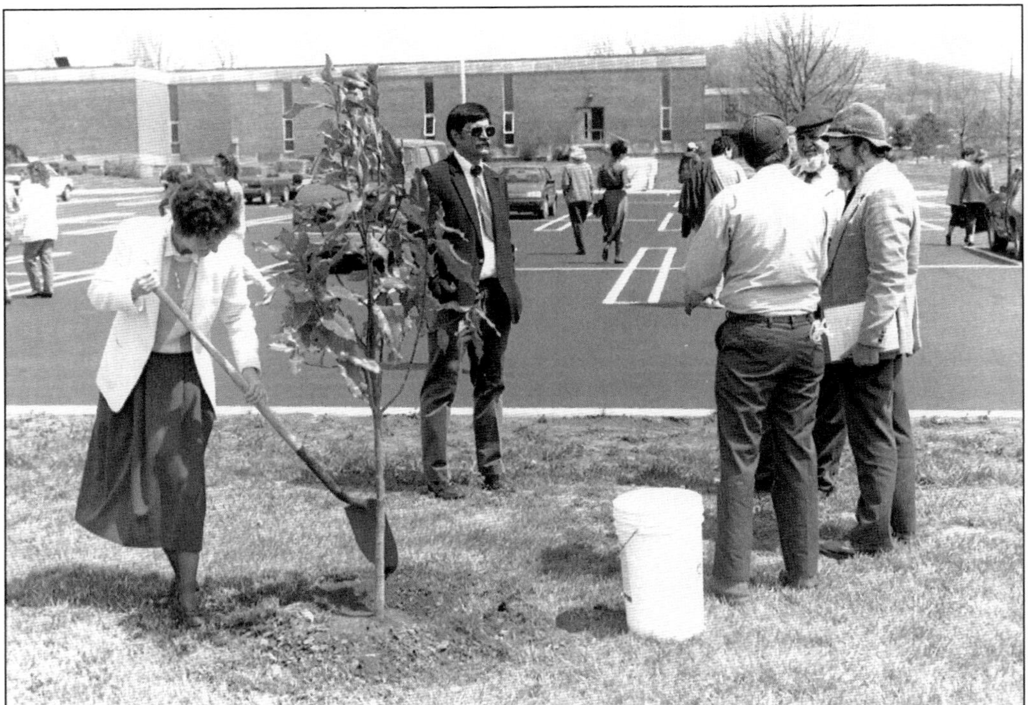

Jean Jones provides the finishing touches to a tree planted on Arbor Day while the director of buildings and grounds, Rick Lee (center), and others pay little attention to her efforts.

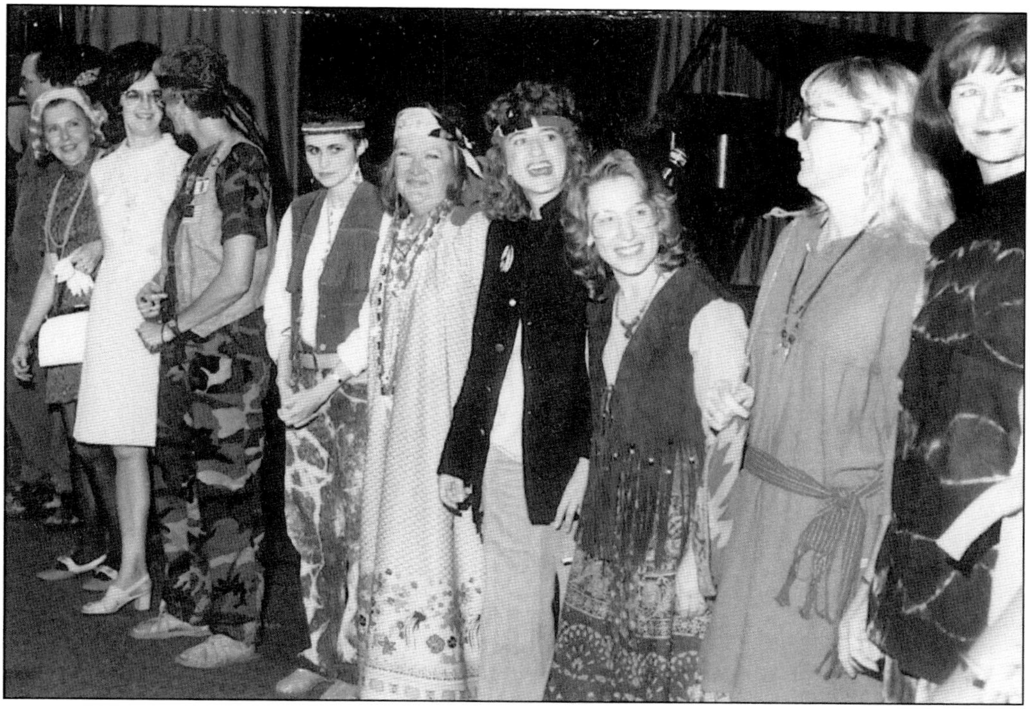

Hippie Day 1989 was a colorful and fun event. Faculty members posing during in-service are, from left to right, Carolyn Allred-Winnett, Jean Garmon, Elner Hamner, Joni Brooks, Bea Curry, Elaine Newcomb, Susan Raines, Toni Meredith, and Juanita Davis.

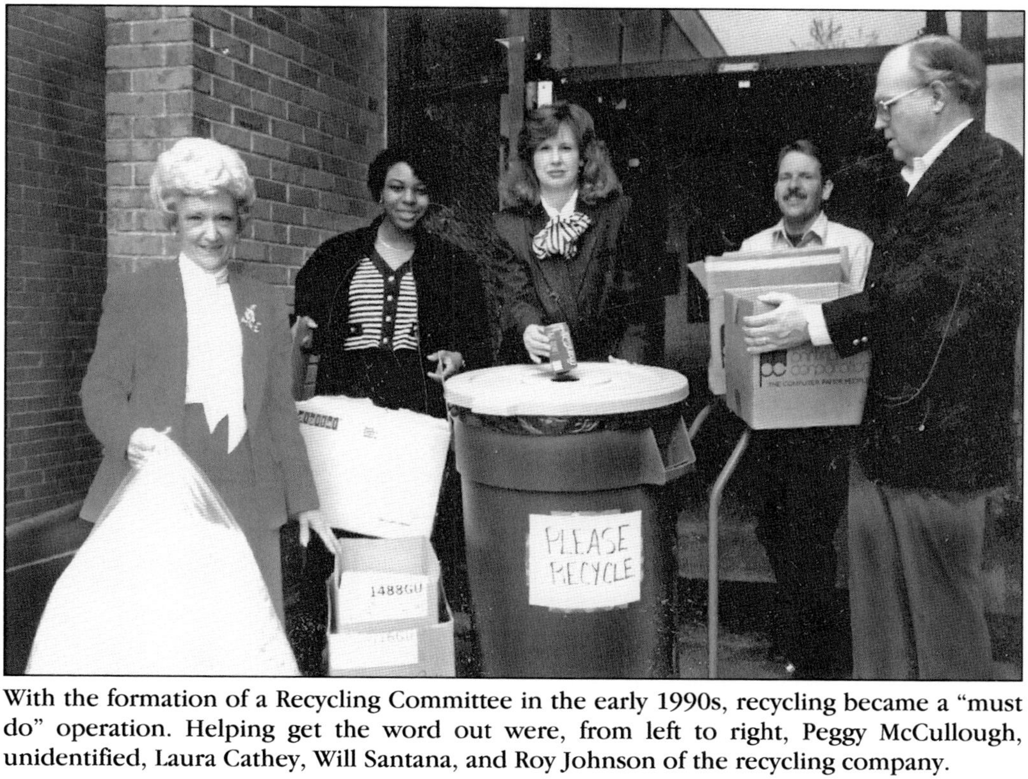

With the formation of a Recycling Committee in the early 1990s, recycling became a "must do" operation. Helping get the word out were, from left to right, Peggy McCullough, unidentified, Laura Cathey, Will Santana, and Roy Johnson of the recycling company.

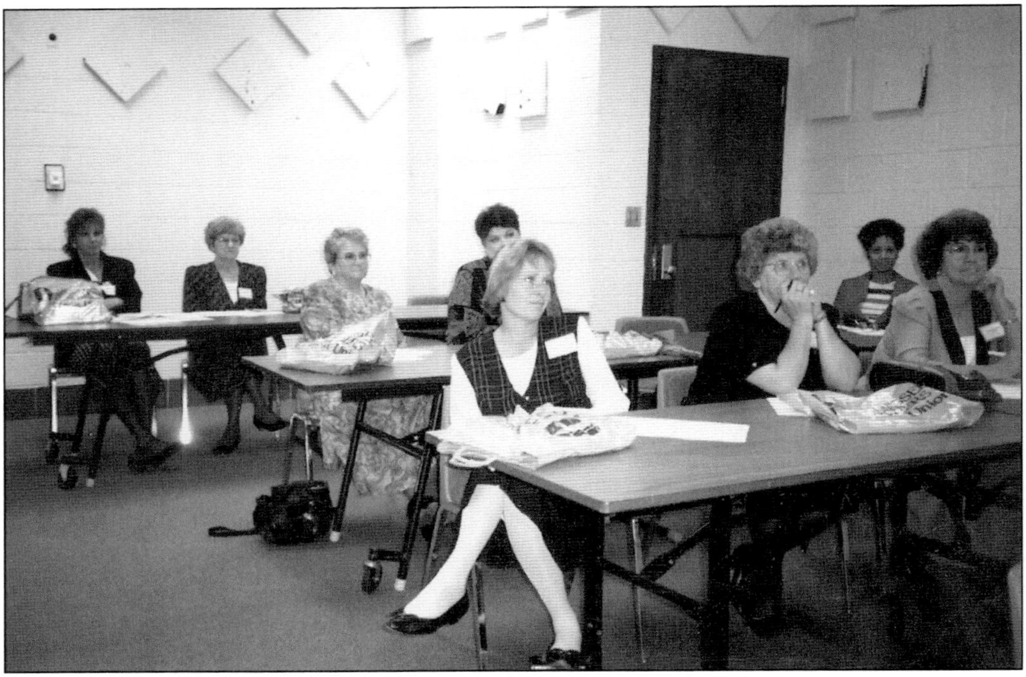

Several staff members attended the American Association of Women in Community Colleges meeting in 1996. From left to right are Laura Cathey, Faye Daniels, Sara Lindsey, Lisa Trimble, Nancy Scott, unidentified, 3Lillian Hayes, and Naomi Rosson.

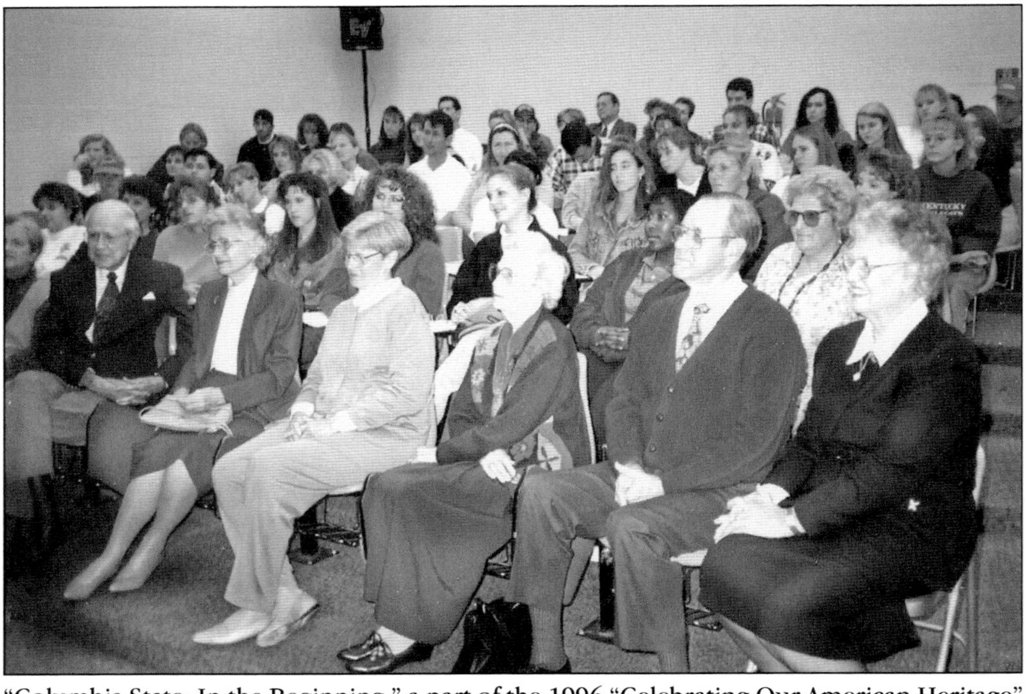

"Columbia State: In the Beginning," a part of the 1996 "Celebrating Our American Heritage" series, was attended by some of the original staff members. From left to right of the front row in this picture are John Dillingham and his wife Marie, Jean Hurt, Frances Williams and her husband, and Ava Eaton.

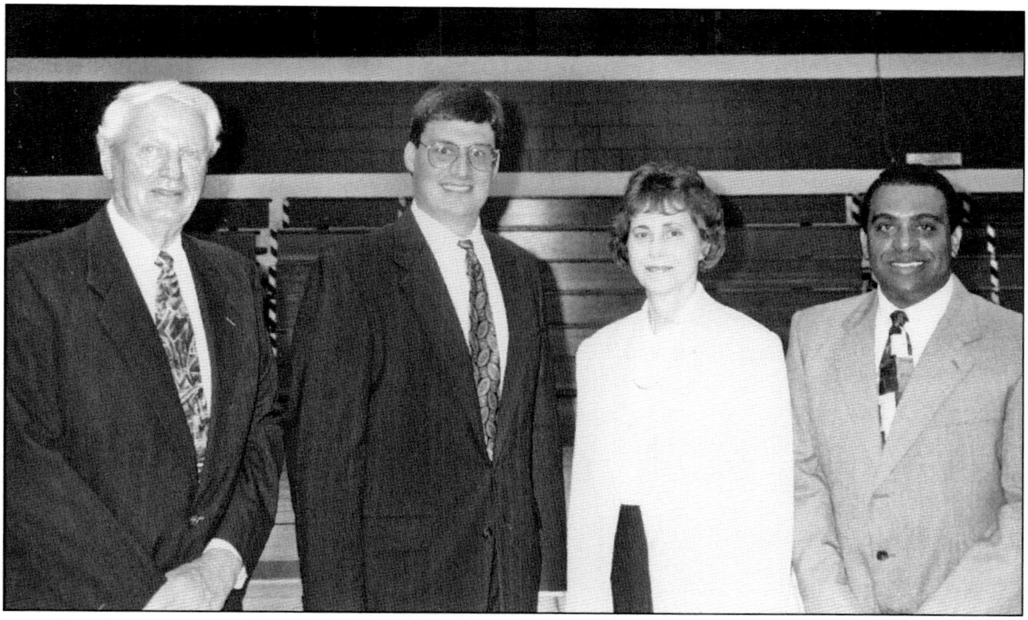

David Wilson, an Olympic gold-medal swimmer, spoke to a student assembly in 1996. From left to right are President Sands, Wilson, Dean of Instruction Betty Kyger, and Dean of Student Services Johnny Williams.

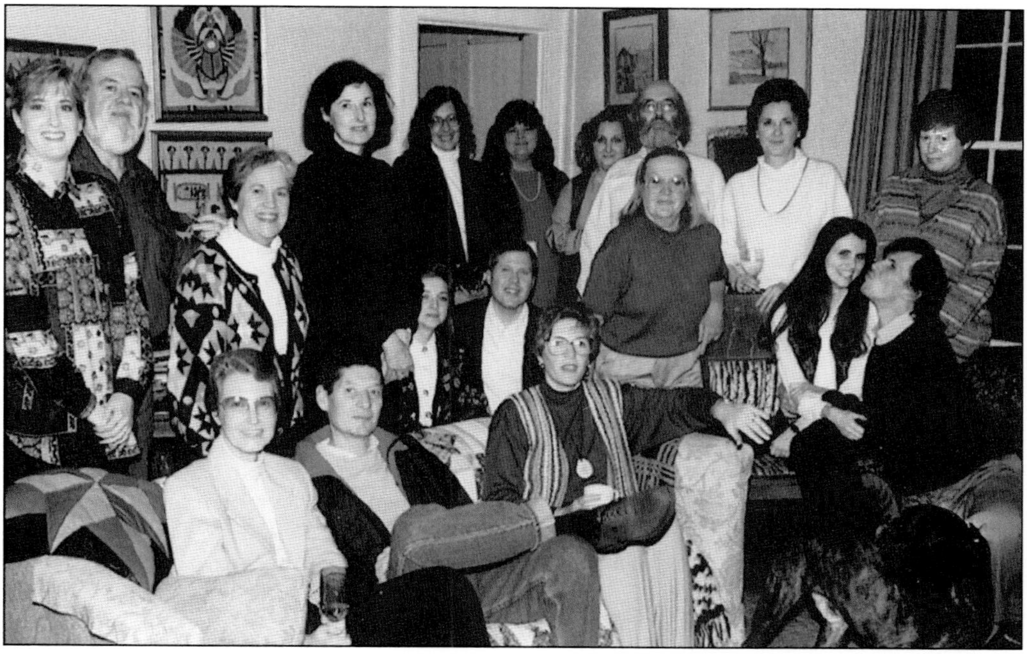

A momentous occasion was the engagement party of two faculty members, Joni Brooks and Stuart Lenig. From left to right are (seated) Ginny and Mart Austin, Debra and Barry Gidcomb, Elizabeth McDow, Bea Curry, and the honorees Joni and Stu; (standing) Linda Brunton, Lewis and Lil Moore, Claudia Andrews, Jane Senefeld, Beverly Mitchell, Susanna Holmes, Jim Senefeld, Jean Jones, and Louise Katz. Prince is standing on the floor.

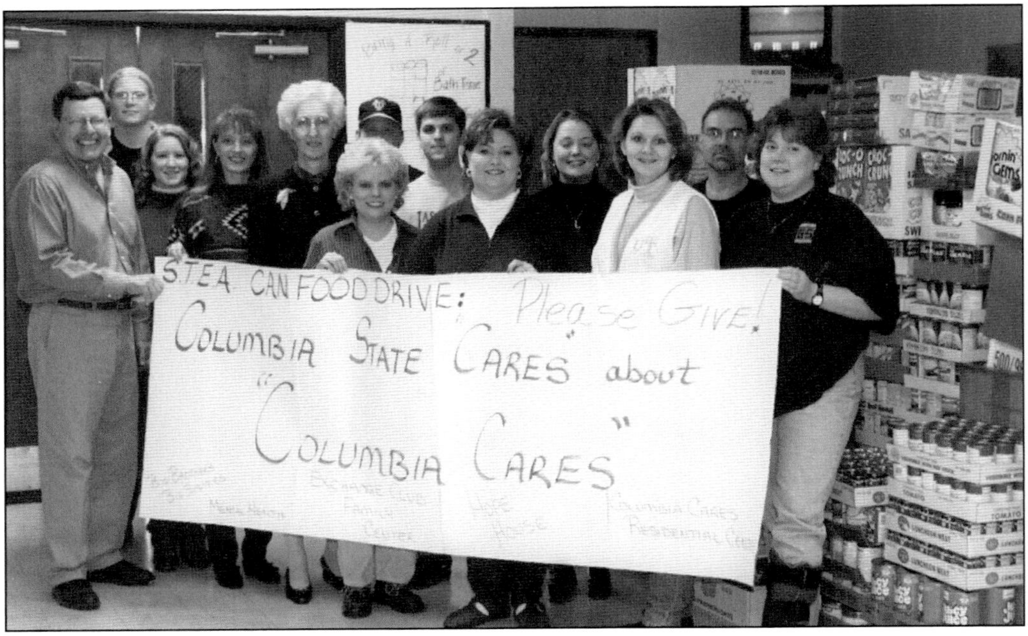

The 1998 Food Drive provided food for local organizations. Faculty sponsors were Aubrey Flagg (left) and Ricky Martin (second from right). President Hawkins is pictured fifth from left.

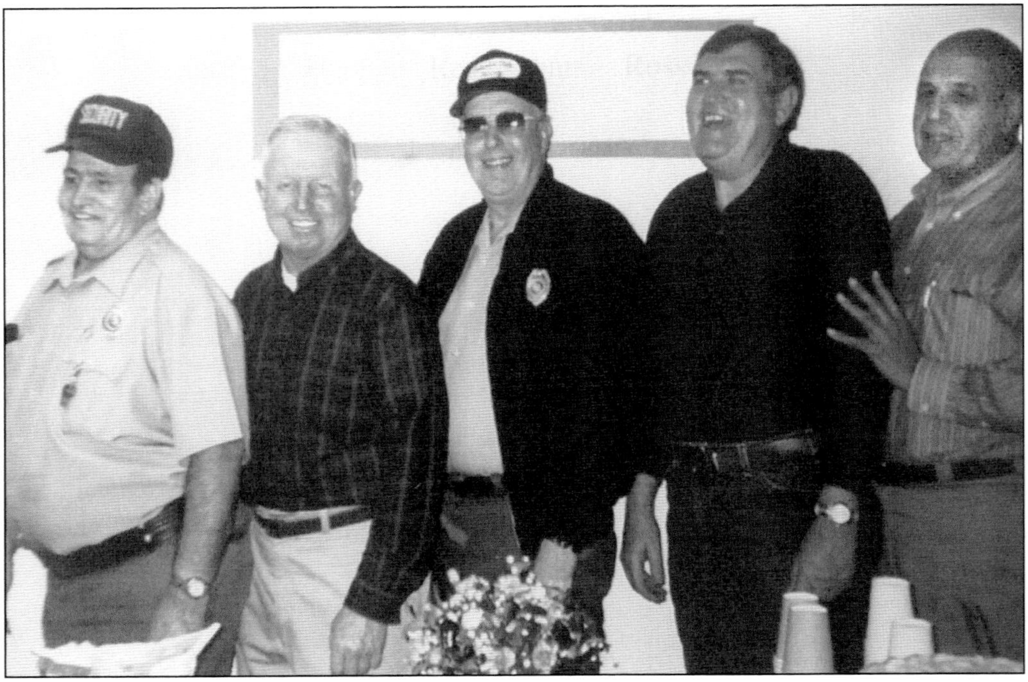

Columbia State security personnel gather for the retirement celebration of Ross Ayres. From left to right are Henry McKennon, Pat Hickman, Ayres, John Hill, and John Kirk.

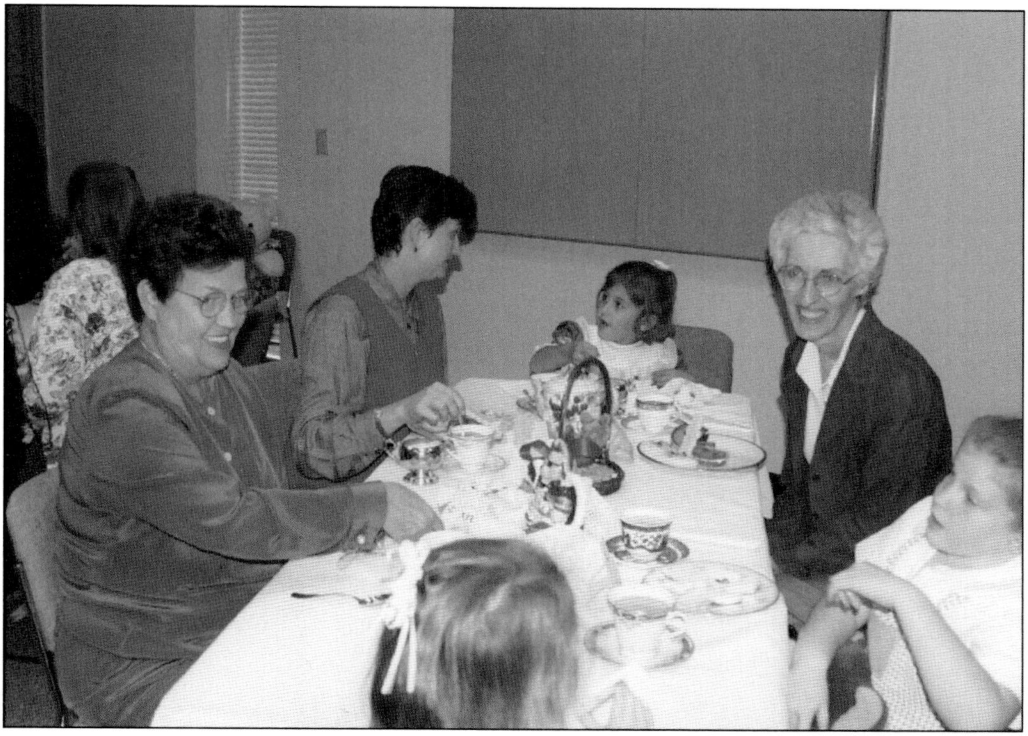

Culture Fest 1998 offered the "Teddy Bear Tea" for children ages four to seven. Mr. Teddy Bear, story telling, teddy-bear crafts, and refreshments were a joy for the children. President Hawkins (right), who attended one of the teas, enjoys refreshments with Susan Cothran (left) and Susan's granddaughter, seated at the end of the table.

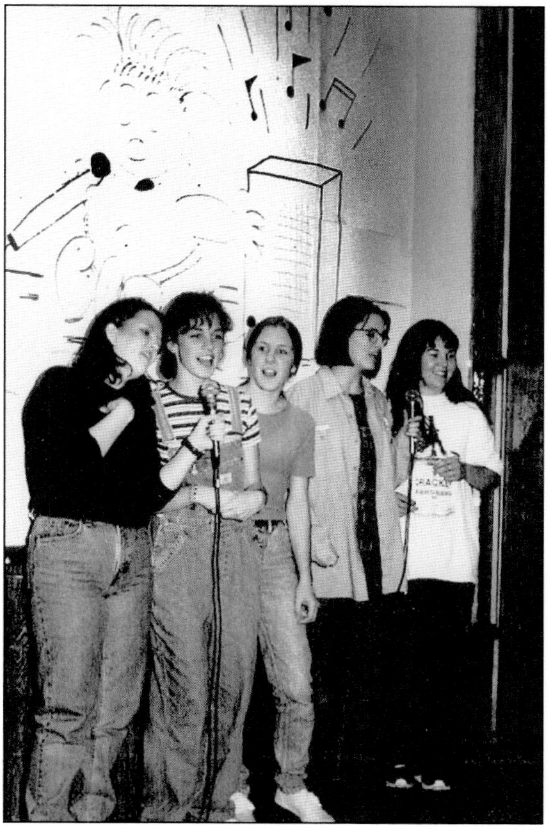

Karaoke has always been a popular student activity.

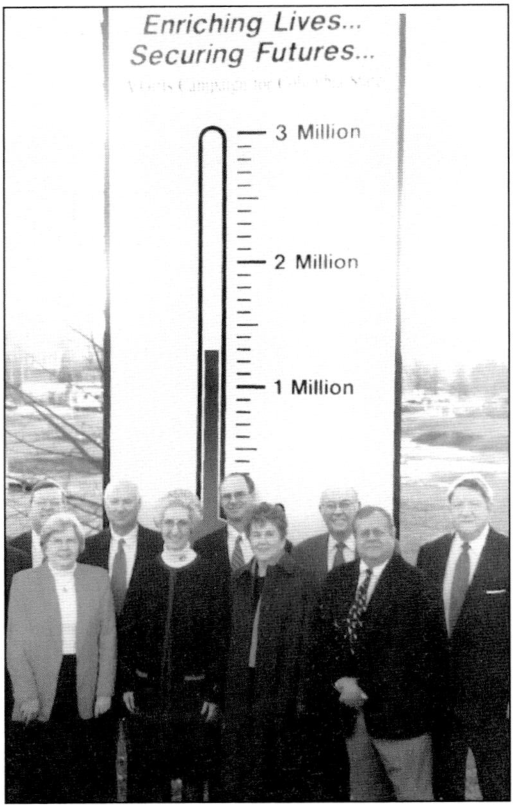

The "Enriching Lives . . . Securing Futures" gifts campaign raised over $3 million, primarily for student scholarships. The campaign began in 1999. Pictured in front of the sign are campaign executive committee members. From left to right are Charles Sanders, Carolyn Allred-Winnett, Jim Criswell, President Hawkins, Marc Lively, Sydney McClain, Jim Sloan, Roger Witherow, and Waymon Hickman.

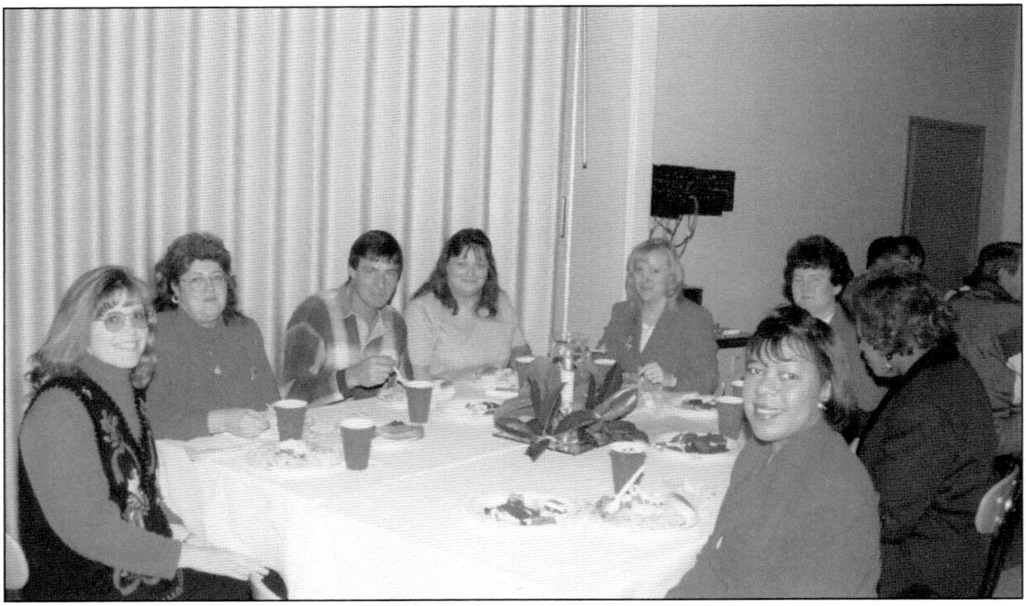

Each December, employees celebrate at a Christmas luncheon. Seated around the table from left to right are Linda Boshers, Wanda Moore, Barry Brown, Cindy Runnels, Sonja McCormick, Betty Yates, Deborah Armstrong, and Sharon Bowen.

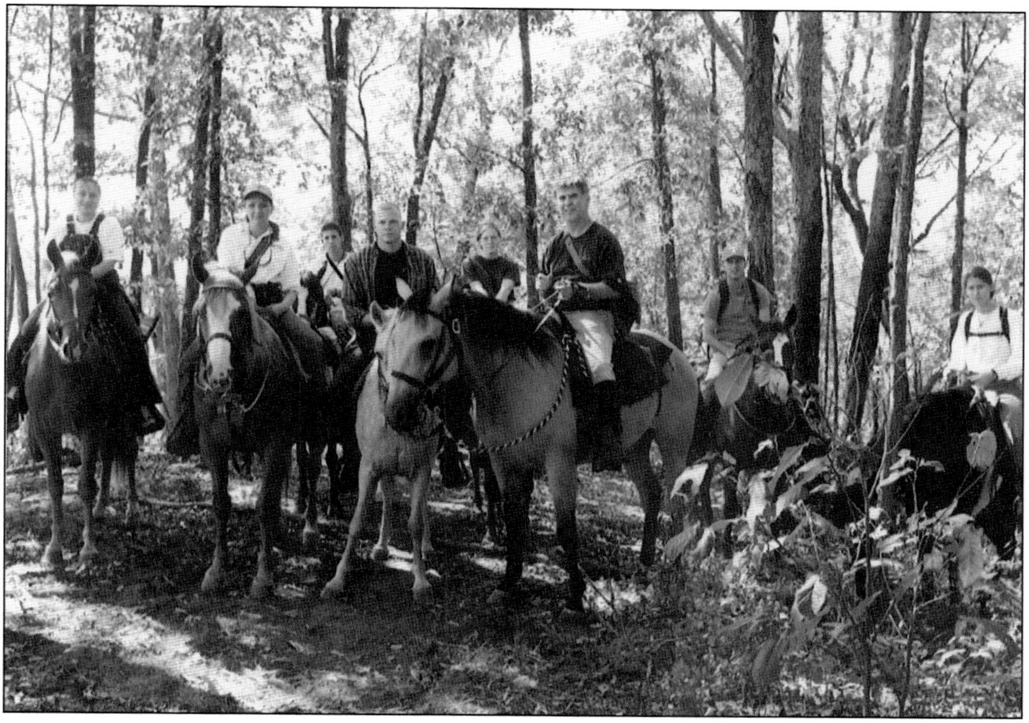

In 2000, Bill Andrews and students went on a field trip to the Hernando de Soto Trail on the Tennessee/North Carolina border.

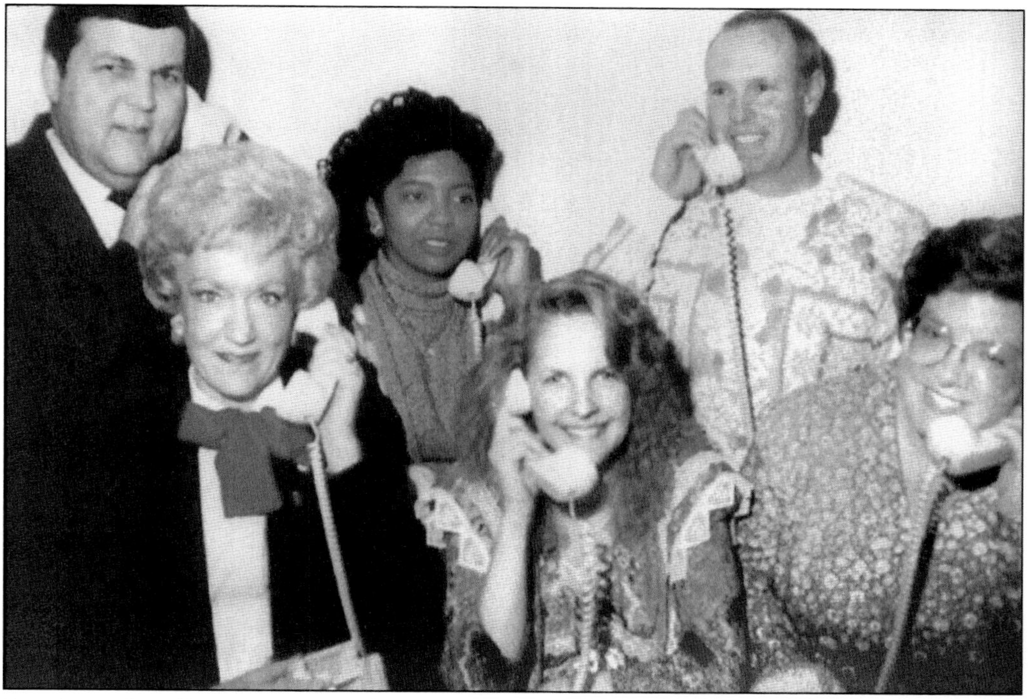

Faculty and staff participate in phone-a-thons to raise funds for scholarships. Calling their friends and neighbors during the 2000 phone-a-thon are, from left to right, Charles Sanders, Peggy McCullough, Christa Martin, Eve Jones, Ron Dinwiddie, and Kay Luttrell.

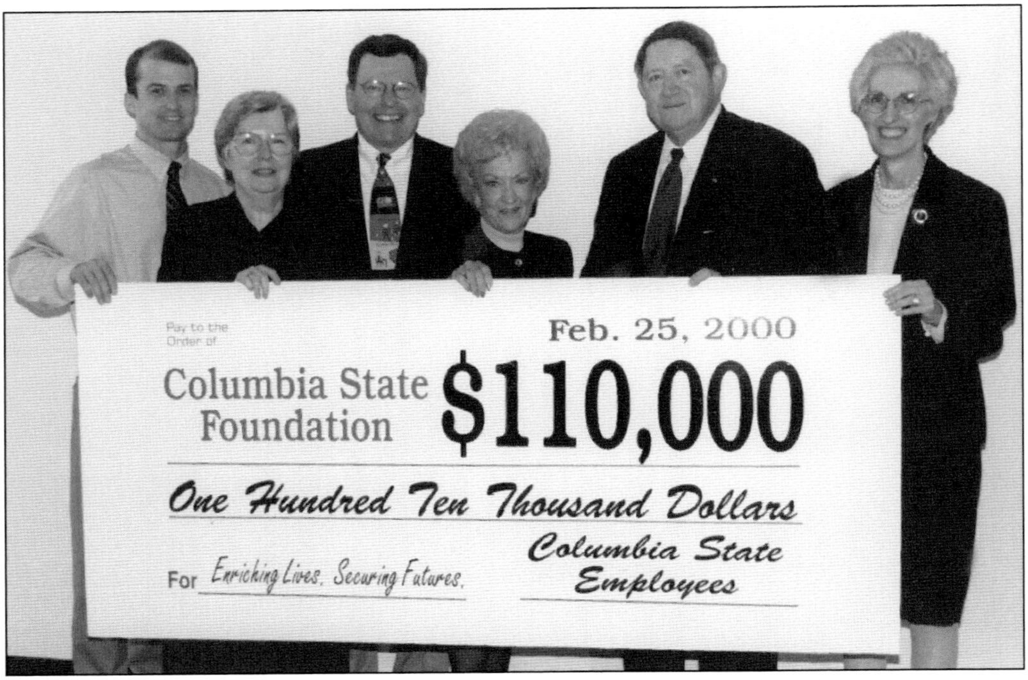

Columbia State employees contributed $110,000 to the "Enriching Lives . . . Securing Futures" gifts campaign. Pictured from left to right during the campus celebration in 2000 are Dusty Doddridge, campus chair Carolyn Allred-Winnett, Aubrey Flagg, Peggy McCullough, Columbia State Foundation president Waymon Hickman, and President Hawkins. Doddridge, Flagg, and McCullough were chairs for the professional staff, faculty, and support staff, respectively.

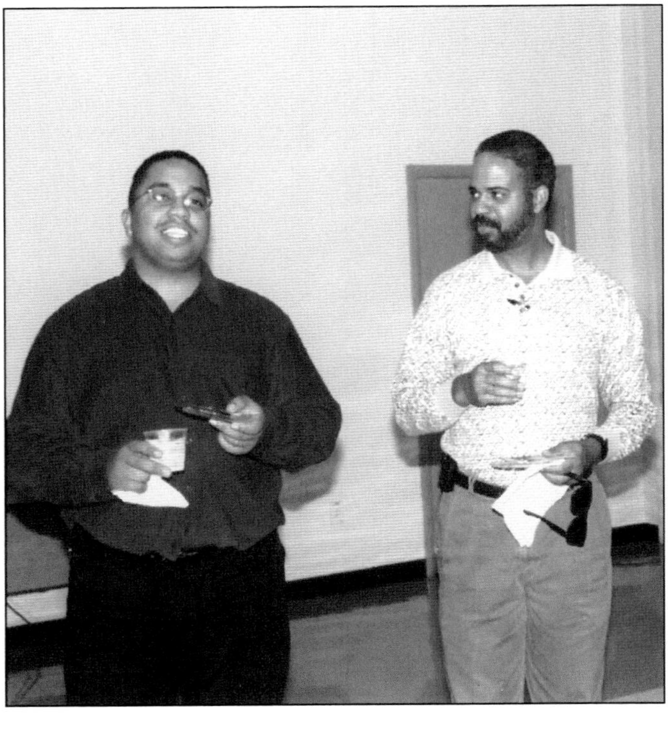

Trent Ogilvie (left) and Lynn Ross enjoy refreshments at the gifts campaign celebration.

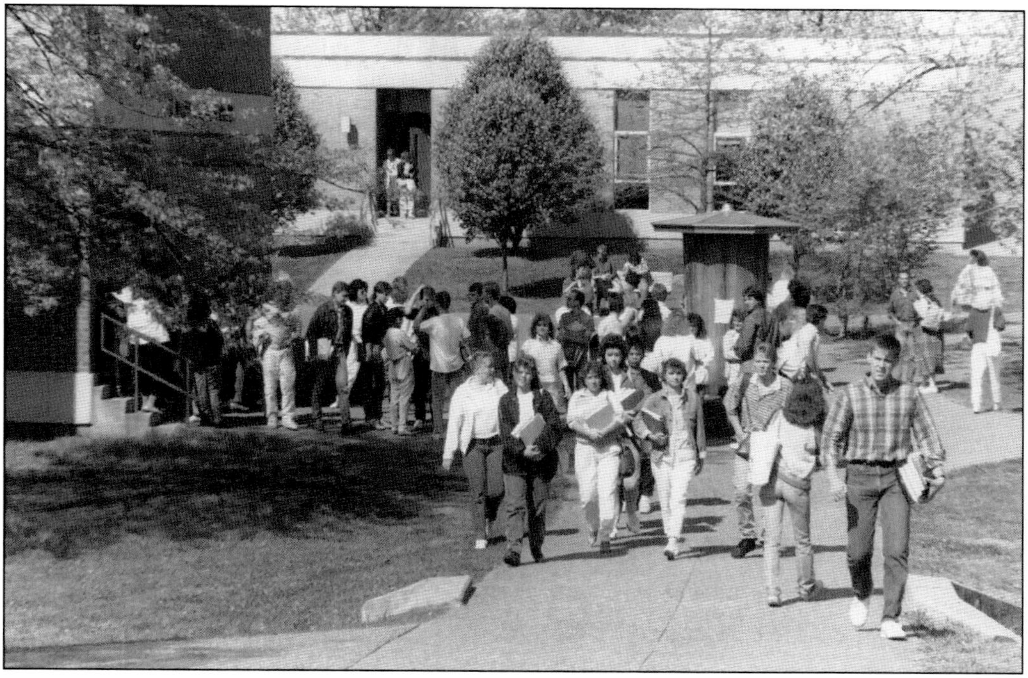

The kiosk is one of the favorite student gathering places on campus. To the left is the Warf Building and in the background is the Walter Building.

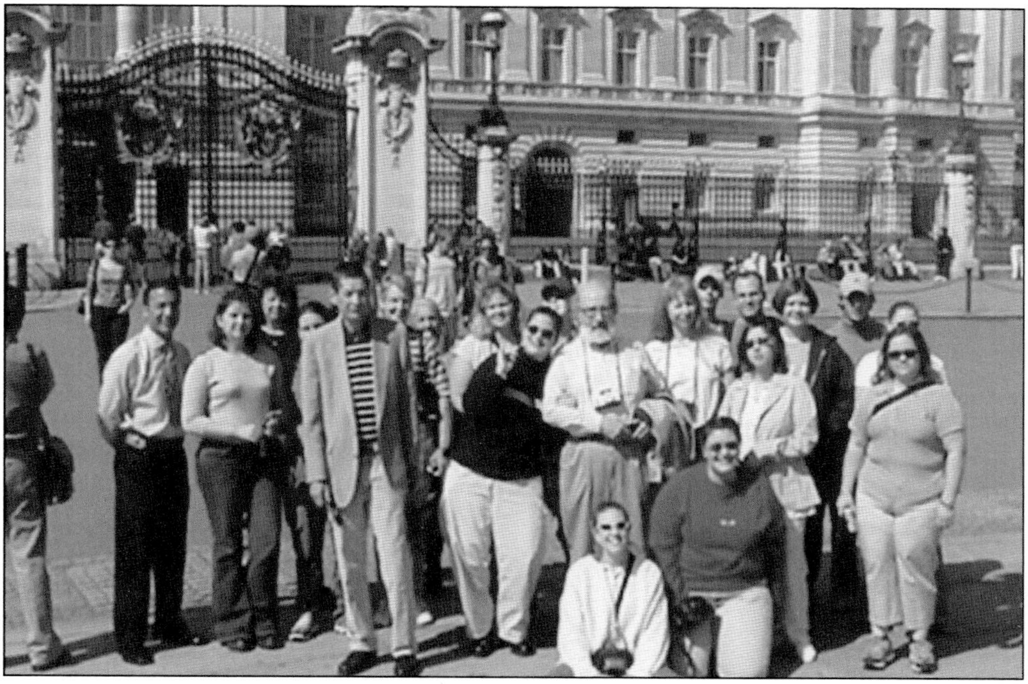

Each year, members of the faculty accompany students on an overseas trip. Thus far, trips have been taken to Greece, England, Italy, and France. Pictured in front of Buckingham Palace on the 2001 trip are the students who participated. The group was accompanied by faculty members Mart Austin and James Senefeld.

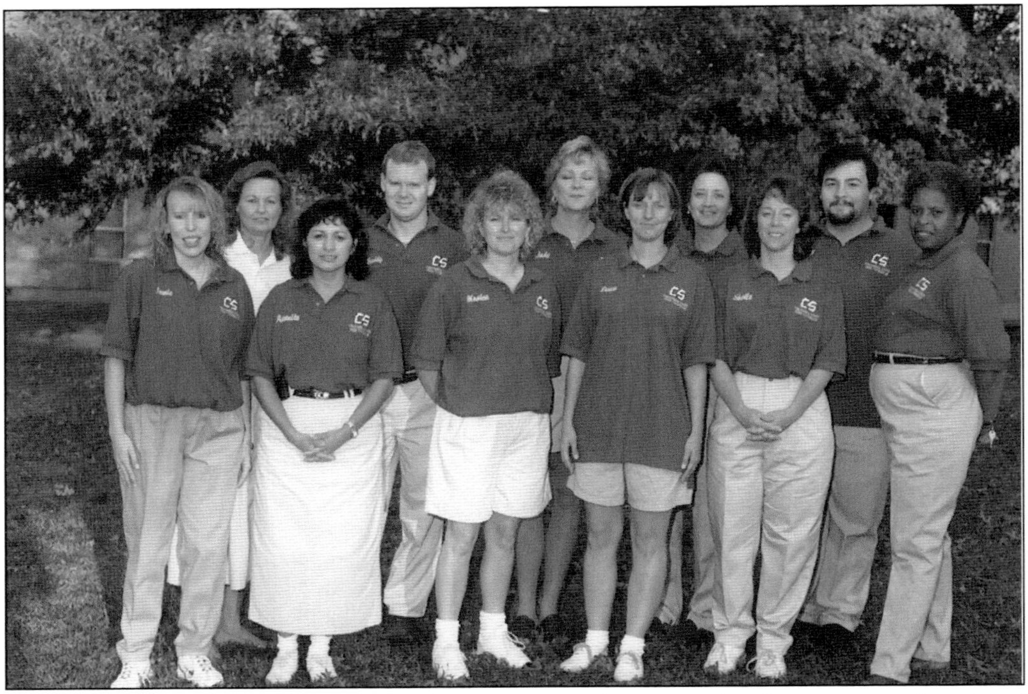

The Student Peer Counselor Program began in 1976 as a result of an Exxon Educational Foundation Grant to provide transitional support to students coming to college for the first time. Selected students were given extensive basic counseling skills training to effectively serve the needs of a diverse student population.

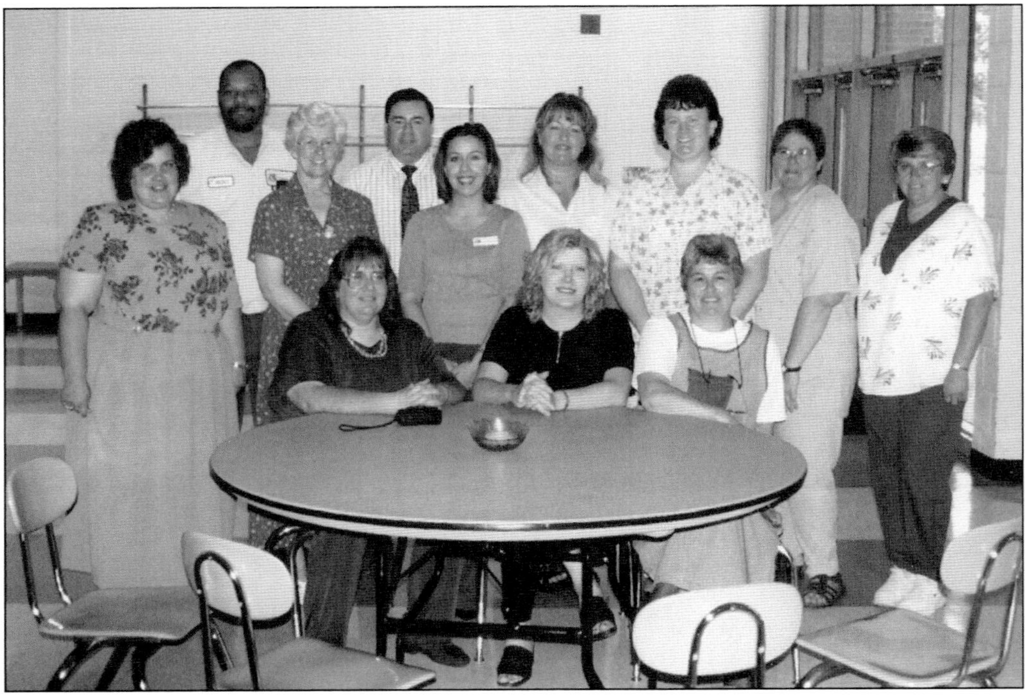

A group of staff members gather in the Jones Student Center to wish Larita Alford (not pictured) well as she leaves for a new job in Bermuda.

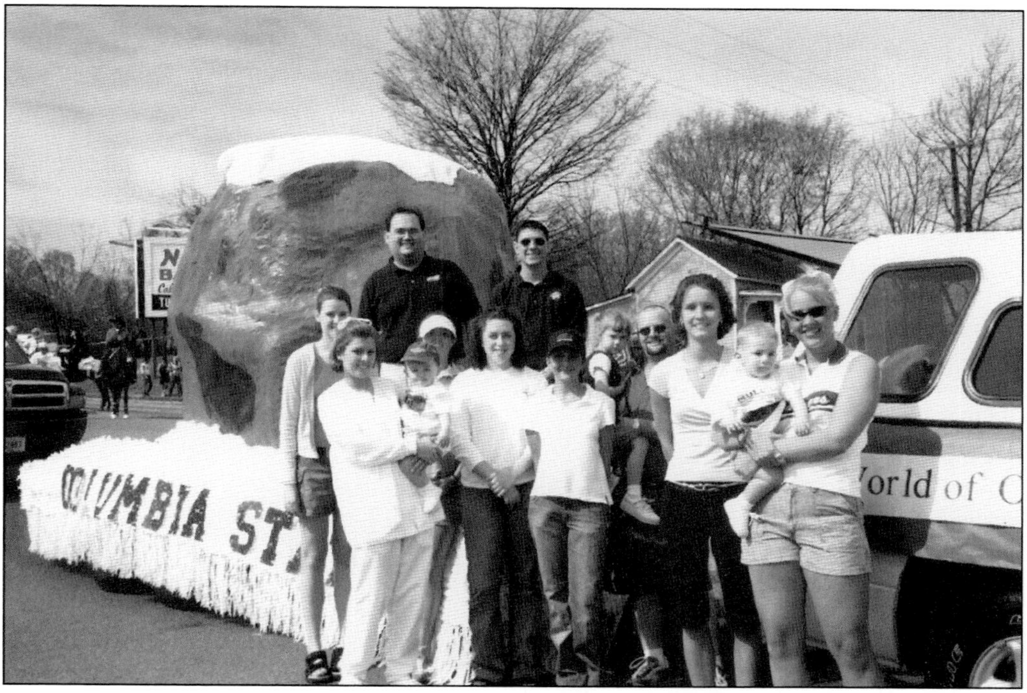

The theme of the SGA entry in the 2001 Mule Day Parade was "A World of Opportunity." From left to right are (front row) Jacki Rickard, Jennifer Peterson holding Seth Scruggs, Meghan Brophy, Miranda Black, Samantha Barnes, Fred Demint and daughter, Rachael Buchanan, and Kristen Lannom holding Zachary Scruggs; (back row) Joey Scruggs and Chris Holland.

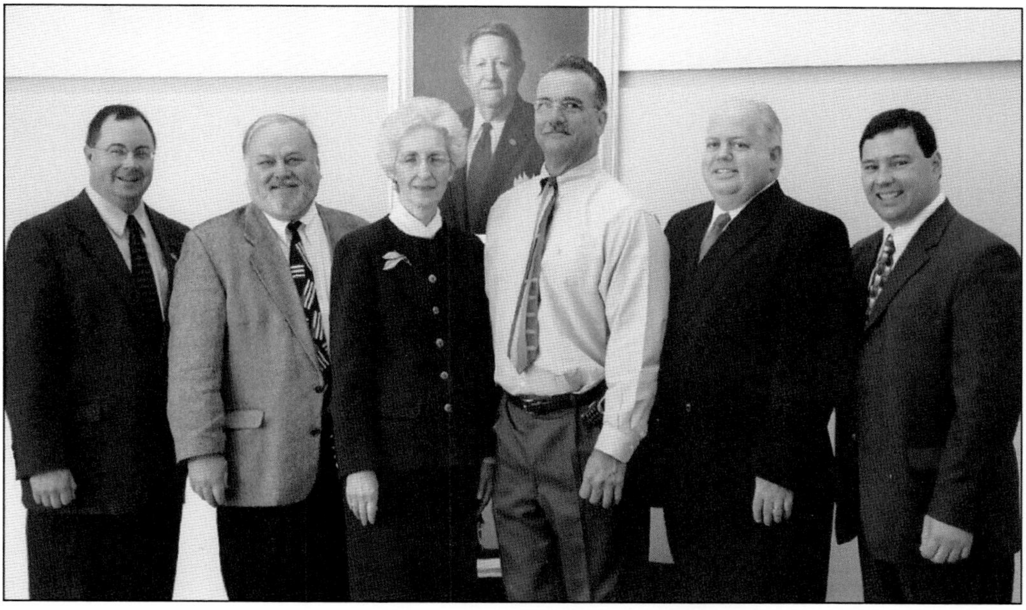

President Hawkins welcomes officials to the Tennessee Criminal Justice Language Academy opening session in March 2002. From left to right are State Rep. and alumnus Tom DuBois, Dist. Atty. Gen. Mike Bottoms, Hawkins, Language Academy instructor Jose Alentado, Governors Highway Safety Program manager Randall Smith, and Language Academy director Paul Rosson.

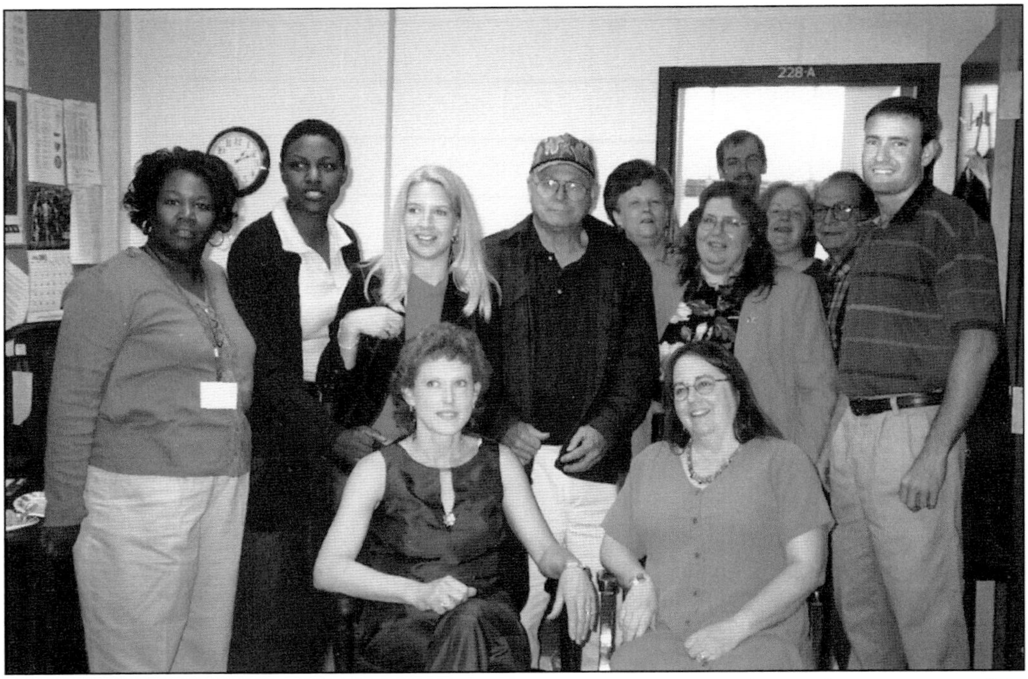

Holiday and end-of-the-year luncheons have always been a popular tradition. Pictured in May 2003 are employees on the second floor of Warf. From left to right are (seated) Kay Geving and Karen Kendall-Fite; (standing) Yolanda Neal, Meredeth McCoy, Lisa Rutledge, Monte Bayless, Jo Cathey, Freda McClain, James Smith, Mary Lou Baker, B.I. Naddy, and Ricky Hardison.

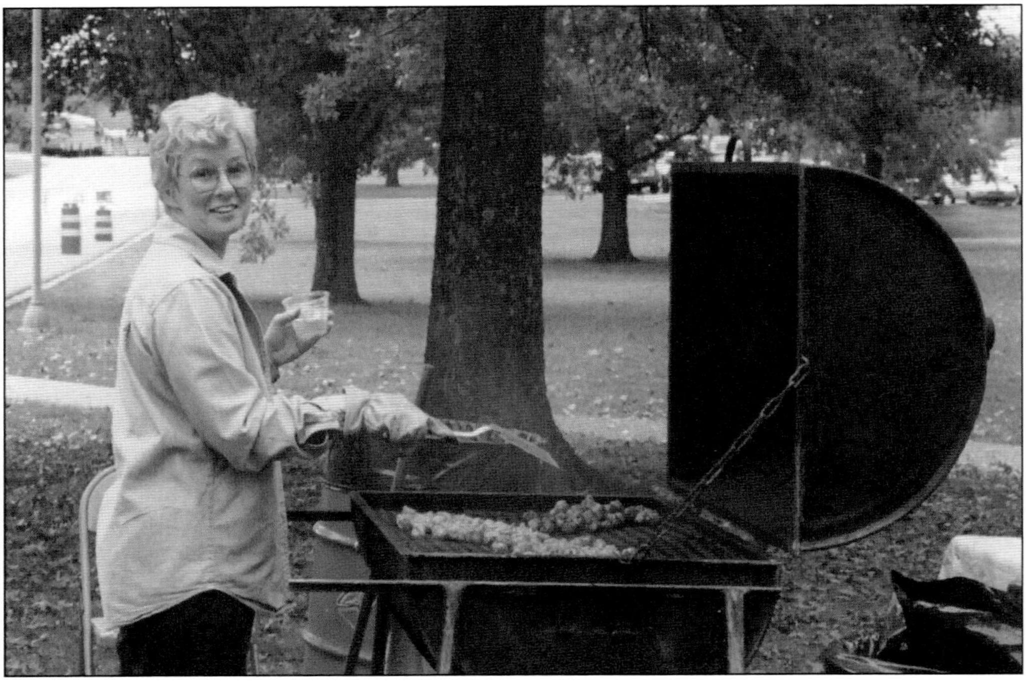

Dr. Cathy McDonald, vice president for academic affairs, cooks sausages for visitors at Culture Fest.

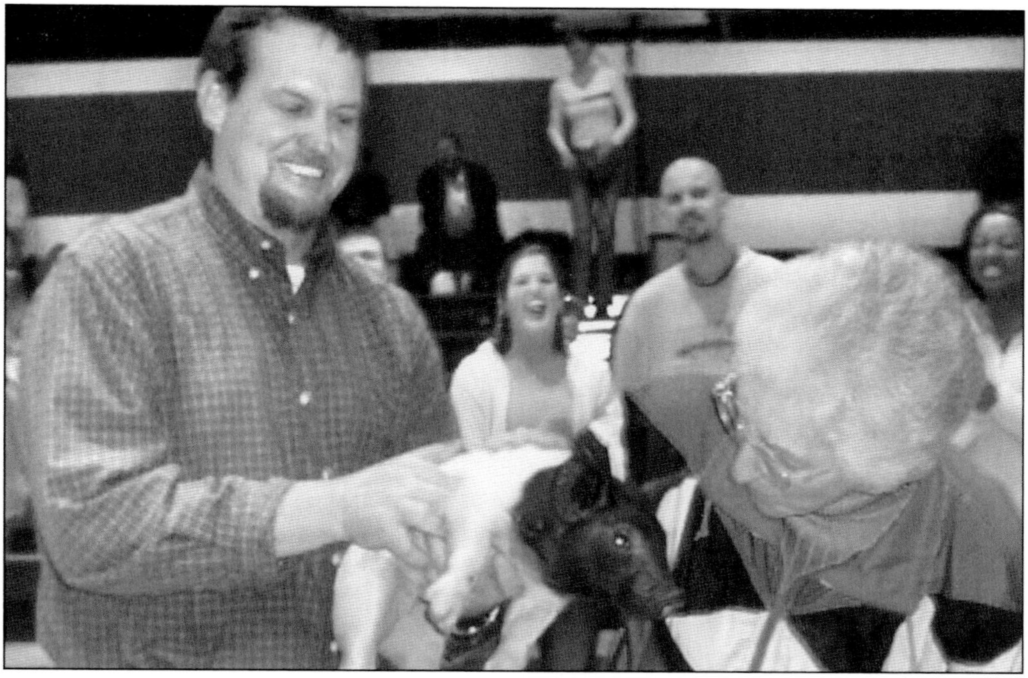

Each year a contest, organized by the SGA, determines whom on the faculty or staff will get to kiss a pig at homecoming. Pres. Rebecca Hawkins received the "honor" in 2003.

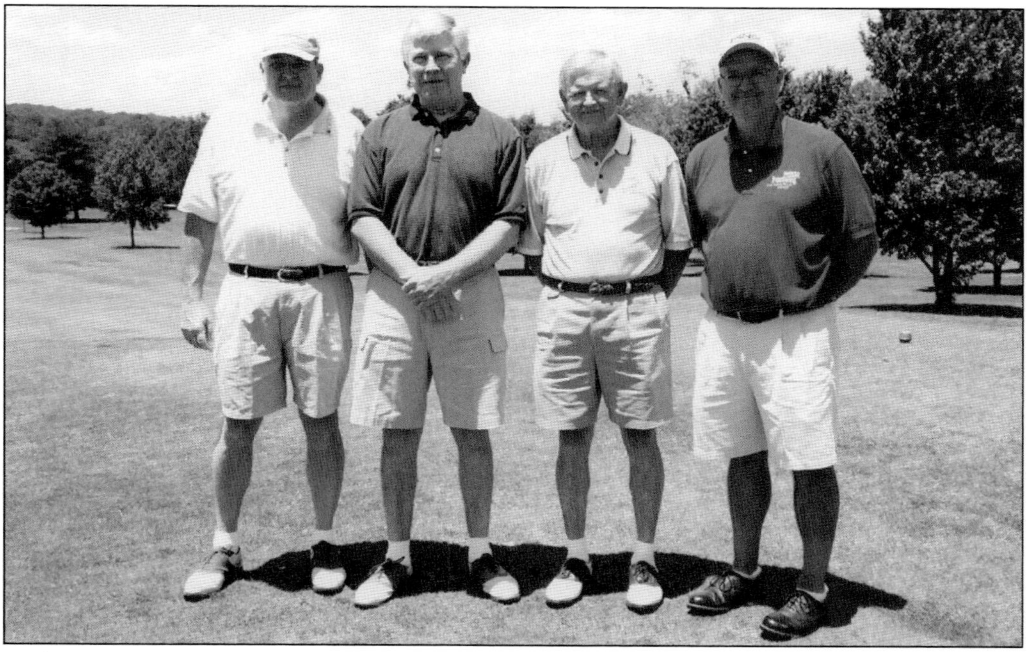

Each year, two golf tournaments are held to help raise funds for scholarships and other CoSCC Foundation activities. The James R. Moon Golf Classic in Lewisburg, now in its eighth year, provides scholarships for Marshall County students. The Columbia Rock Products and Industrial Contractors Golf Classic in Columbia is now in its 12th year. Pictured is one of the teams in the 1993 Columbia Classic. From left to right are Stan Breeden, David Forrester, Dean Dickey, and Mike Potts.

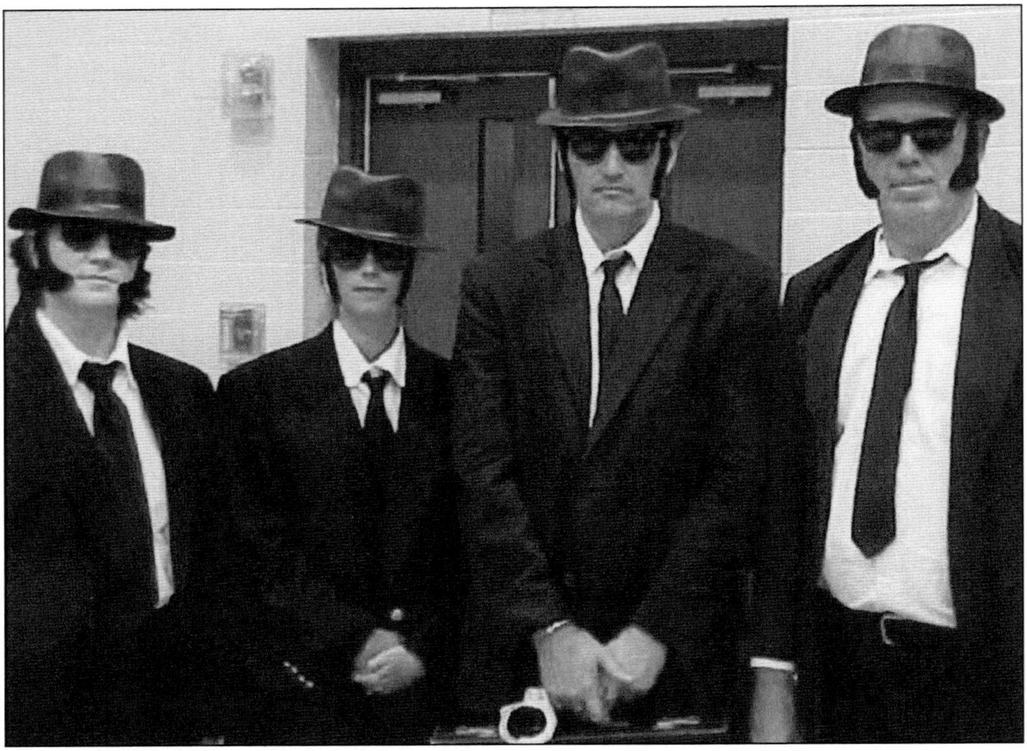

The "Blues Brothers" represent Columbia State at an American Heart Association event. From left to right are Dina Phelps, Kadi Lehnhart, Paul Jennings, and Dan Opalewski.

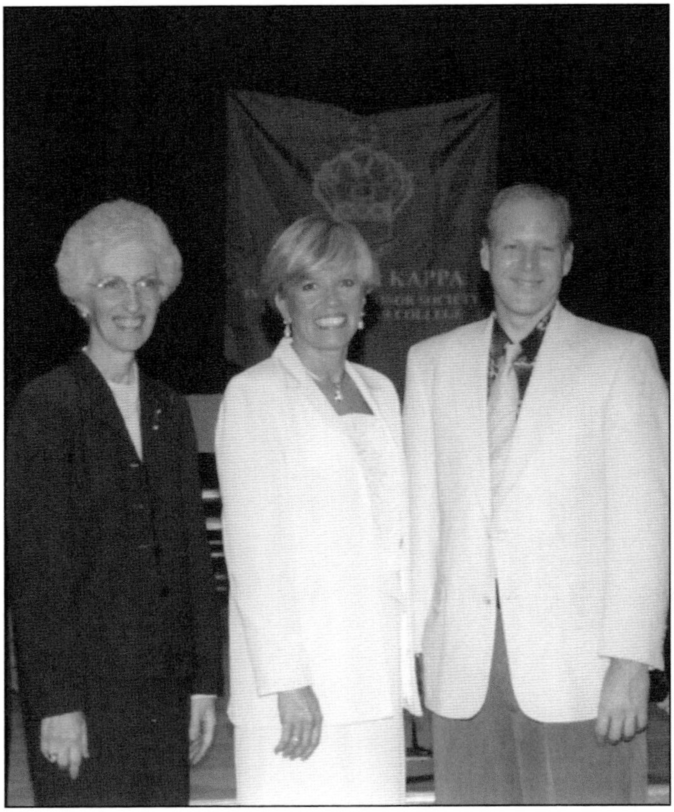

President Hawkins (left), Jan Whitley, and Skyler Ross, both Phi Theta Kappa advisors, attended the 2002 induction ceremony.

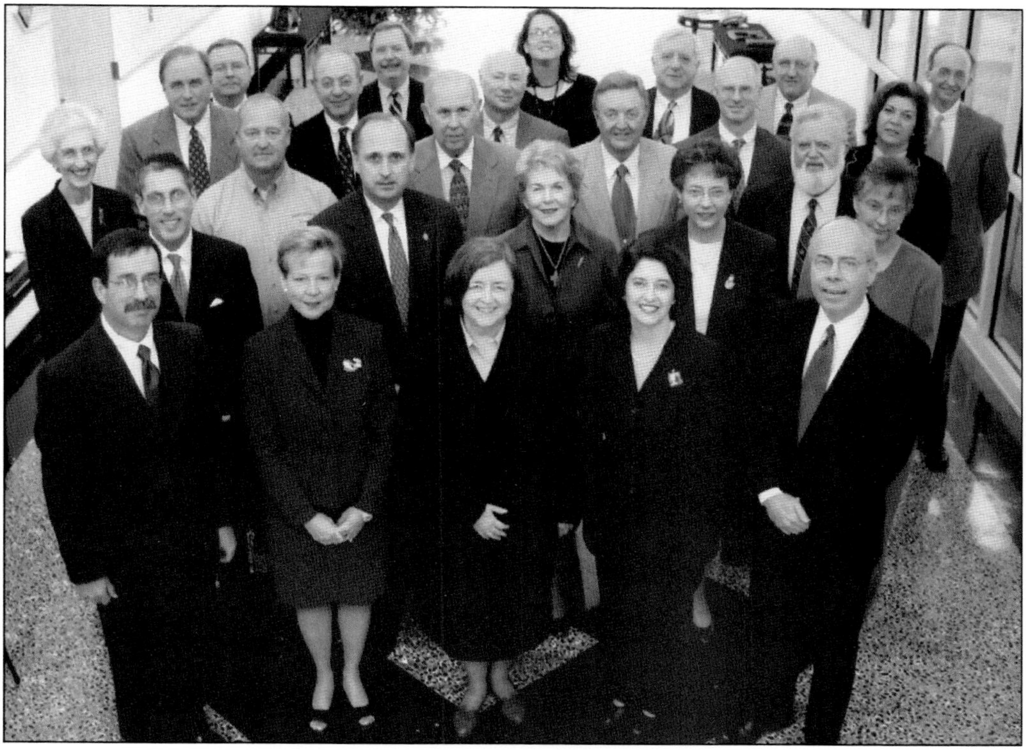

Pictured is the Columbia State Foundation for 2003–2004.

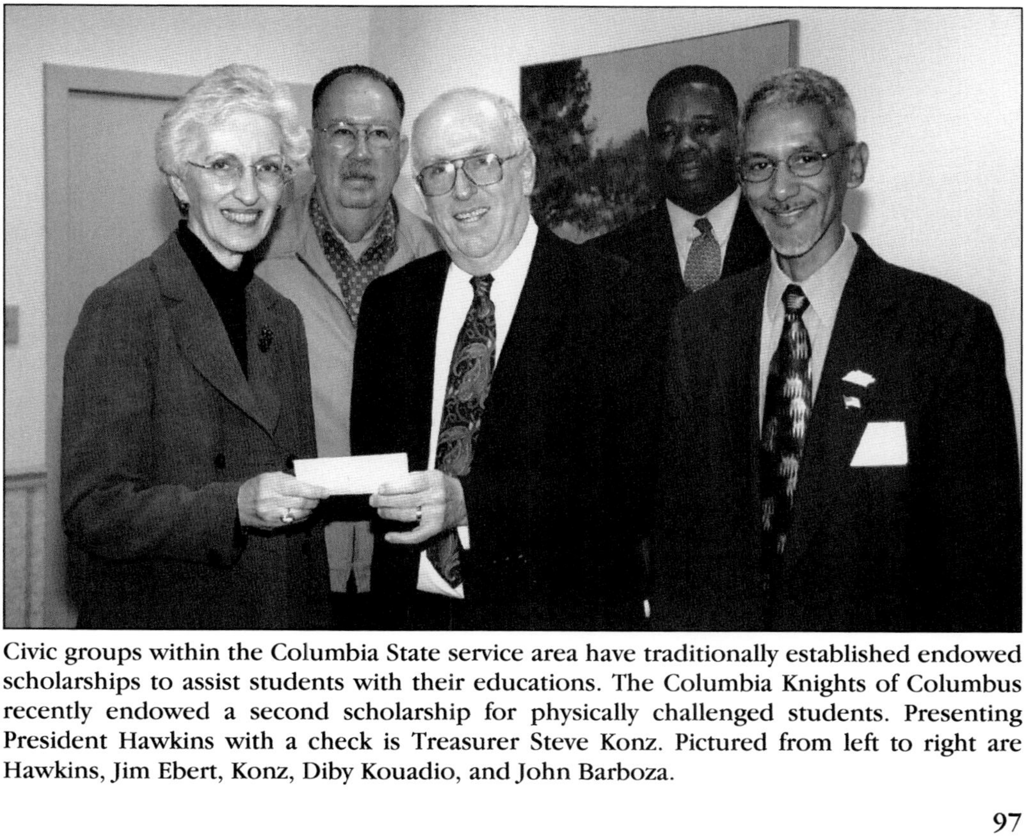

Civic groups within the Columbia State service area have traditionally established endowed scholarships to assist students with their educations. The Columbia Knights of Columbus recently endowed a second scholarship for physically challenged students. Presenting President Hawkins with a check is Treasurer Steve Konz. Pictured from left to right are Hawkins, Jim Ebert, Konz, Diby Kouadio, and John Barboza.

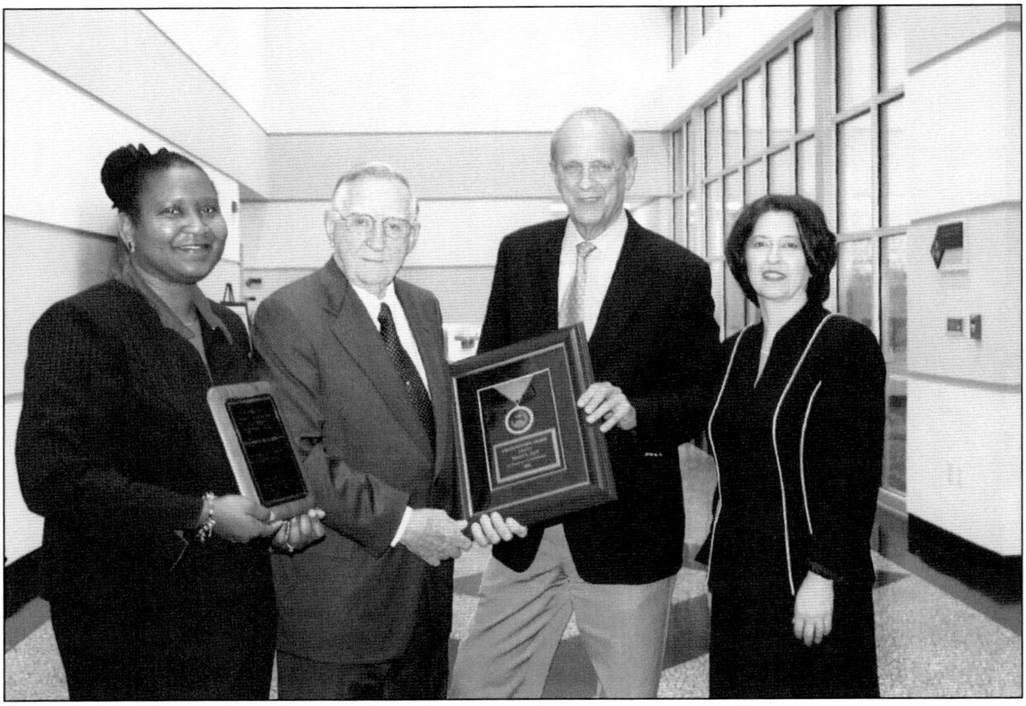

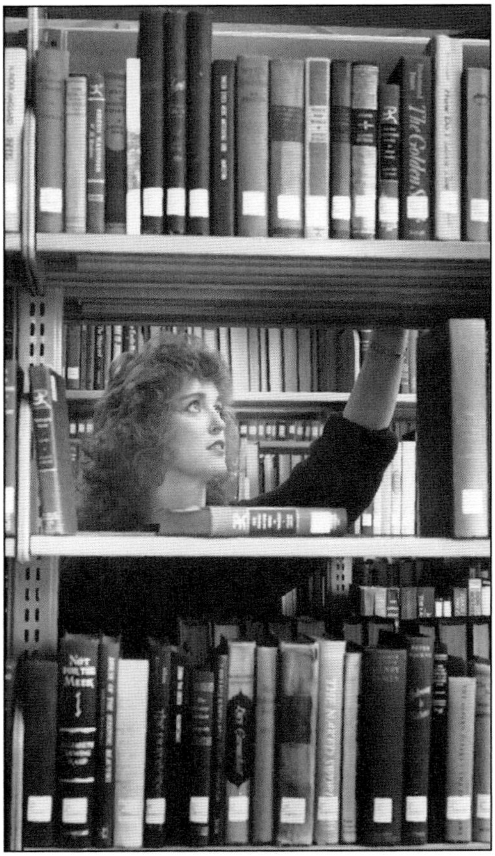

Dr. Harold S. Pryor was honored with the Chancellor's Award for Excellence in Philanthropy on March 9, 2004, following the Columbia State Foundation quarterly board meeting. Elizabeth Crutcher, CPS, was also recognized as the Outstanding Columbia State Alumnus of the Year 2003. From left to right are Crutcher, Pryor, TBR chancellor Charles Manning, and Gayle Mathis, president of the CoSCC Alumni Association.

Angela Hay is performing the faculty's preferred student activity of gathering information for a class assignment.

Four

The Arts

Columbia State has hosted many cultural activities over four decades. In addition to annual plays, musical programs, and art exhibits that originated on campus, there have been frequent visits by notable persons and performance groups. Groups such as the National Players, the National Opera Company, the Nashville Symphony, and the Fisk Jubilee Singers have thrilled their audiences. Notable speakers not pictured in this book included Virginia Spencer Carr, Dr. Dorothy Brown, Ralph Nader, David Haberstam, Peter Jenkins, Bill Monroe, Francis Robinson, and Bob Sheffer. Monologuists have brought to life such personalities as Mark Twain, Sojourner Truth, William Faulkner, Edgar Allen Poe, and Lyndon Baines Johnson.

Other cultural activities have included "Celebrating Our American Heritage," multicultural festivals, and Perceptions, *a literary magazine.*

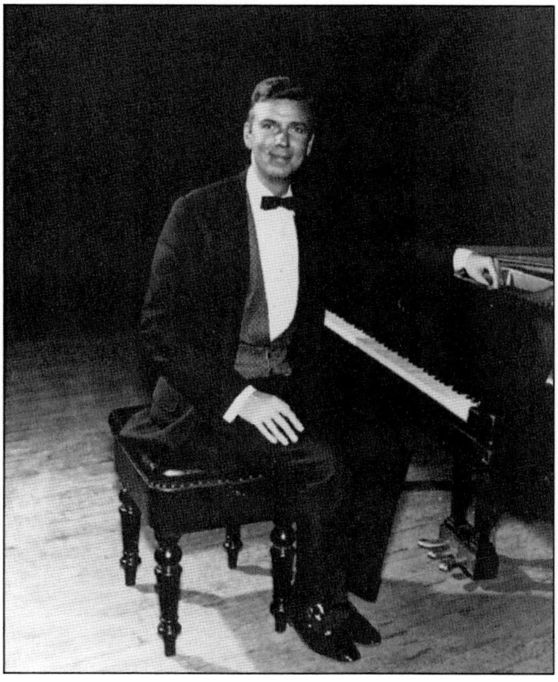

The first special performance at Columbia State was that of pianist Greg Colson. Colson entertained his audience at the Memorial Building, playing music from classical to pop to jazz. After each break in the performance, he re-entered the stage with a different, brightly colored vest. Following the performance, faculty and staff were able to visit with Colson at a reception at the home of Dean James Clark and his wife Winifred.

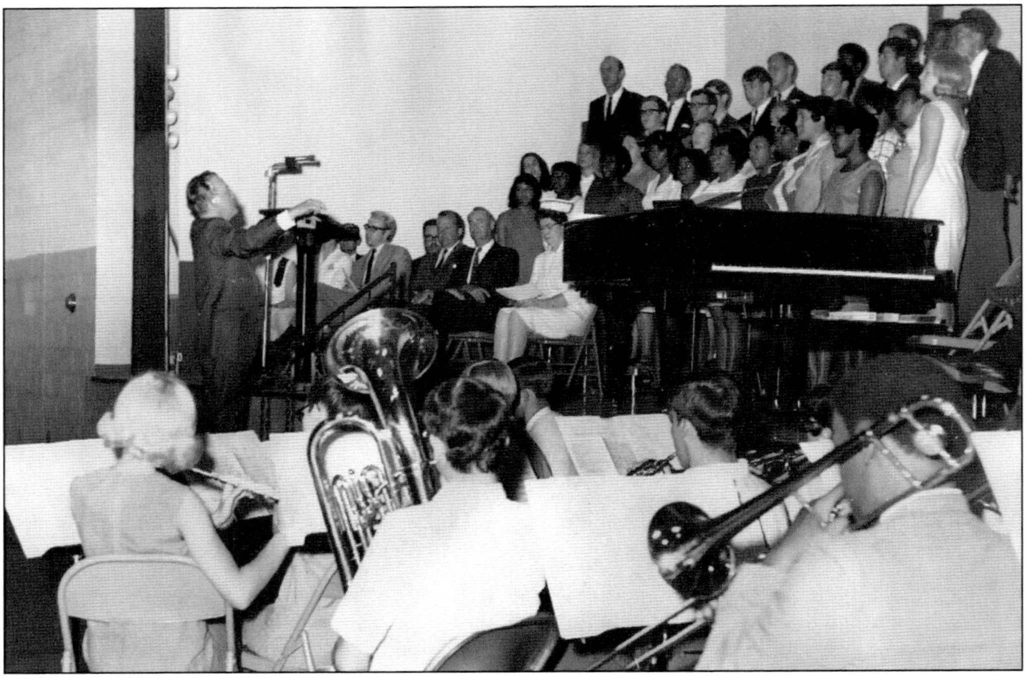

The Columbia State band and chorus, directed by Howard Lawrie, perform at the first Awards Day ceremony on May 14, 1969.

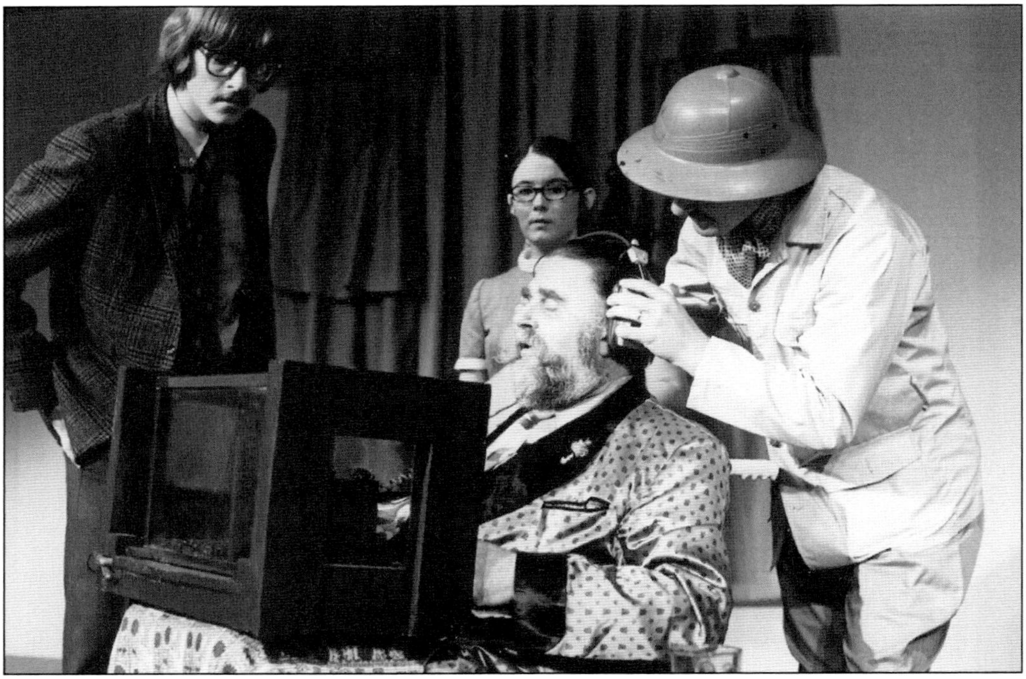

The Columbia State Drama Club was organized in 1967. Members received training in acting, stagecraft, makeup, and lighting. Between 1967 and 1971, the Drama Club produced *Bus Stop*, *You Can't Take It With You*, *The Weatherman*, *Spoon River Anthology*, and *The Man Who Came to Dinner*. Sam Martin, an instructor of history, is the bearded "man who came to dinner."

Fred Becker, Columbia State's first music teacher, portrays the "Man of Steel" in a campus production.

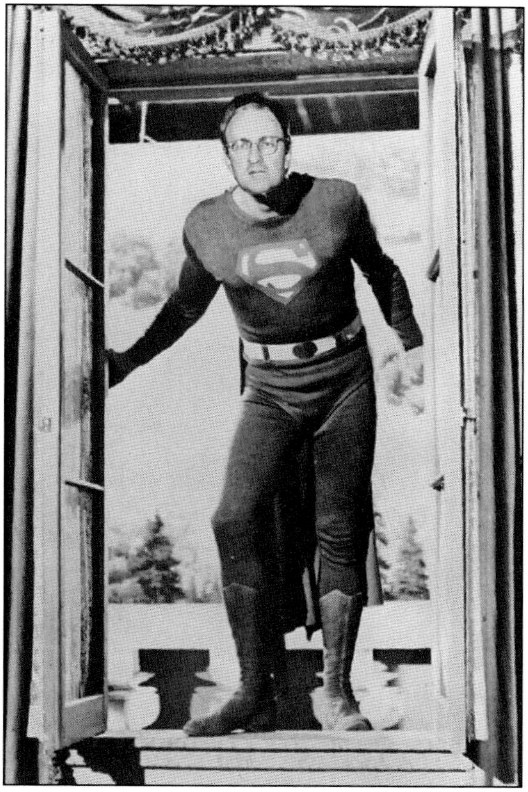

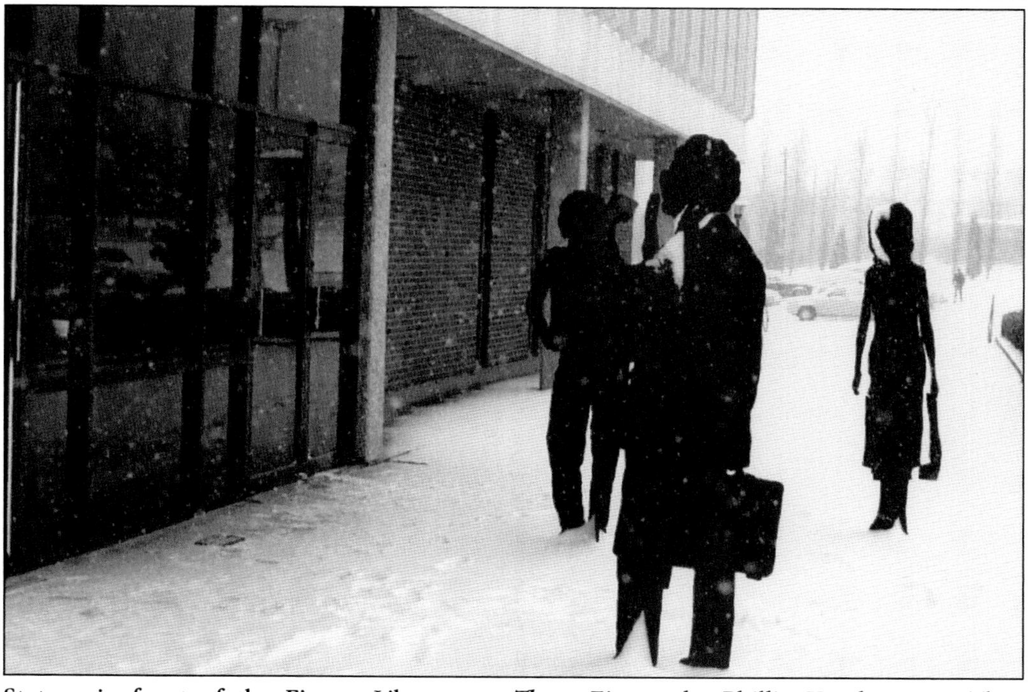

Statues in front of the Finney Library are *Three Figures* by Phillip Vander Weg. They were made possible by a grant from the Tennessee Arts Commission and the Columbia State Foundation.

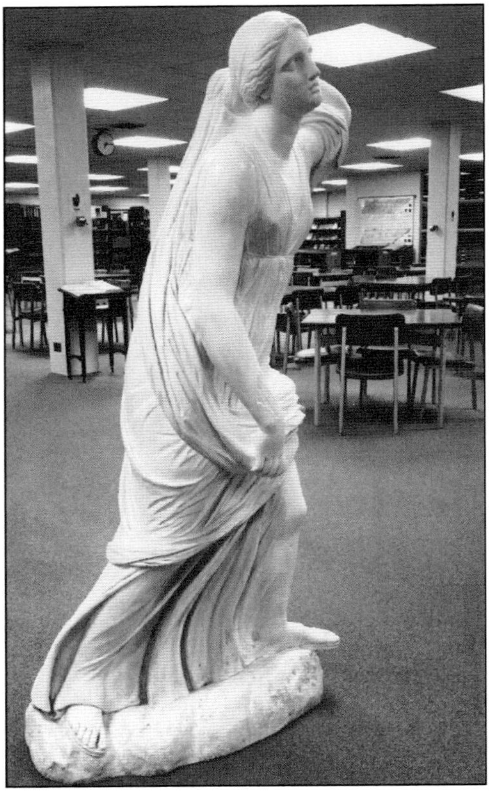

In 1978, the college received a gift of 13 plaster casts of statuary from the Metropolitan Museum of Art in New York on a permanent loan. The collection consists of four statues, six busts, and three bas reliefs. Pictured is one of those casts, *A Niobid*, which dates to about 100 B.C., possibly by Skopas.

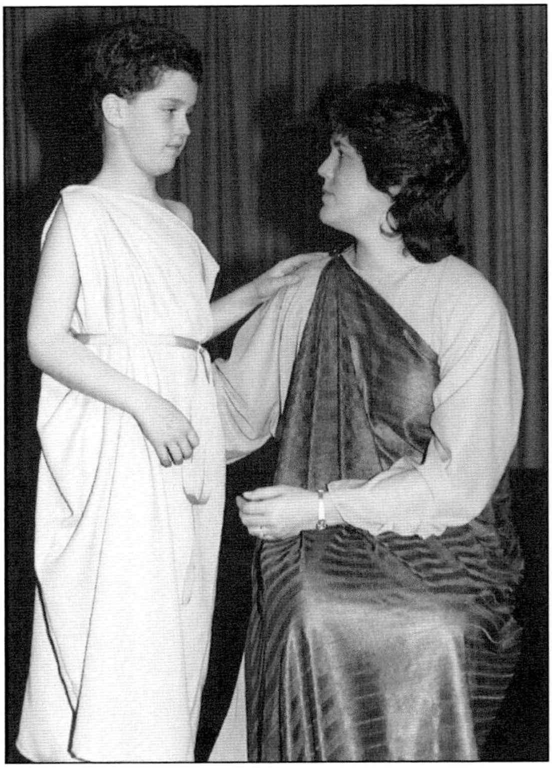

Trojan Women was produced in 1983 by the Columbia State Drama Club. Pictured are Lauri Kaye Bolton and Jimmie Jones.

Wilma Dykeman, noted historian and novelist, cast "a tall shadow" as author-in-residence. Dykeman, state historian for Tennessee, spent a week at Columbia State giving lectures to students and the general public. Dykeman authored the novels *The Tall Woman*, *The Far Family*, and *Return the Innocent Earth*. She was the graduation speaker in 1980.

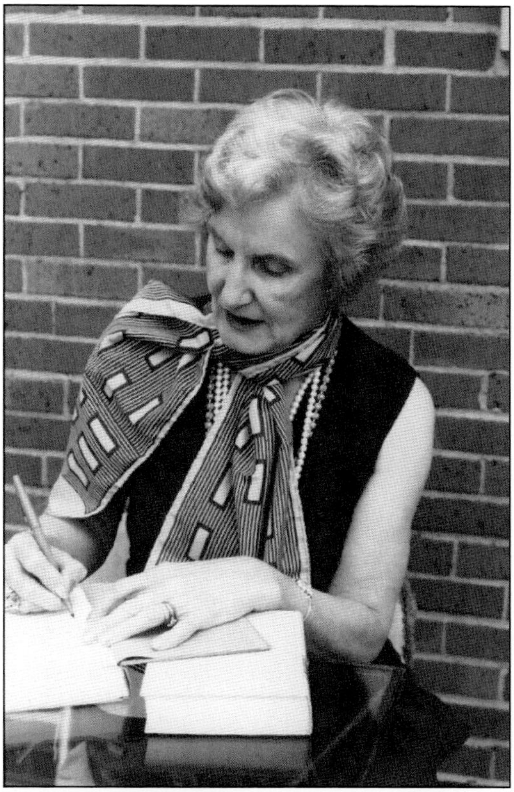

Famous comic Jerry Clower did a benefit for the athletic department in 1984. Clower is pictured with Van Jones (left) and Paul Sands.

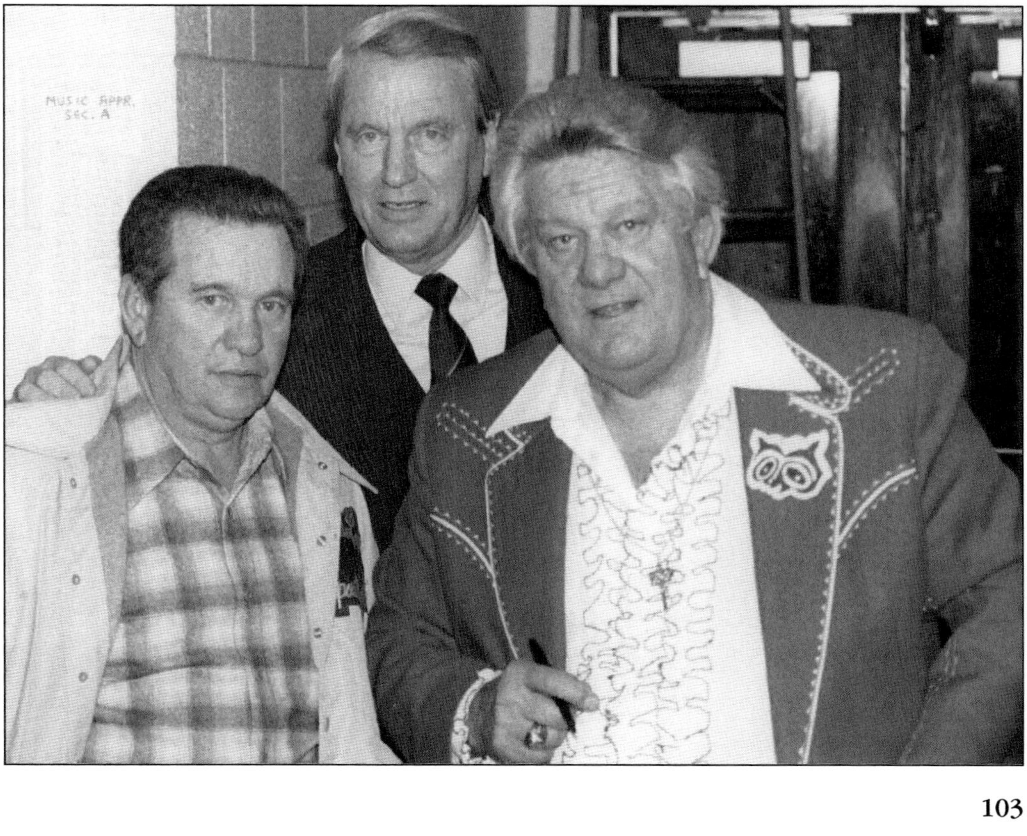

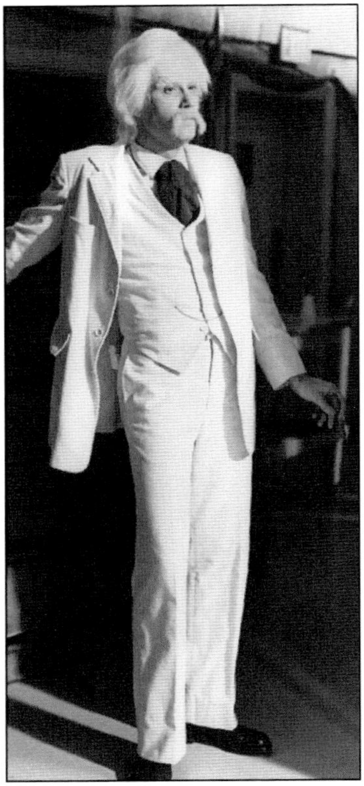

Will Stutts came to Columbia State several times to present his one-man show on Mark Twain. He also delivered monologues on other famous figures such as Walt Whitman, Clarence Darrow, and Edgar Allan Poe.

The Outlook Speaker Series, sponsored by the Lyceum Committee, has hosted several interesting personalities. Pictured with President and Mrs. Pryor is Gen. William Westmoreland (right).

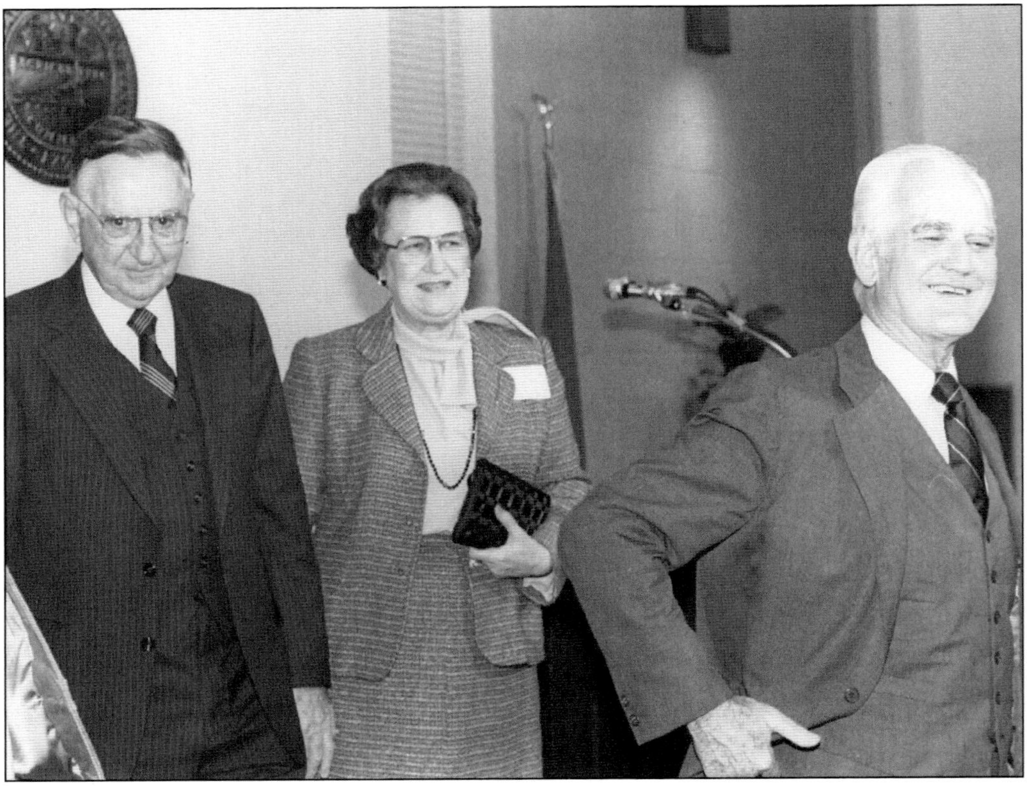

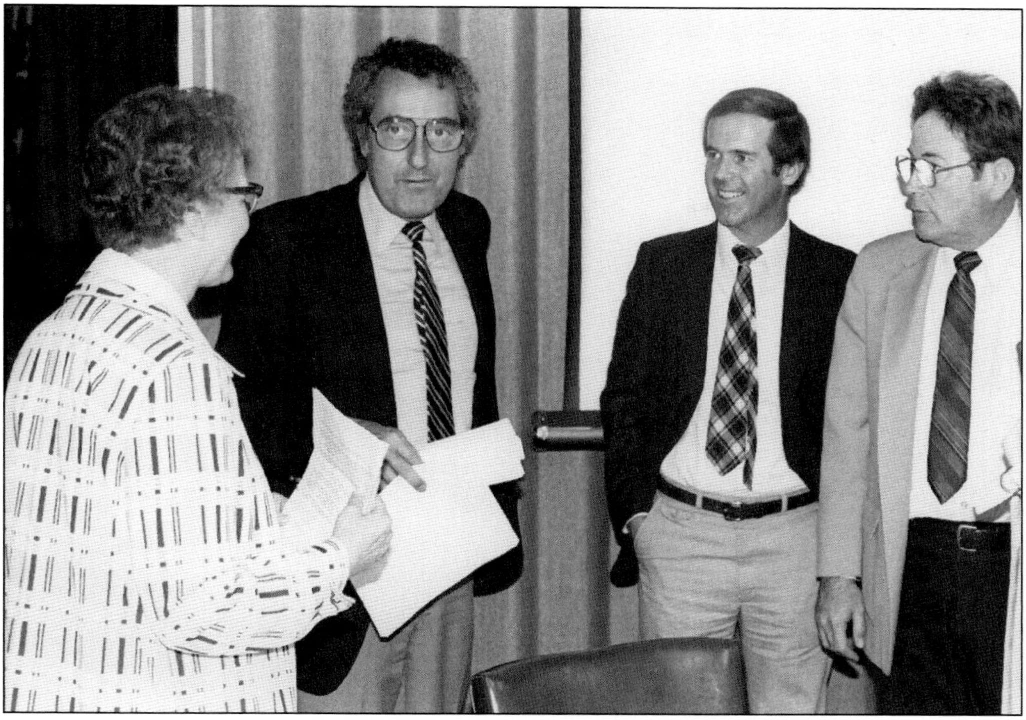

News commentator Richard Valeriani was one of the speakers in the Outlook Series. Pictured with Valeriani are, from left to right, Gabes Hubert, Bill Andrews, and Tom Wesley.

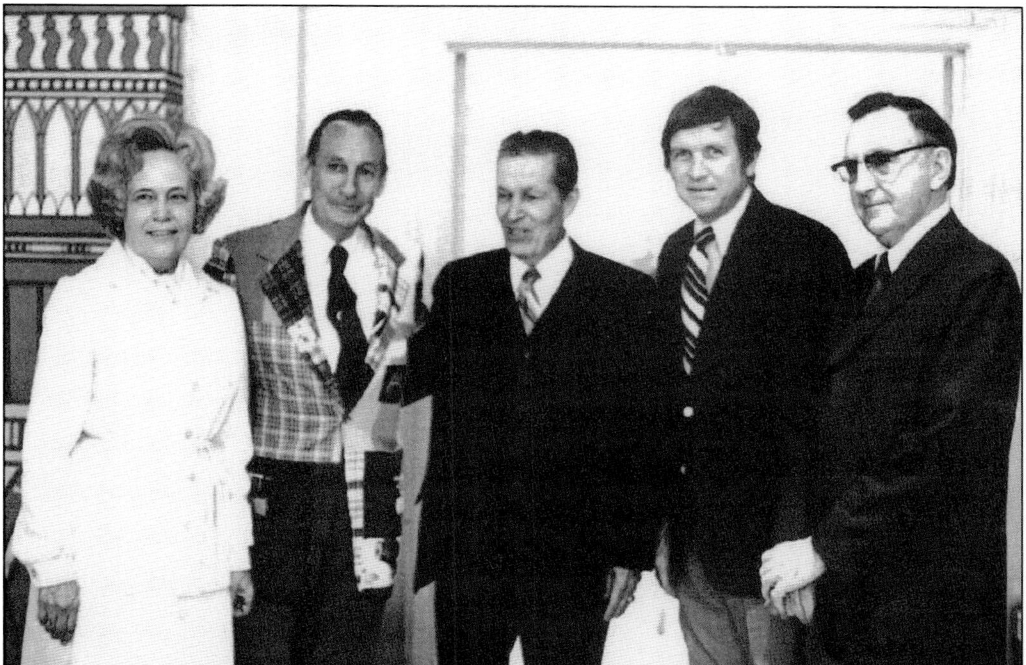

Nationally recognized sportscaster Lindsey Nelson, a graduate of Central High School, appeared in the Outlook Speaker Series. From left to right are Mrs. Taylor Rayburn, Nelson, County Judge Taylor Rayburn, Johnny Majors, and President Pryor.

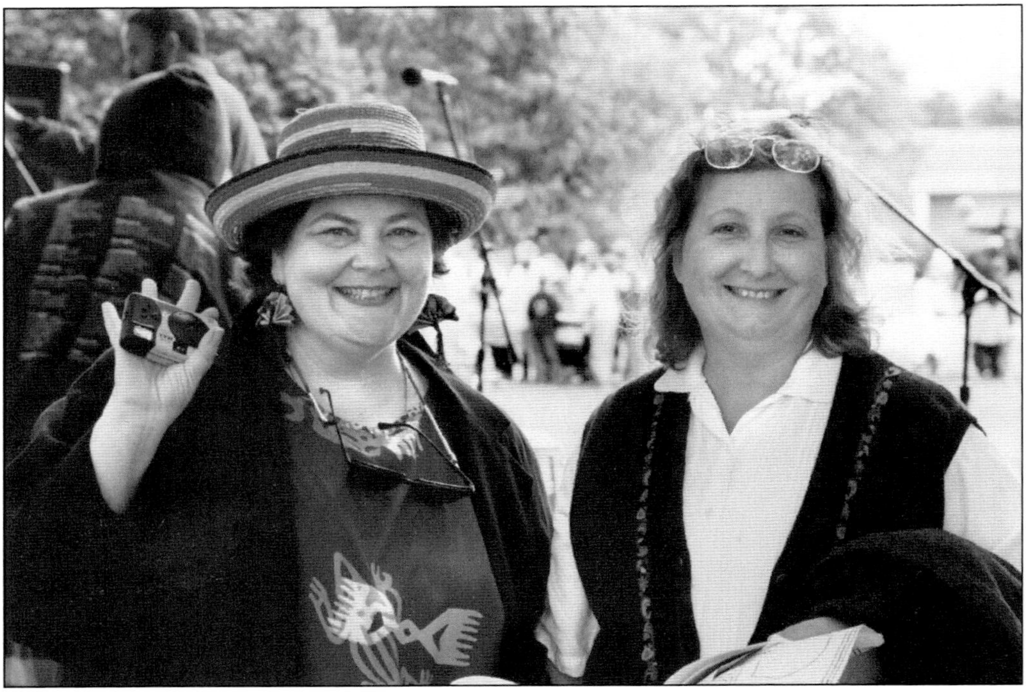

Beverly Mitchell (left) and Susanna Holmes, both of the English department, were the organizers of the Multicultural Festival, later named Culture Fest.

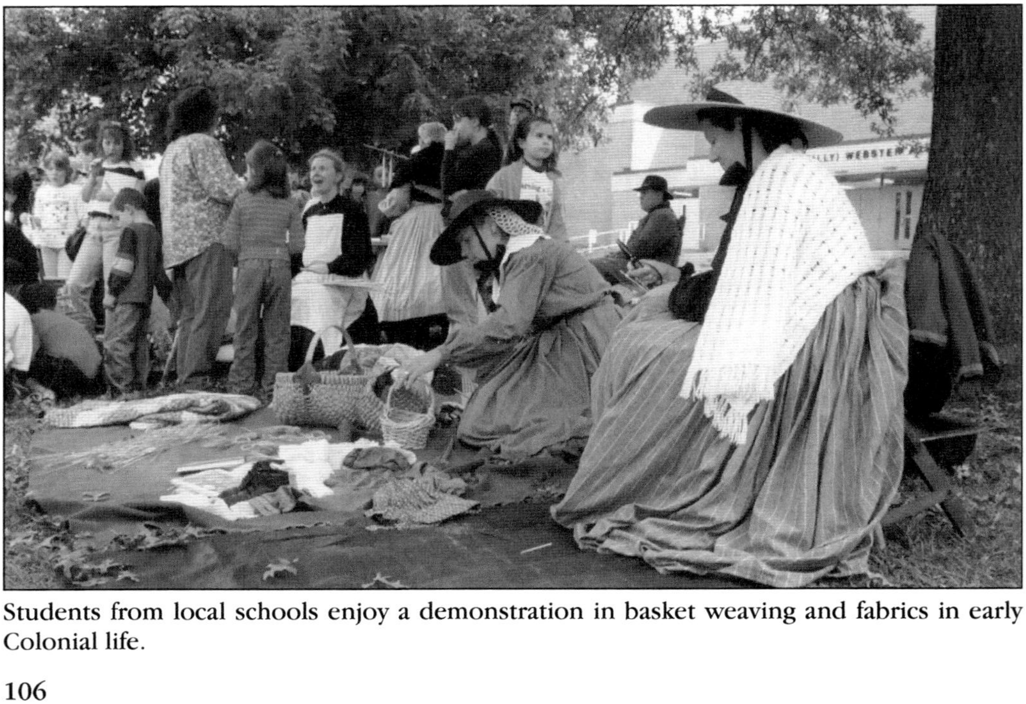

Students from local schools enjoy a demonstration in basket weaving and fabrics in early Colonial life.

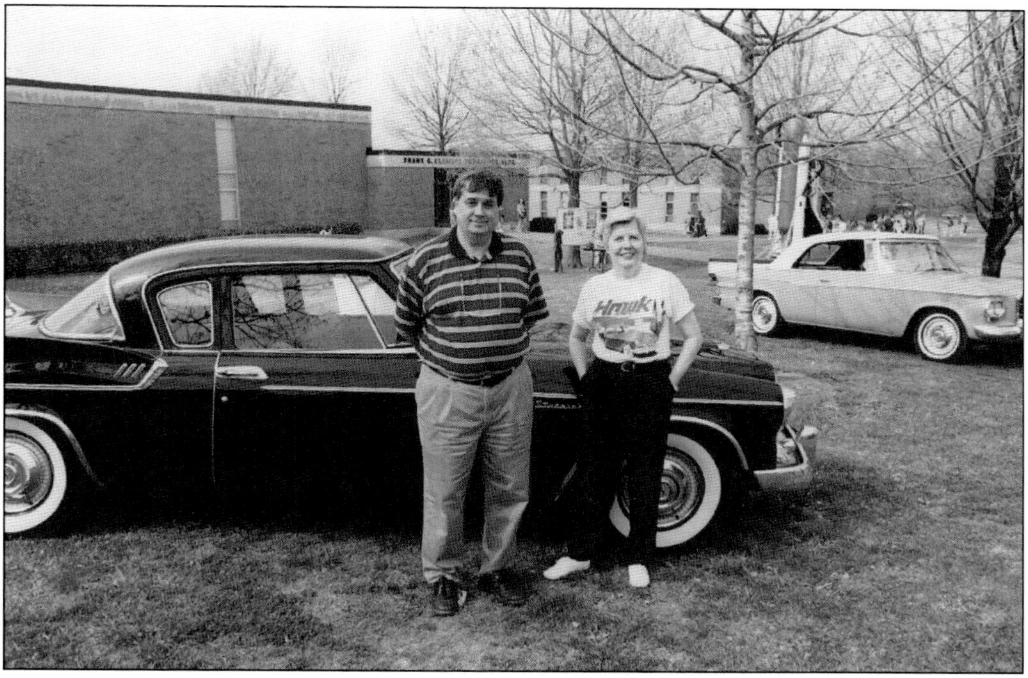

The year 1996 was the 100th anniversary of the American automobile industry. Carolyn Allred-Winnett and Phil Matlock stand in front of the Frank G. Clement Humanities Building with two of Carolyn's Studebakers, a 1960 Hawk and a 1962 Lark Convertible, during the 1996 Multicultural Festival. These cars were only six and four years old, respectively, when Columbia State opened. In the background is a model of the space shuttle.

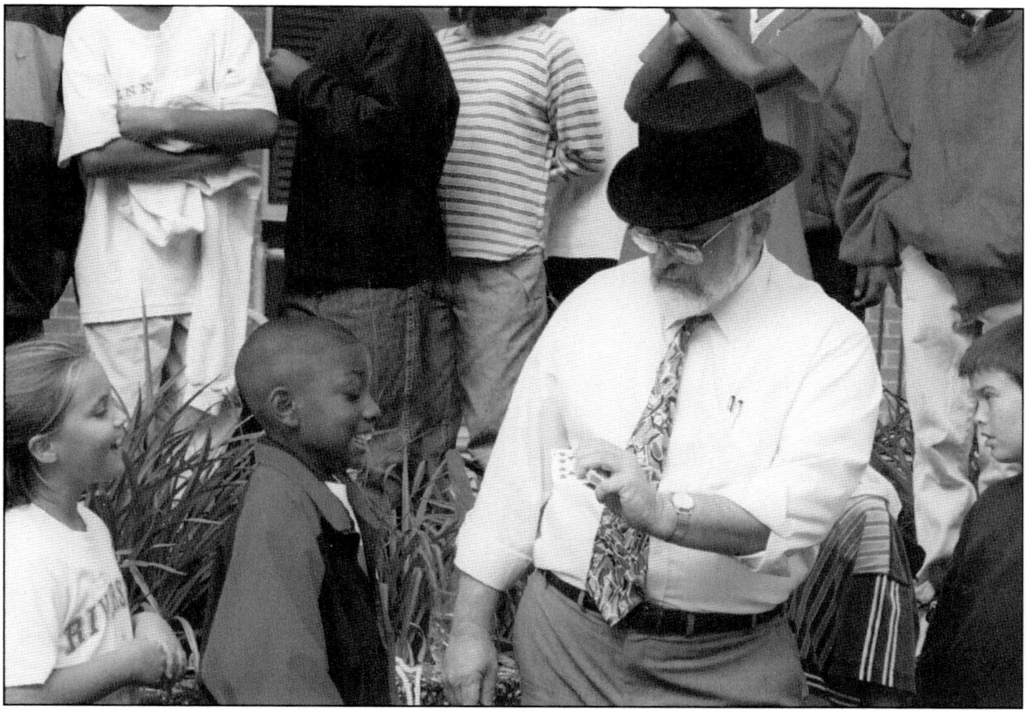

Jim Murchison performs magic tricks for astonished children at the Multicultural Festival.

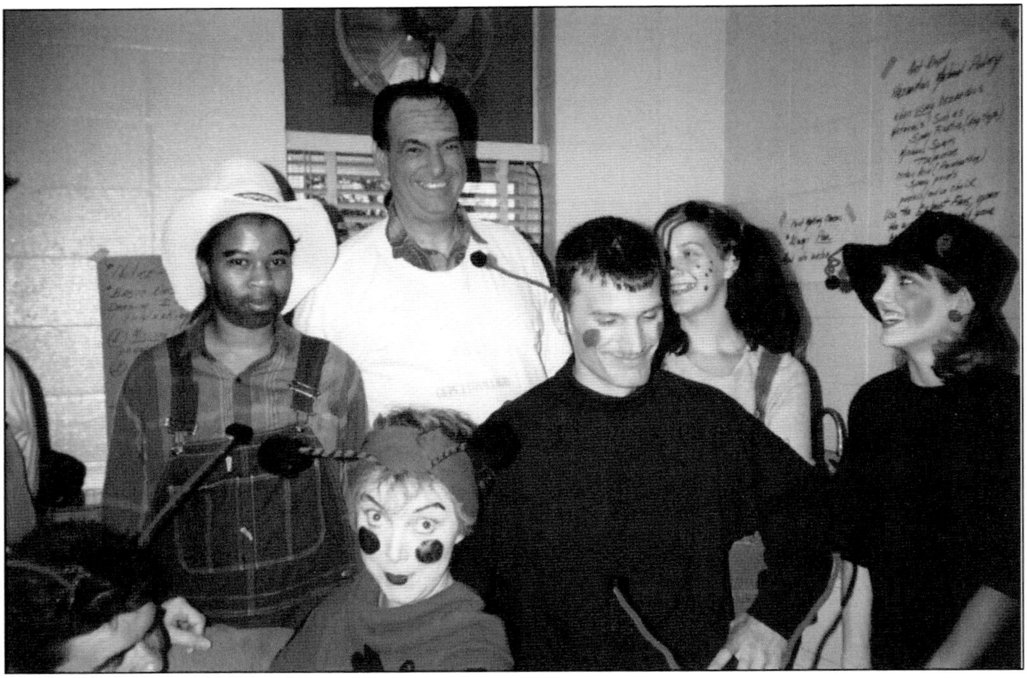

Pinosio was written and directed by Beverly Mitchell of the English department. Preparing to go on stage are, from left to right, Antoinette Gaines, unidentified, Bo Bollinger, David Miller, Ashley Foster, and unidentified.

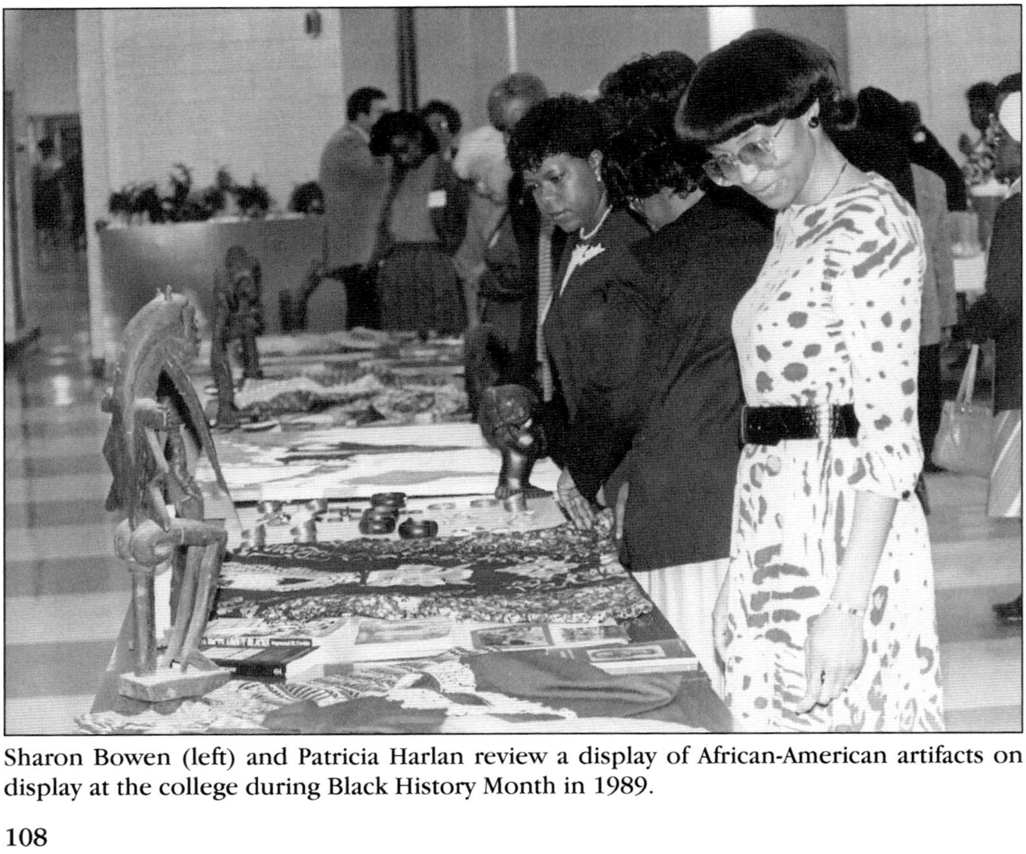

Sharon Bowen (left) and Patricia Harlan review a display of African-American artifacts on display at the college during Black History Month in 1989.

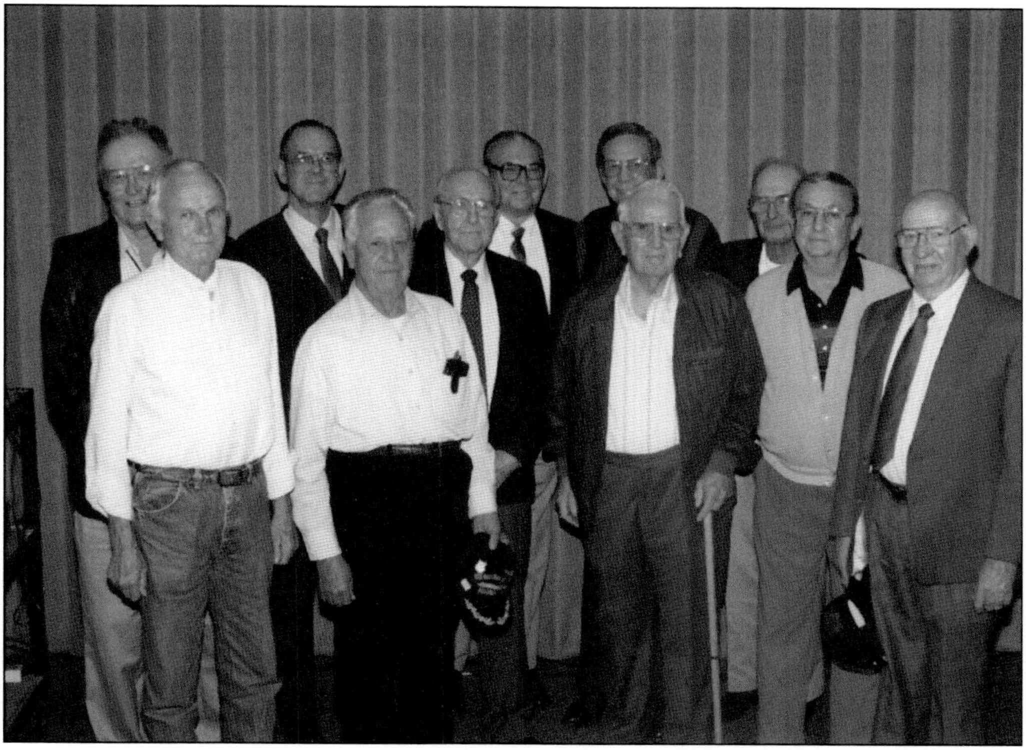

As a part of "Celebrating Our American Heritage" series, veterans of Philippine Campaigns were recognized. Pictured from left to right are (front row) Mack Counts, Melvin Anderson, Charles Alexander, Thomas Williams, Fisher Oakes, and Bill Voss; (back row) Glenn Stevenson, James D. Williams, Charles Yokley, Charles Brown, and Ivie West.

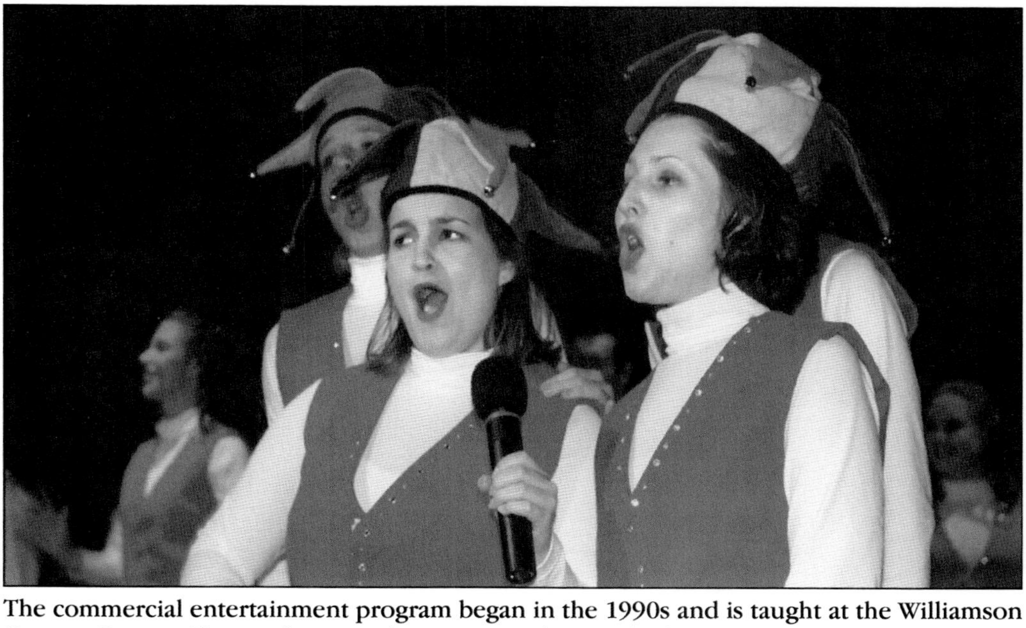

The commercial entertainment program began in the 1990s and is taught at the Williamson County Center. The students perform a special annual Christmas program. Pictured are Tracy Hill (left) and an unidentified friend.

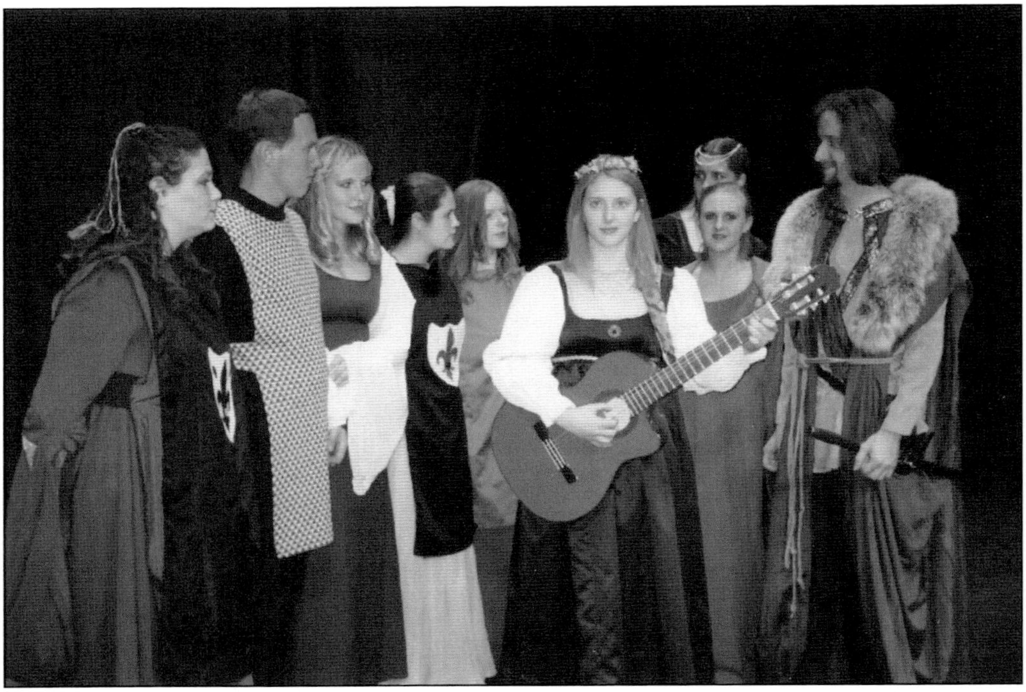

Here students perform *Romeo and Juliet* in the Cherry Theater in 2002. The play was directed by Beverly Mitchell. Performing are (from left to right) Jessica Cooper, Josh Holloway, Sabrina Ardry, Erin Pruett, Sarah Hathaway, Kate Neff, Nicole Loveless, Marie McBride, and R.J. Polito.

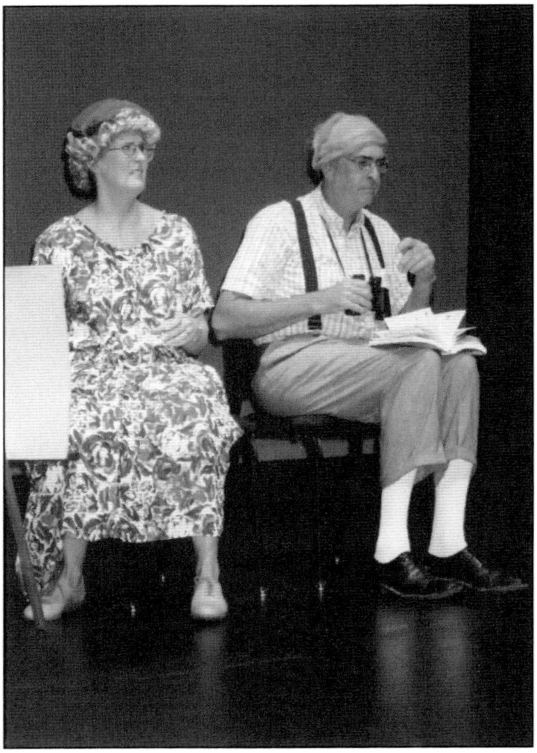

Judy Smith of the nursing department and theater and media technician Bo Bollinger perform the comedy *I'm Herbert* in 2002. This performance was one of three in "A Night of One Acts," which was organized by the Geste Club.

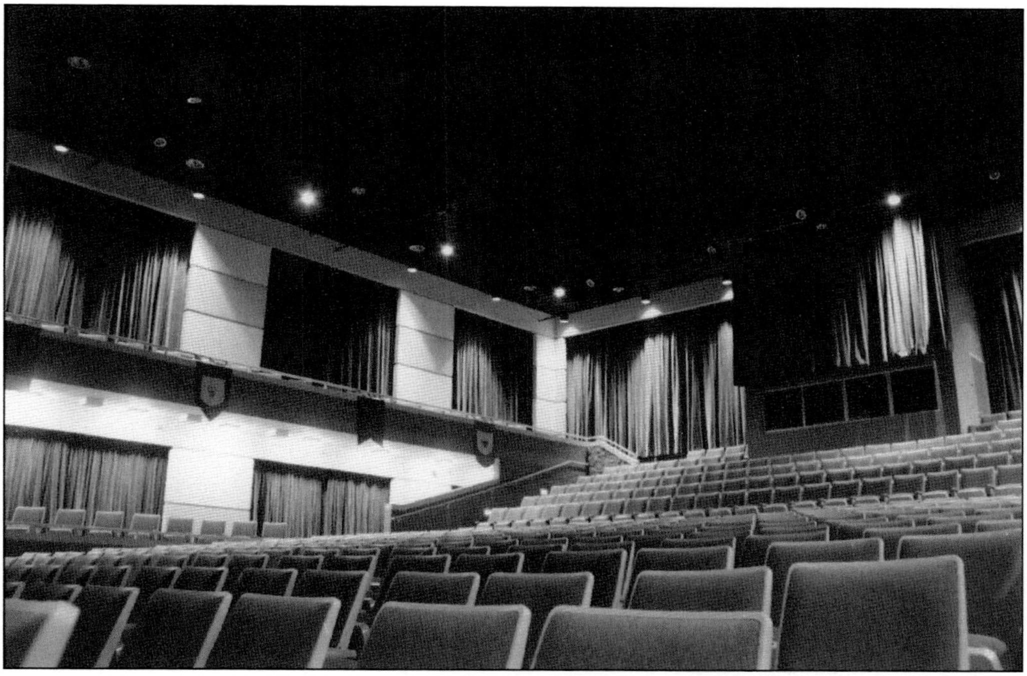

The 500-seat Cherry Theater, in the Hickman Building, was dedicated to Kenneth and Ramona Cherry in 2002. The theater and backstage area is equipped for almost any type of stage production. With the completion of the Cherry Theater, the annual "Performance Series" brings many cultural opportunities to the college and community.

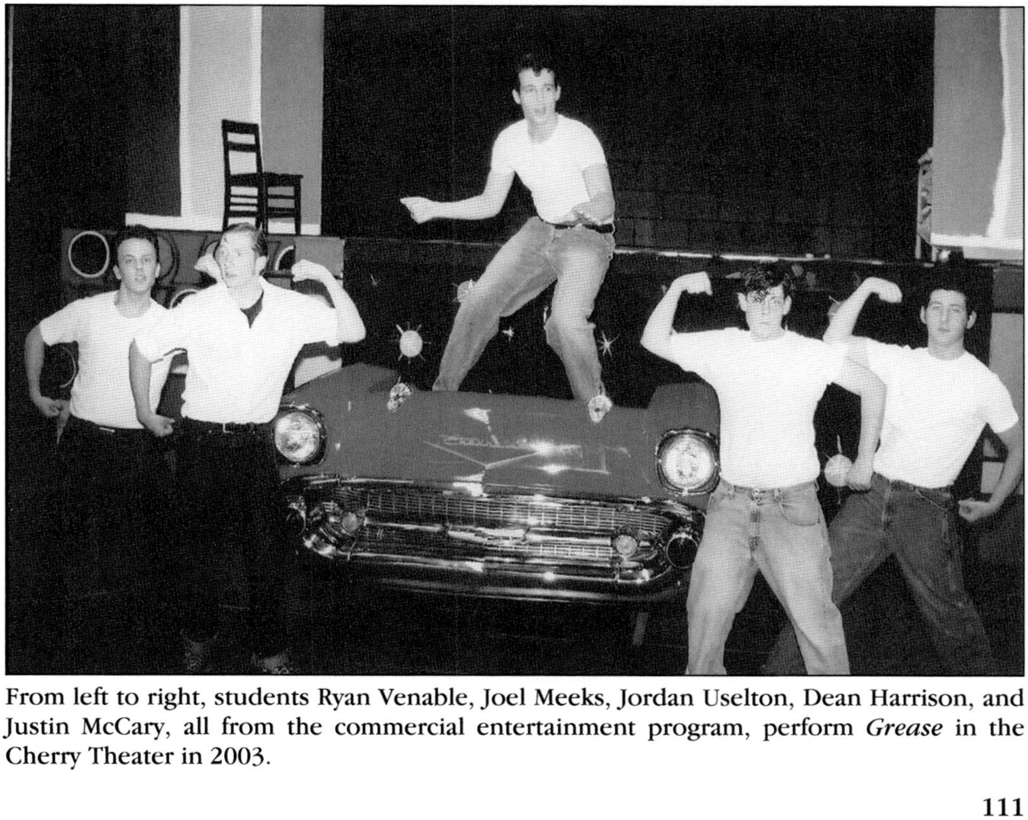

From left to right, students Ryan Venable, Joel Meeks, Jordan Uselton, Dean Harrison, and Justin McCary, all from the commercial entertainment program, perform *Grease* in the Cherry Theater in 2003.

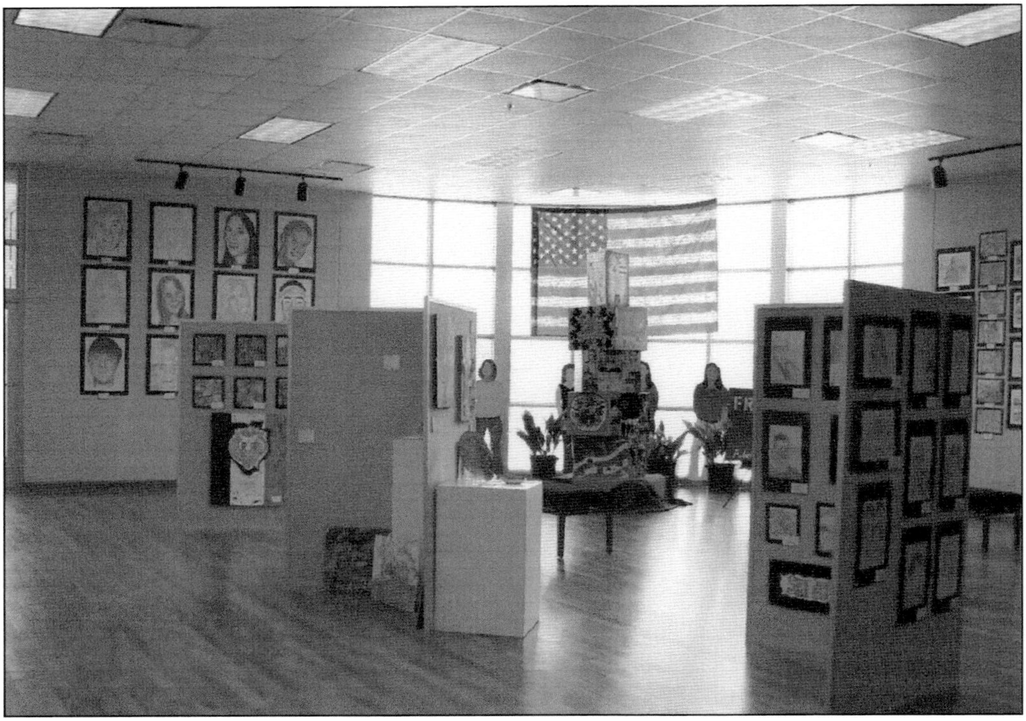

The Pryor Art Gallery is named for LaRue V. Pryor, wife of Columbia State's first president. The gallery is in the Hickman Building and was dedicated in 2002.

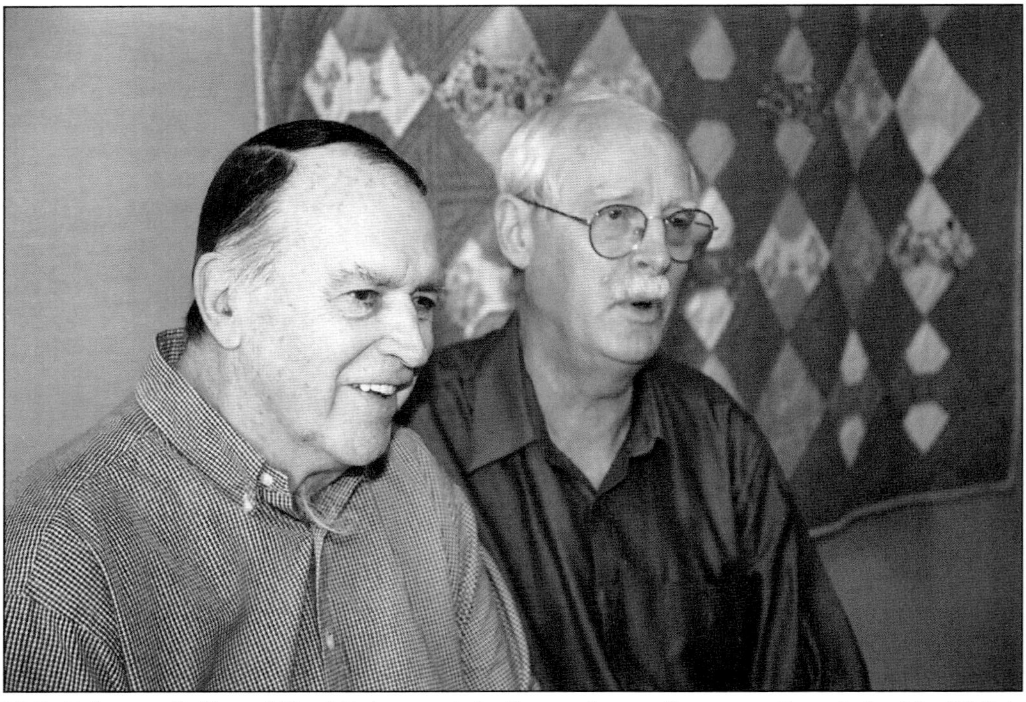

W.O. Johnson (left) and Fred Behrens sit in front of one of many quilts stitched by W.O.'s mother. The quilts were on display in the Pryor Art Gallery in 2003.

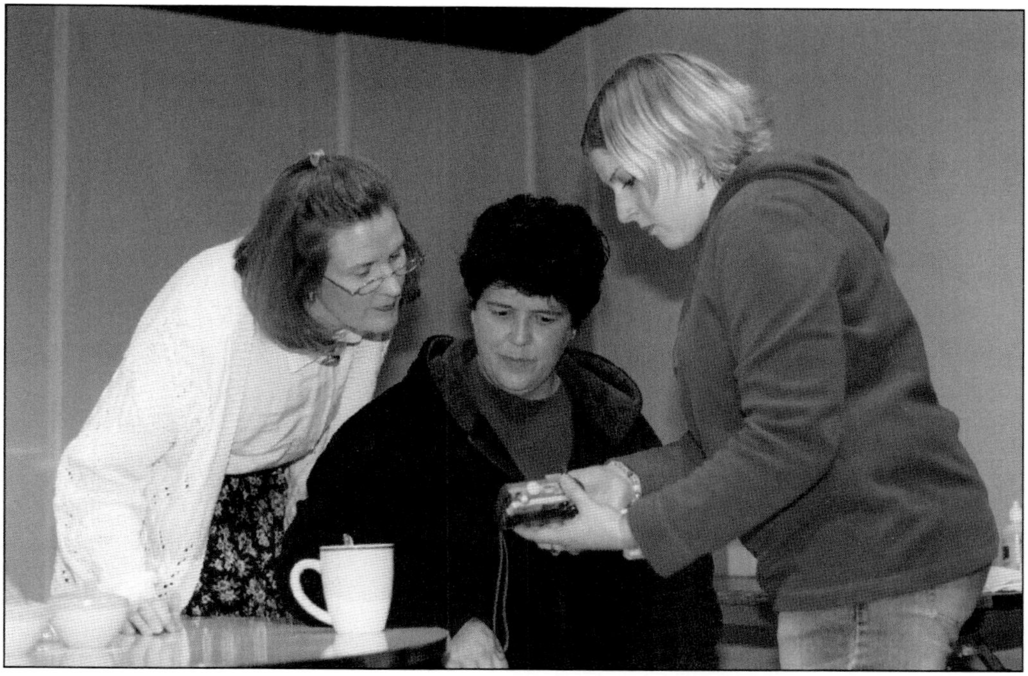

Judy Smith (left) and Lauri Kaye Burns (center) receive instructions from Terry Ruth Winnett, Columbia State sophomore and director of the play *'night Mother*. Judy teaches in the nursing department, and Lauri Kaye is an alumnus and theatre student at Middle Tennessee State University.

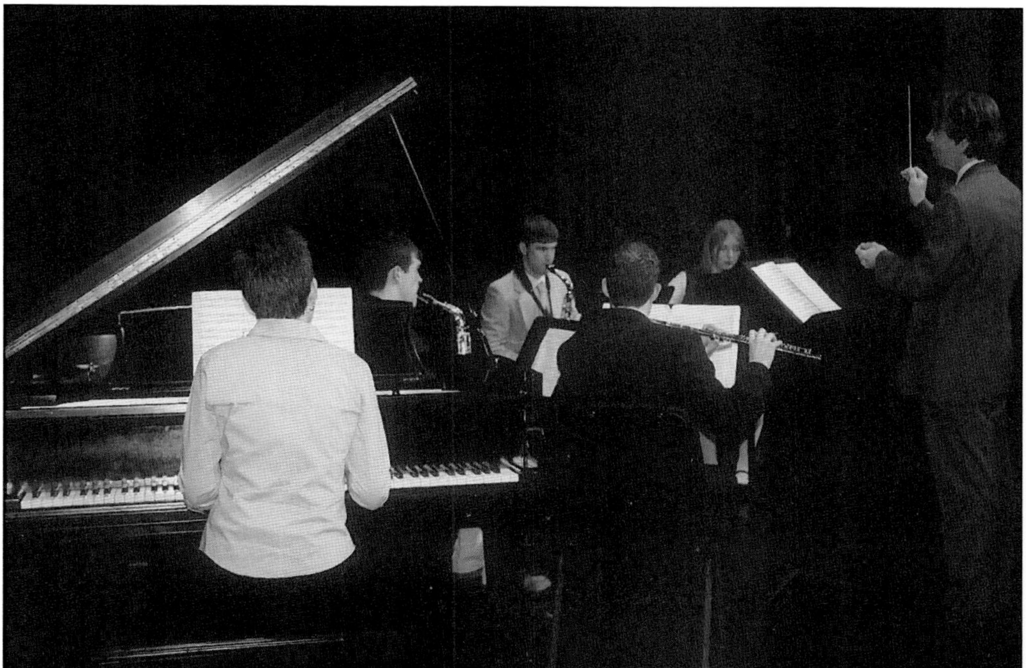

The Columbia State String Ensemble, conducted by Mark Lee, performs each year at graduation and other special events.

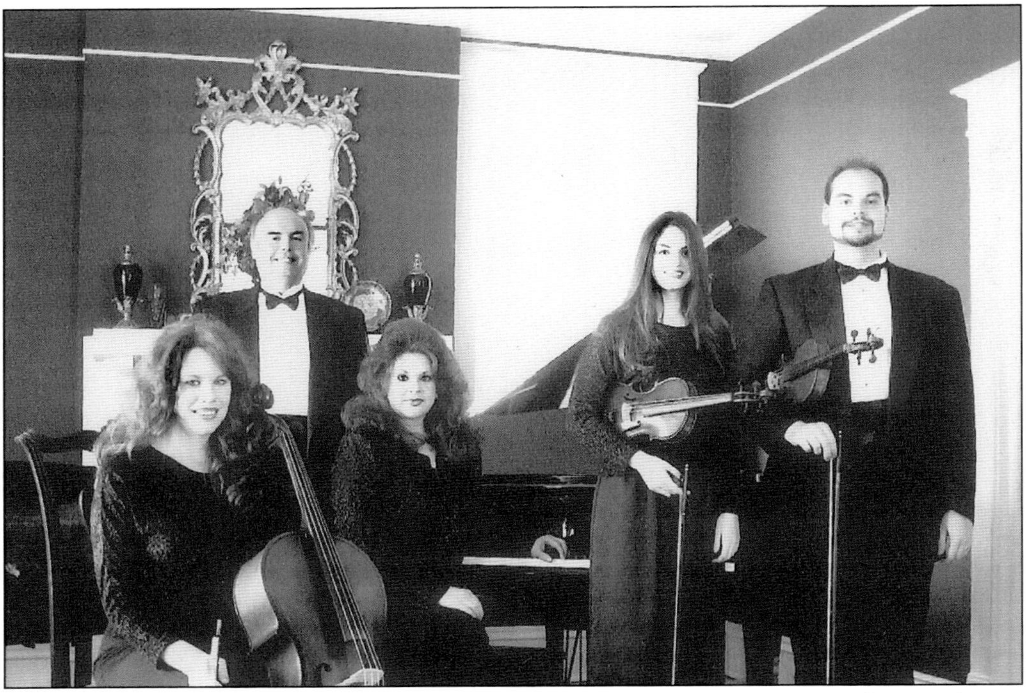

Pictured here are family members of the Lewis Chamber Strings. From left to right are Elizabeth Lewis, cello; Mel Lewis, narrator/technician; Beverly Lewis, director/pianist; Margaret Lewis, violin; and Matt Lewis, violin. Matt is a Columbia State alumnus and an employee at the Lewisburg Site.

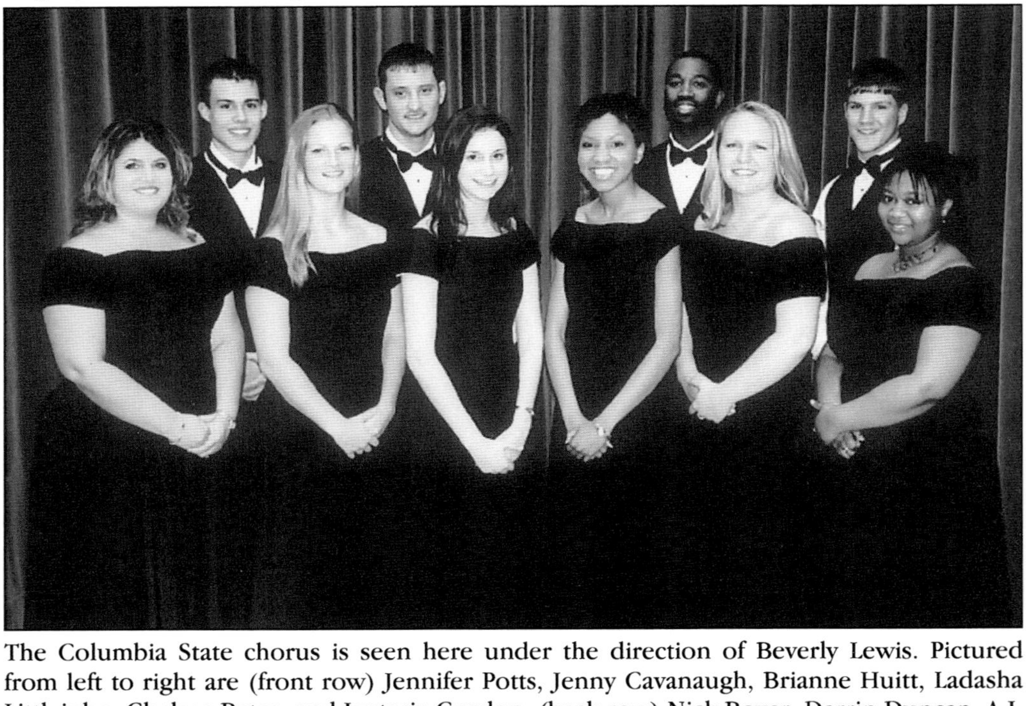

The Columbia State chorus is seen here under the direction of Beverly Lewis. Pictured from left to right are (front row) Jennifer Potts, Jenny Cavanaugh, Brianne Huitt, Ladasha Littlejohn, Chelsea Bates, and Lysteria Gordon; (back row) Nick Boyer, Darrin Duncan, A.J. Anderson, and Kenny Heiser.

Five

ATHLETICS

A group of Tennessee community colleges, acting without state authorization, joined with existing private junior colleges to form a new intra-state athletic conference. The Tennessee Junior College Athletic Association (TJCAA) was formed in May 1968. Columbia State, a charter member, has enjoyed considerable success in all areas of team competitions.

Through 2003, baseball teams won 15 TJCAA championships and participated in six national tournaments. Men's basketball teams won three state championships and advanced to three national tournaments. Women's basketball teams won three state titles and went to one national tournament. Women's tennis teams won three state championships and participated in two national tournaments. Men's tennis teams won two state championships and went to one national tournament. One golf team won a state title.

Athletic facilities include a gymnasium that houses a weight room and indoor track, a quarter-mile outdoor track, tennis courts, a baseball field named for Dave Hall, a softball field, a soccer field, and natatorium.

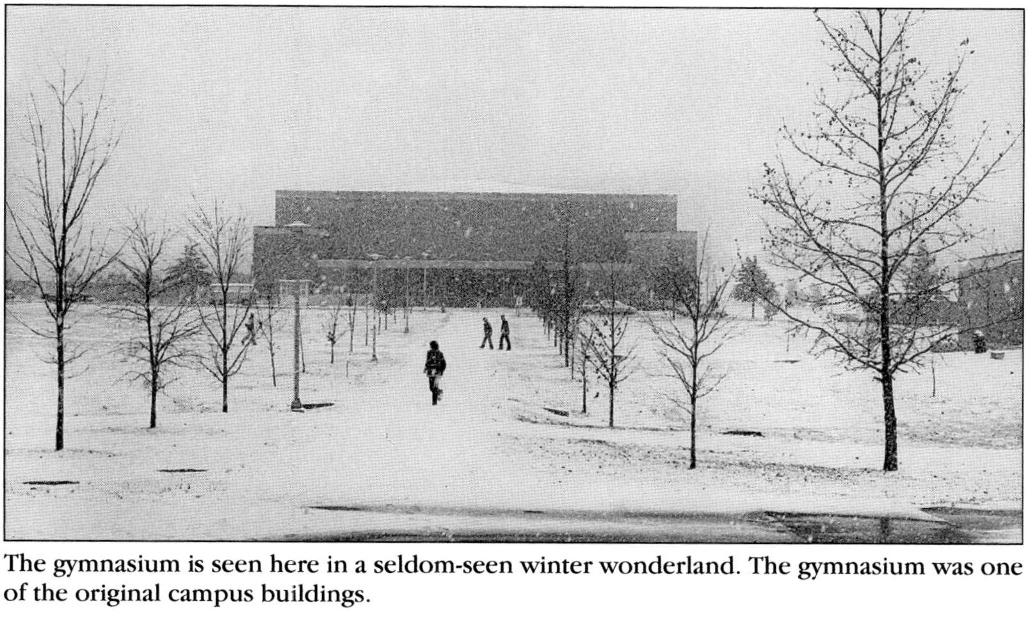

The gymnasium is seen here in a seldom-seen winter wonderland. The gymnasium was one of the original campus buildings.

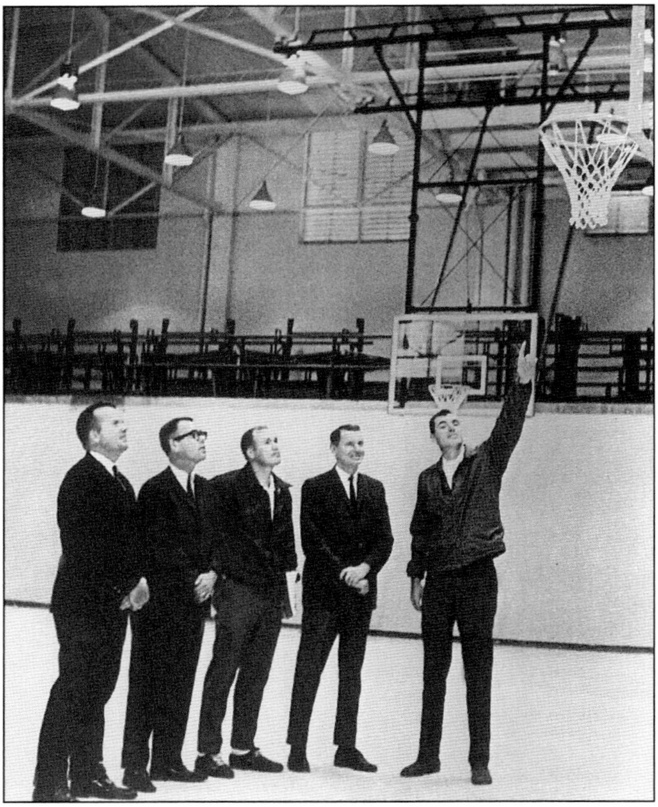

The first coaching staff inspects the new gym. From left to right are Lewis Moore, tennis; John Thomas, golf; Dave Hall, baseball; Paul Sands, athletic director; and Bennett Jent, basketball.

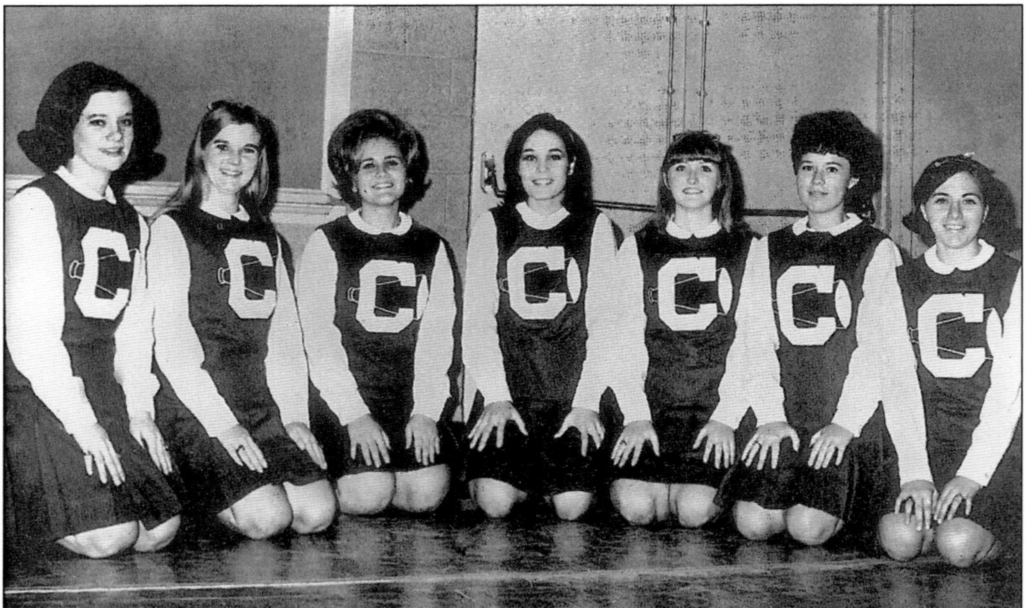

Columbia State's 1967–1968 cheerleaders were (from left to right) Linda Davis, Linda Garbarina, Sandy Hines (captain), Elaine Harris, Gail Norman, Sheila Mash, and Beth Henry.

The peak of school spirit was homecoming, complete with a bonfire, new pep band, dance, and the crowning of the 1968 queen, Dianne Potts, who was escorted by Billy Chappell.

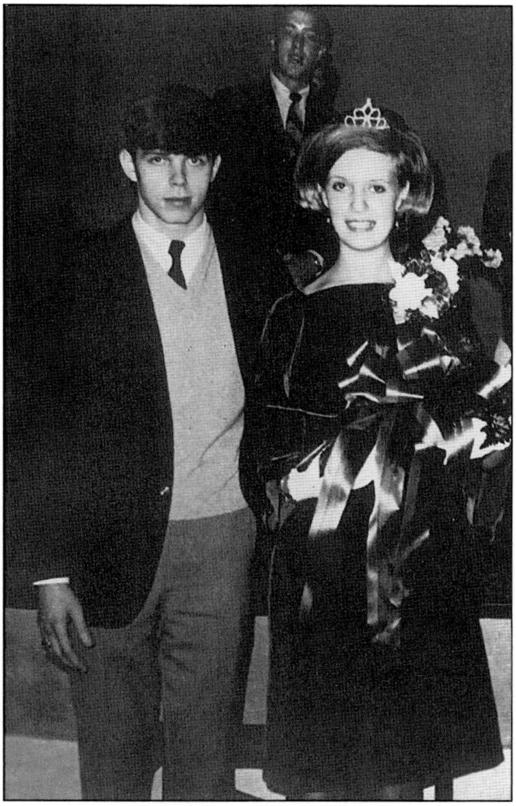

The 1968–1969 Charger basketball team, under Coach Bennett Jent, finished a successful year with an exciting season-ending 86–85 win over arch-rival Martin College. From left to right are (front row) Mike Royster, manager; James Claiborne; Phil Lovell; Richard Caulfield; Ronnie Saunders; Louis Connor; and Pete Johnson, manager; (back row) Larry Brewer; Donnie Crenshaw; Herb Luker; Ronald Warf; Virgil Beasley; and Ricky Luna. Brewer and Connor later became Columbia State head coaches.

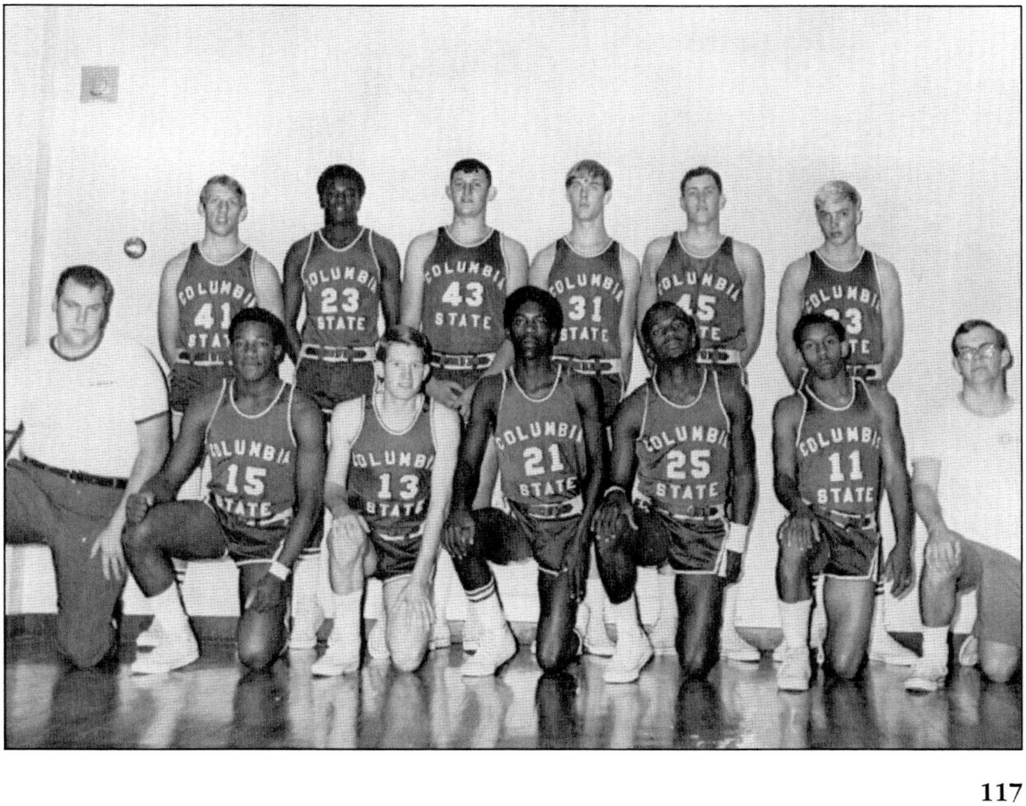

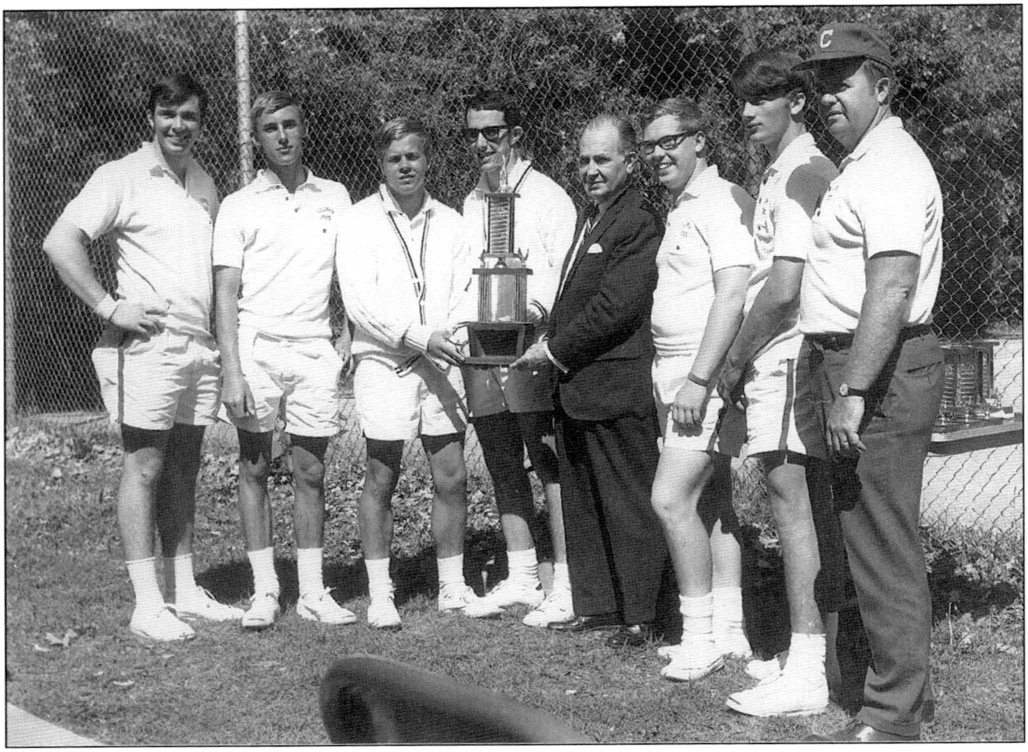

Columbia State's first TJCAA tennis champions are pictured here in 1969. From left to right are Louie Johnston, Dale Truitt, Roger Witherow, Pitts Hinson, the TJCAA representative, Jeff Powell, Johnny Edwards, and Coach Lewis Moore.

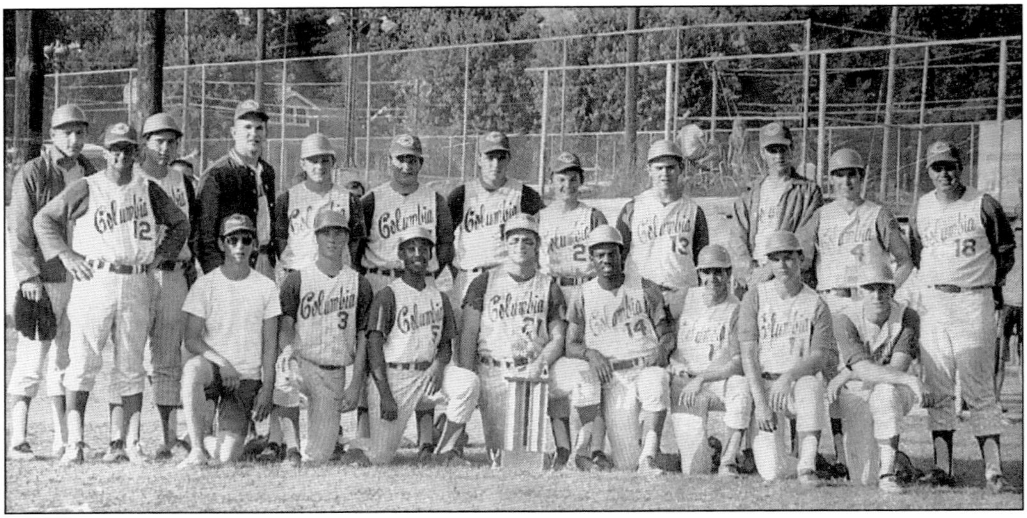

The 1970 Chargers were champions of the TJCAA and finished third in the National Junior College Athletic Association (NJCAA). From left to right are (front row) Butch Newell, Don Rhoton, Larry Jones, John Kyle, Ronnie Saunders, Lynn Alford, Don Harrison, and Don Cook; (back row) Butch Hinshaw, Coach Jim Painter, Eddie Echols, Randy Bratton, Ray Moss, Mike Turner, Phil Williams, Larry Patton (MVP), Steve Peterson, David Roberts, Tommy Davis, and Coach Dave Hall.

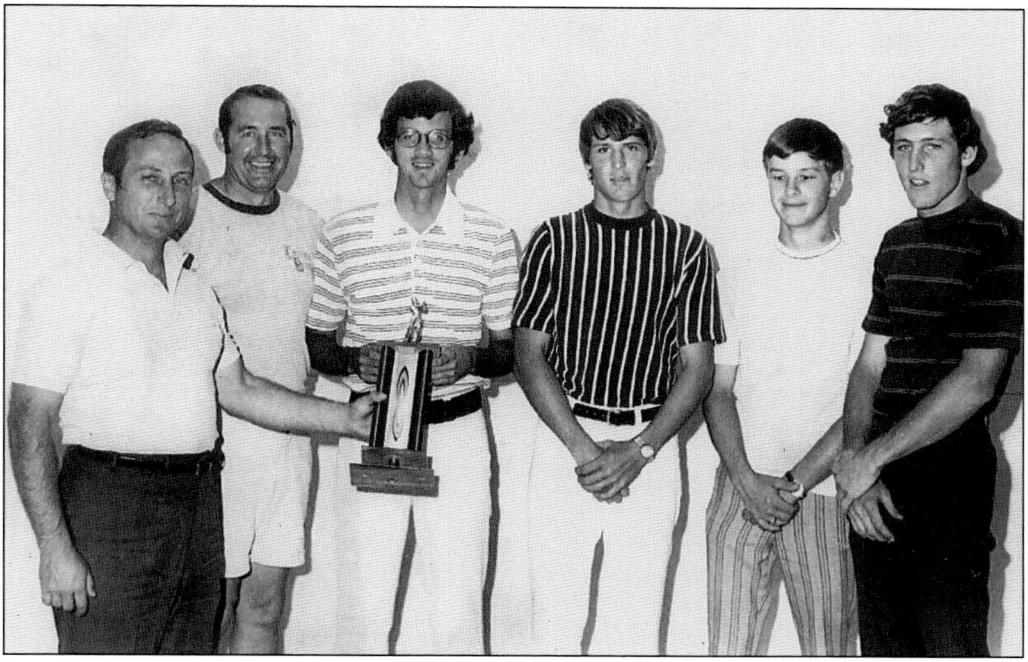

The 1971 golf team, under the leadership of Coach Gene McBee, placed first in the TJCAA tournament. From left to right are TJCAA president March Goodson, McBee, Jeff Swann, Ronnie Thompson, Sonny Reischman, and Gary Wells.

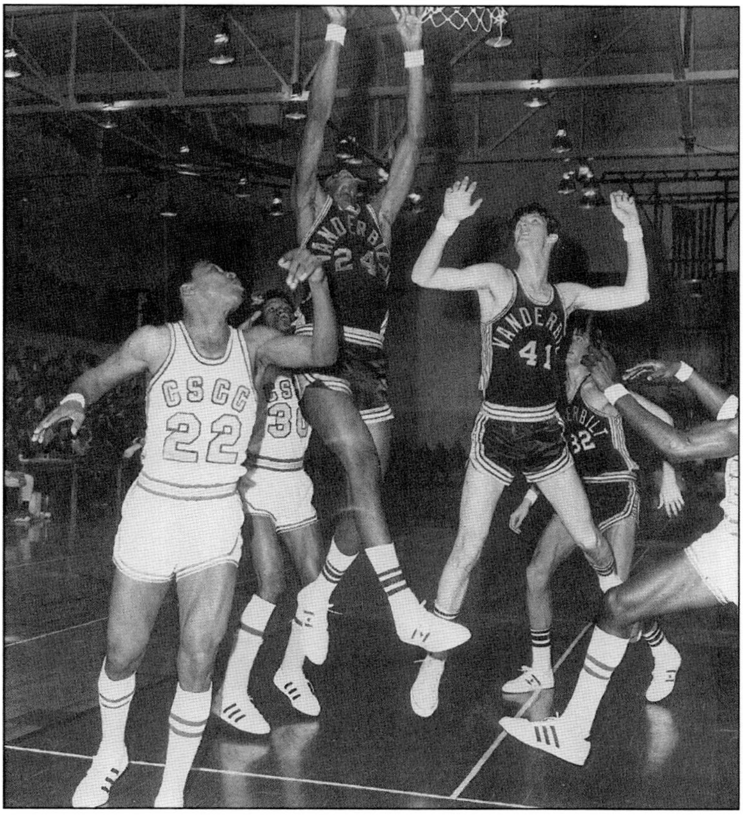

In 1971, the Chargers defeated the Vanderbilt frosh, one of whose players was Columbia Central graduate Lee Fowler. Three years later, Fowler and his teammates were the Southeastern Conference champs.

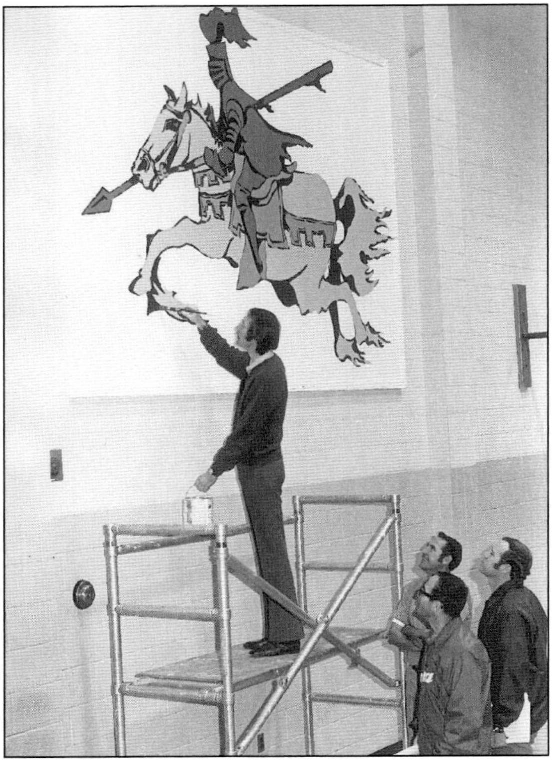

Art instructor Fred Behrens puts finishing strokes to an 8-by-12-foot impression of the Columbia State Charger, the symbol of school spirit. From left to right Coaches Jim Painter, Gene McBee, and Dave Hall admire the artist's work.

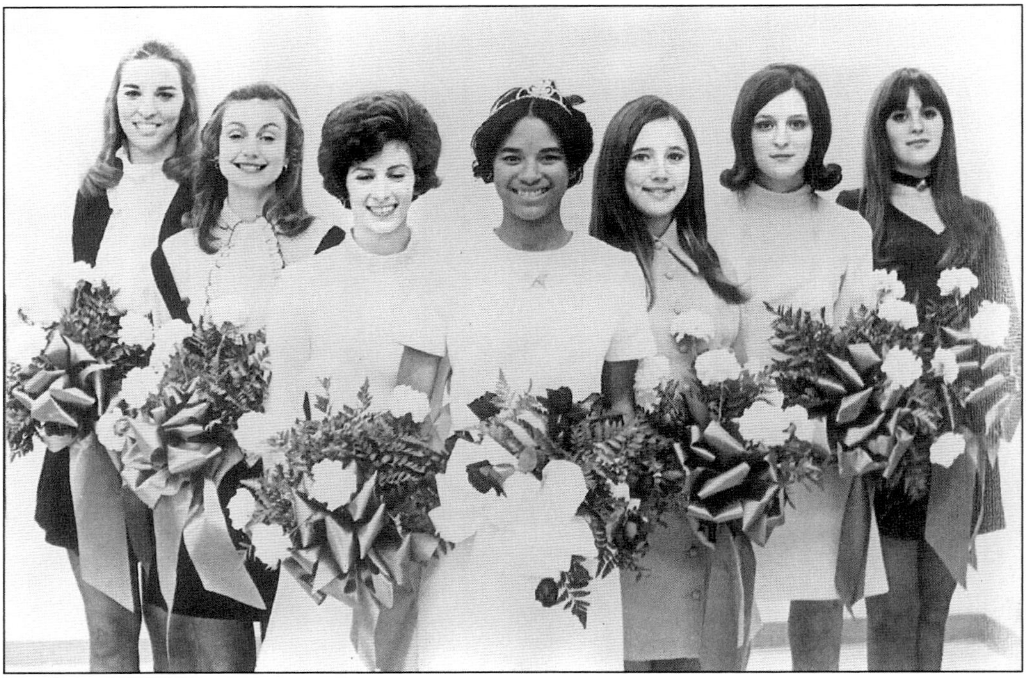

On January 28, 1971, Columbia State celebrated homecoming with a victory. The homecoming court was presented at halftime. Pictured here is the court, from left to right, Lynn Daimwood, Vicki Clower, Janet Huey, Gwen Smith (queen), Maureen Brewer, Janice Ingram, and Diane Loveless.

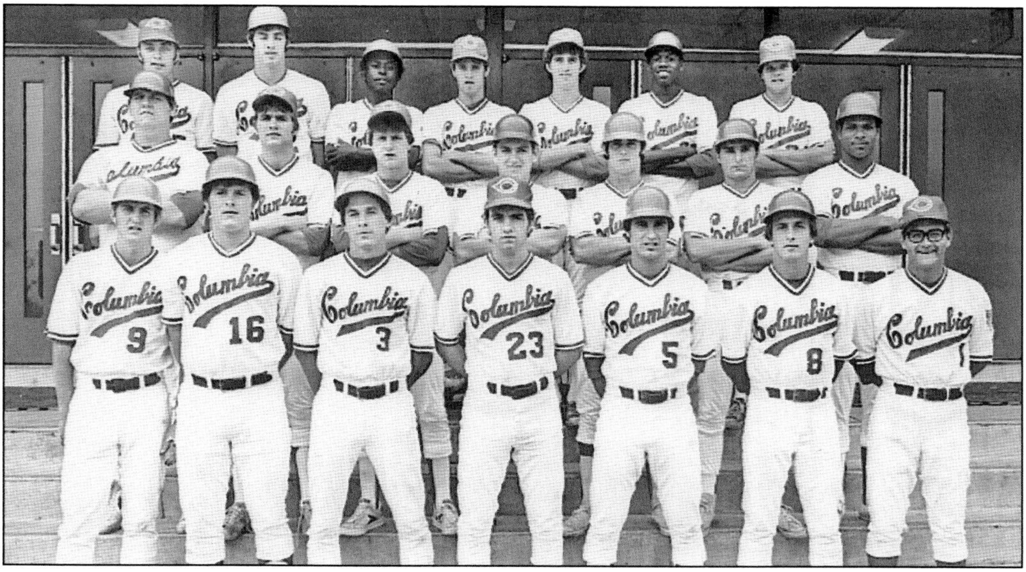

The 1978 Chargers placed first in the TJCAA and finished fourth in the NJCAA tournament. Pictured from left to right are (front row) Perry Thacker, Mike Abbatiello, Jack Reilley, Mark Divinnie, Matt Armenio, Johnny Rowden, and Coach Jim Painter; (middle row) Kenny Cox, Gary Bennett, Davis Swindek, Mike Norment, Wade Max, Scott Rethgren, and Greg Byrd; (back row) Bruce Dorton, Mike Bailey, Ralph Garrett, Steve Scheitel, David Smith, Mike Taylor, and Harley Woody.

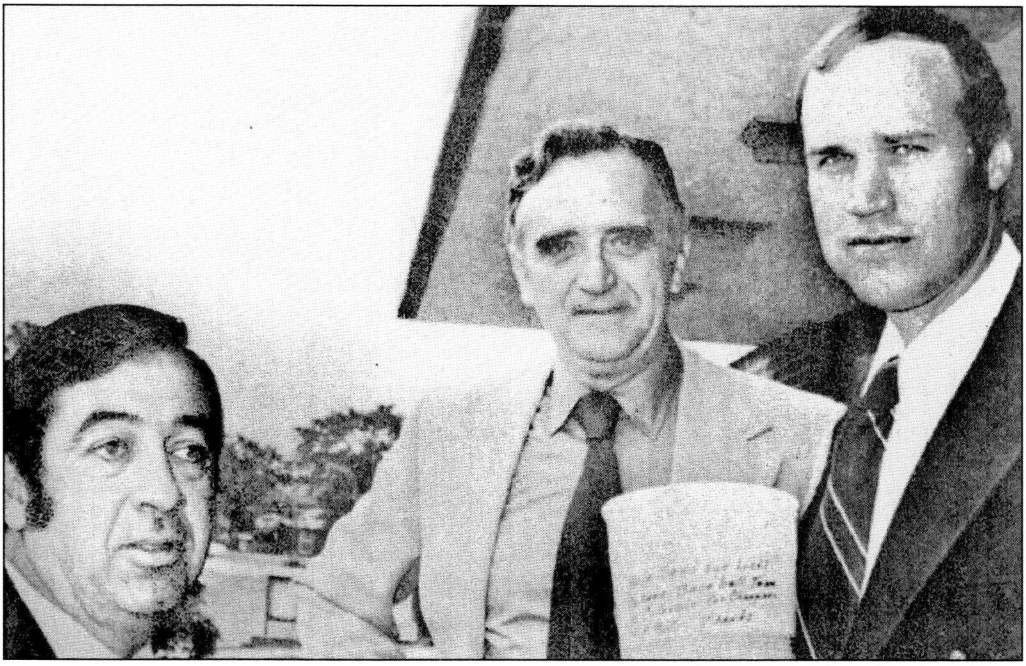

Bill Lawson (left), director of field services, and Dr. U.M. Clemmer (center), chairman of continuing education, check with the athletic director, Dave Hall, before the Chargers depart for Grand Junction, Colorado, for the NJCAA baseball tournament. Hall holds a cup that was used at Oldham's Restaurant to collect funds to help make the air flight to Grand Junction possible.

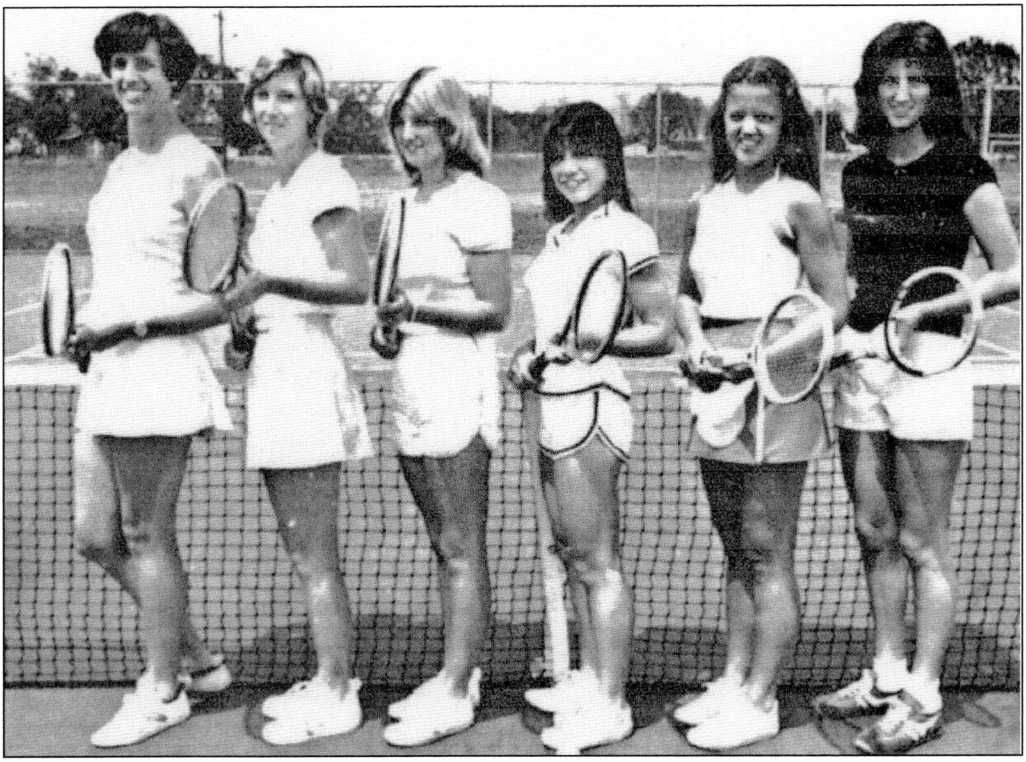

The 1978 women's tennis team was the TJCAA champion and participated in the NJCAA Tournament. Shown here from left to right are Wanda Holloway, Margaret Simmons, Gerrie Norman, Lisa White, Melinda Moore, and Carol Gray.

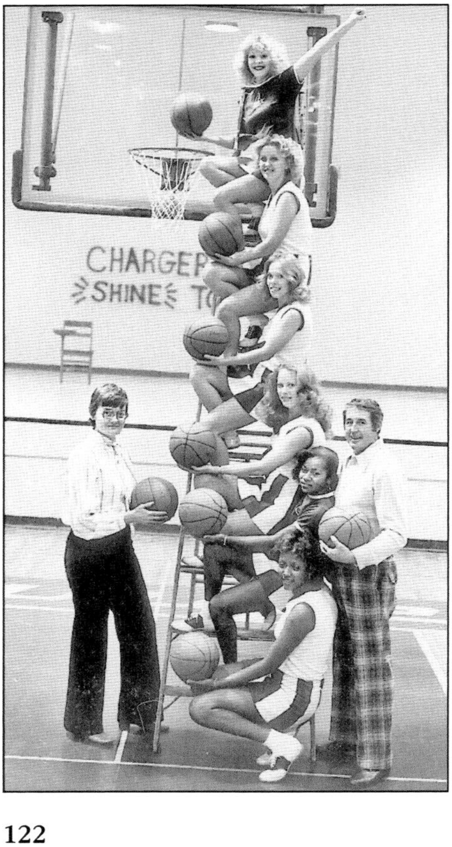

The 1978–1979 cheerleaders are shown with coaches Elner Hamner (left) and Gene McBee. From top to bottom are Sara Skelton, Beverly Meigs, Joni Winters, Sherry Duke, Theresa Cooper, and Alice Watkins.

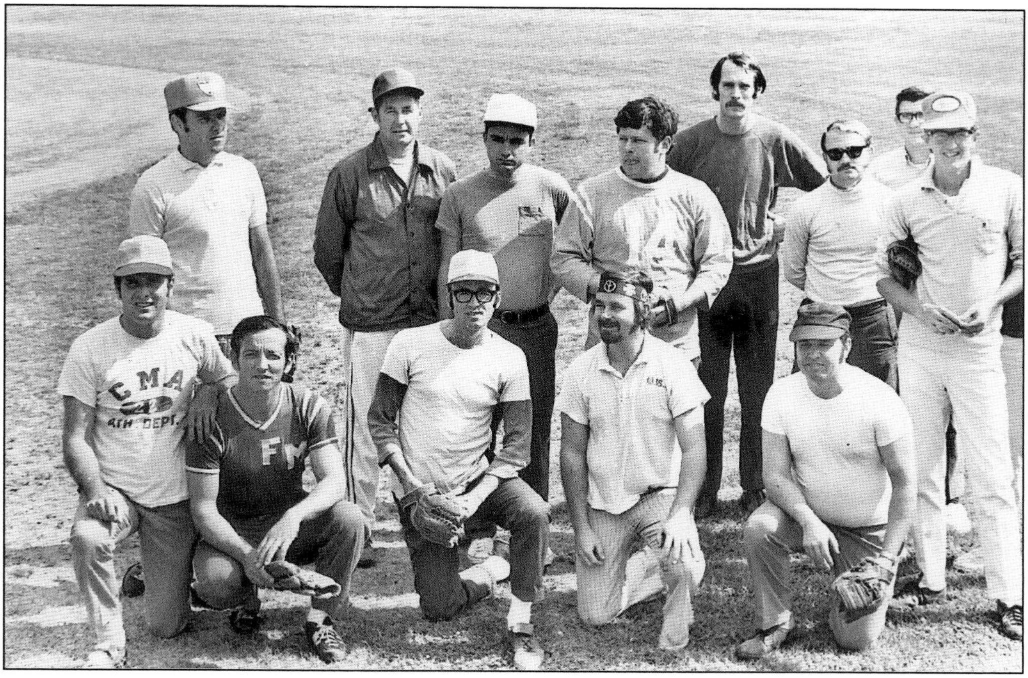

This is the faculty intramural softball team of 1978. From left to right are (front row) Jerry Lindsey, Bob White, Martin Jobe, Rodney Rogers, and John Long; (back row) Robert Simmons, Gene McBee, Ed Murphy, Aubrey Flagg, Fred Behrens, Bob Ruff, Winston Wrenn, and Jim Webb.

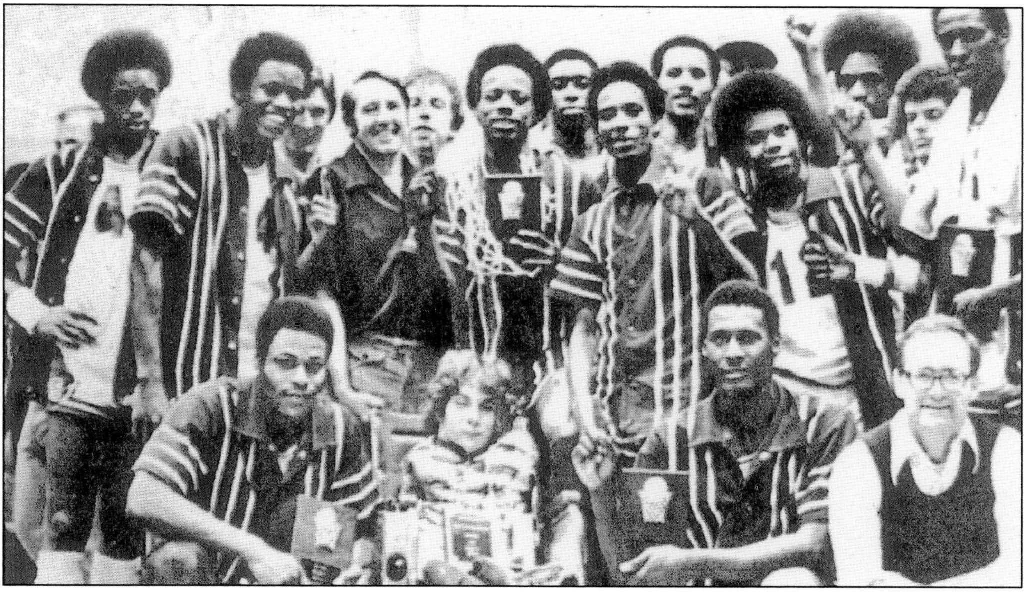

The 1978 Chargers are shown here headed for Hutchinson, Kansas, after winning the Region 7 championship. From left to right are (front row) James Dumes, Roger Rice ("The Voice of the Chargers") Roger Hayes, and Asst. Coach Jim Painter; (back row) Otto Adkerson, Larry Jenkins, Asst. Coach Ronnie Harris, Head Coach Gene McBee, Phil Willard, Ken Offutt, Mgr. Michael Murray, Rusty Poole, Paul Handley, Mgr. William Townsend, Bobby Hines, Oscar Atkerson, and Curtis Webster.

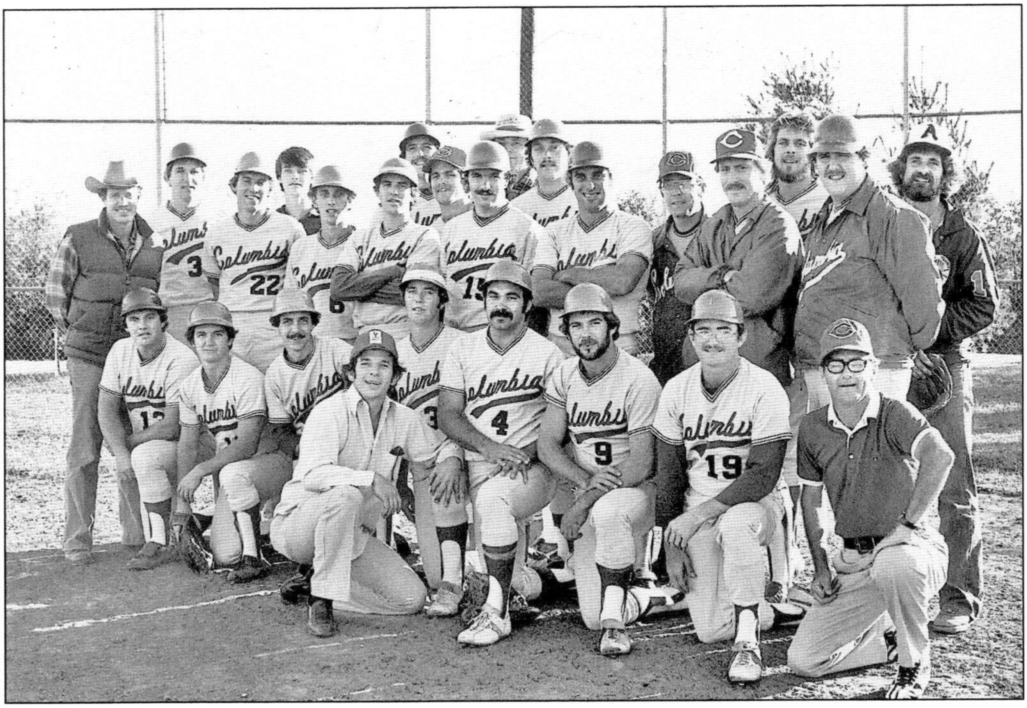

Former baseball players come back for an "Old Timers" game. How many do you recognize?

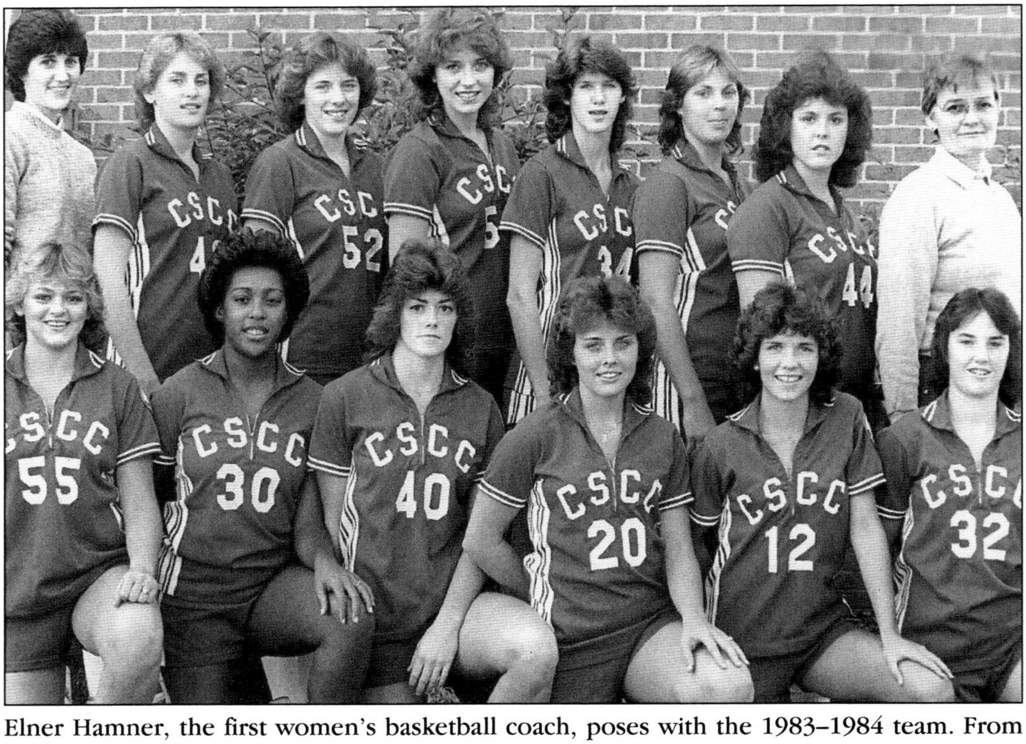

Elner Hamner, the first women's basketball coach, poses with the 1983–1984 team. From left to right are (front row) Rhonda Hill, Senino Turner, Deb Reaves, Anita Farrar, Jana Killen, and Tammy Jones; (back row) Audrey Martin, Sherry Holquest, Cheryl Bouldin, Tobie Flippo, Tracey O'Rear, Leah Loveless, Kim Galbreath, and Coach Hamner.

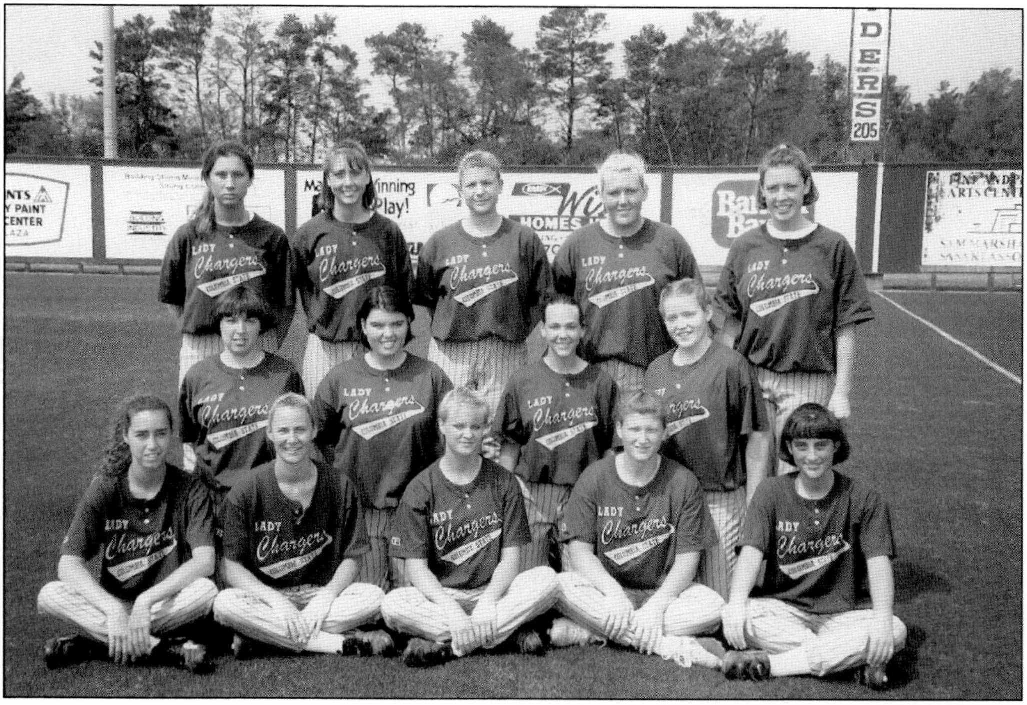

Women's softball was added in 1993 to the existing intercollegiate teams of men's and women's basketball and baseball. The 1997 softball team was TJCAA Western Division champion. Eddie Campbell was the coach. Team members are, from left to right, (front row) Karen Grigsby, Cindy Ferguson, Jannine Cunningham, Wendy Kaier, and Lindsey Armour; (middle row) Heather King, Krystal Allsup, Lisa Hughs, Camille Fitzwater; (back row) Alison Pruitt, Nicole Warren, Ashley Campbell, Laura Beth Ford, and Robyn Cain.

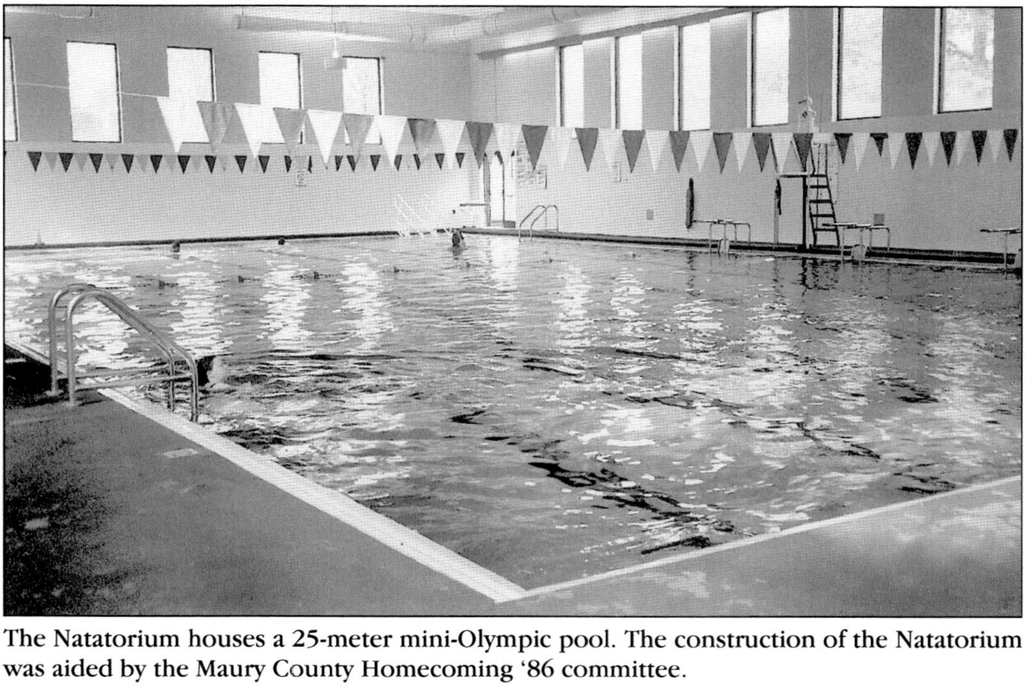

The Natatorium houses a 25-meter mini-Olympic pool. The construction of the Natatorium was aided by the Maury County Homecoming '86 committee.

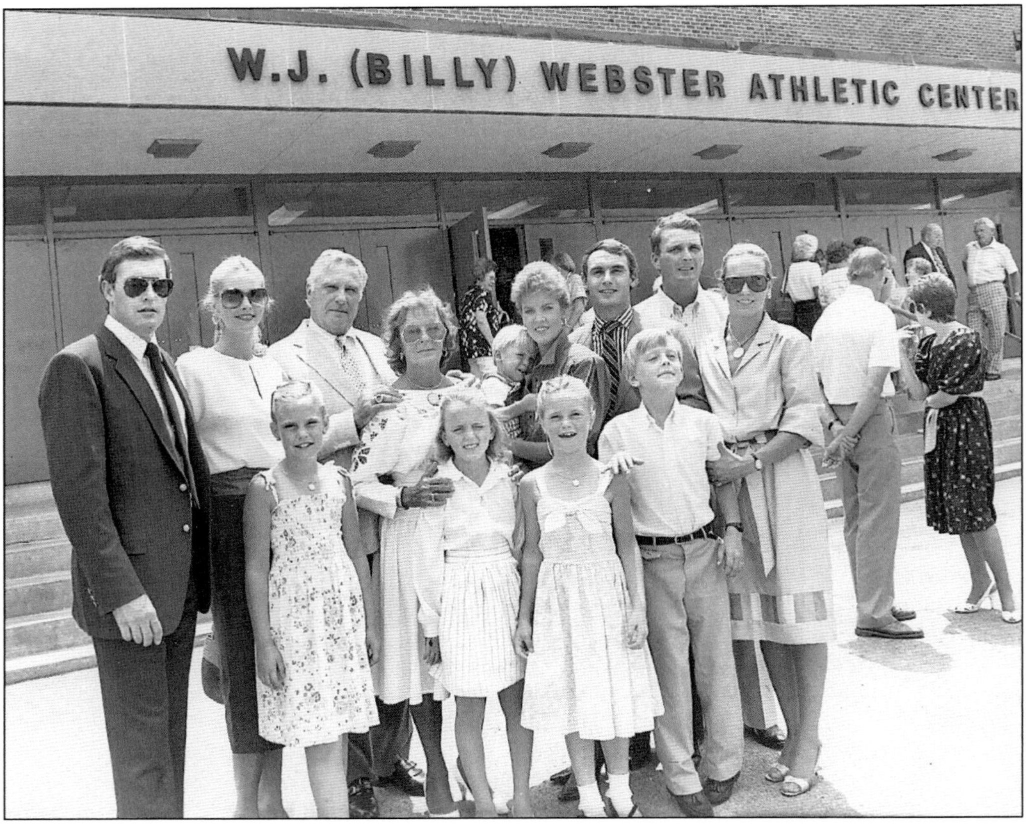

Pictured is the Webster family at the dedication of the W.J. (Billy) Webster Athletic Center.

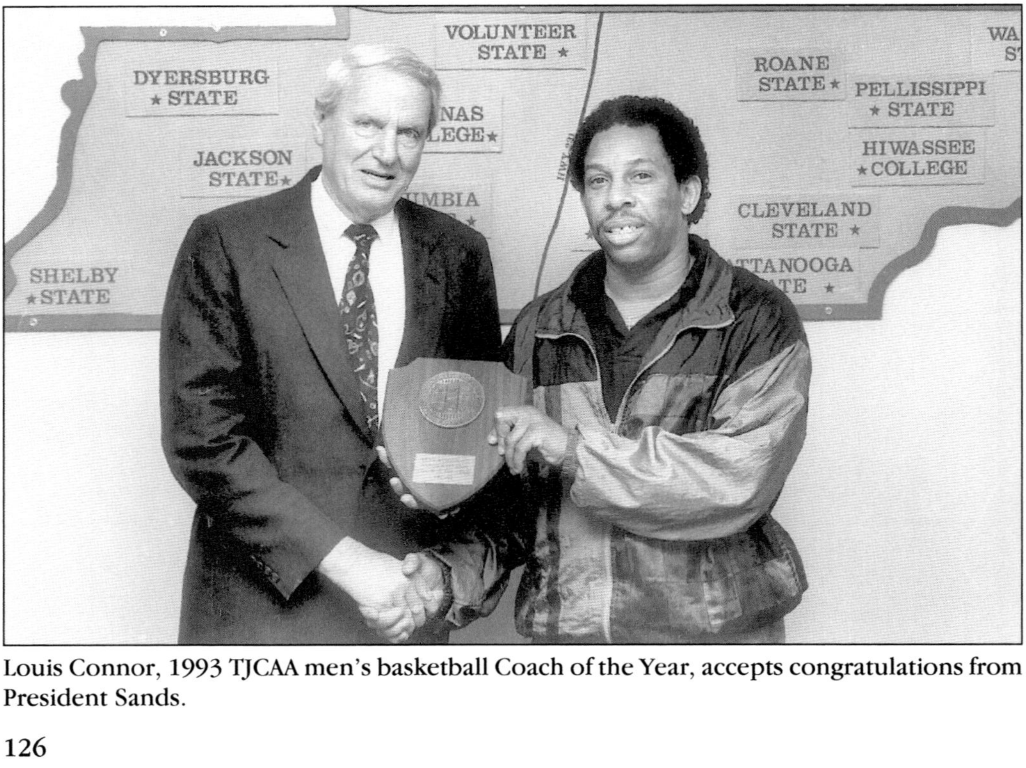

Louis Connor, 1993 TJCAA men's basketball Coach of the Year, accepts congratulations from President Sands.

Baseball coach Jim Painter is shown with daughter Peggy and wife Faye at his induction into the Tennessee Sports Hall of Fame. Paul Sands, Dave Hall, and Larry Brewer are also members of the Hall. Painter was inducted into the NJCAA Hall of Fame following victory number 1,000.

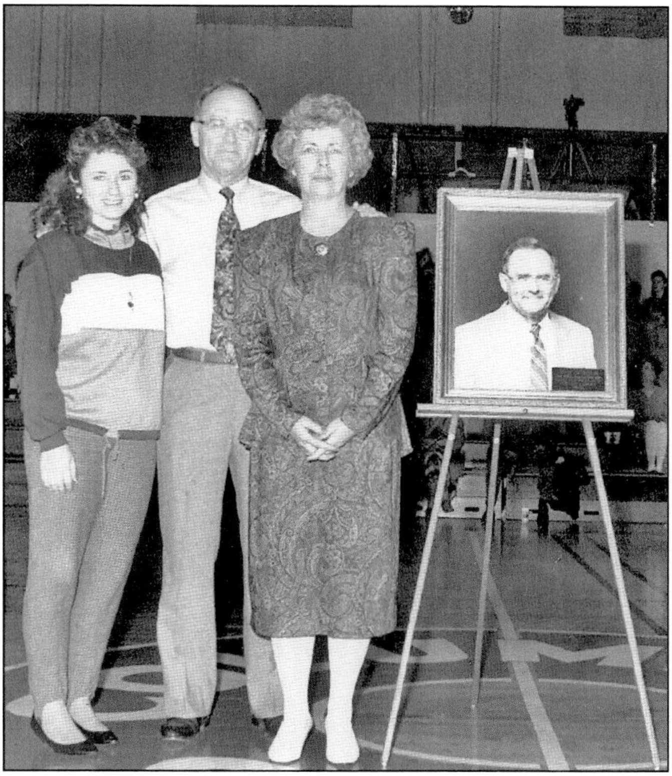

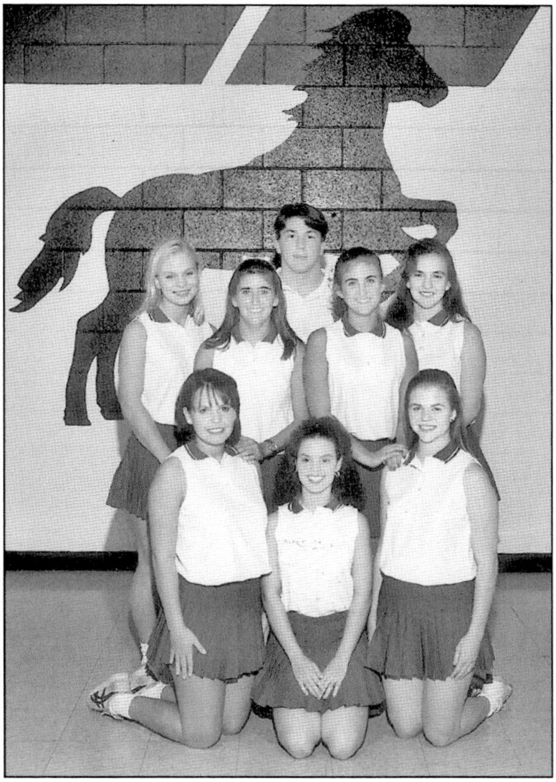

"How lucky can one man be?!" The 1995–1996 cheerleaders are pictured here. From left to right are (front row) Julie Long, Chelle Bradburn, and Stacey Stinson; (back row) Allison Brinley, Susan Shouse, Mica Hartsfield, Amy Melton, and Mandy Satterwhite.

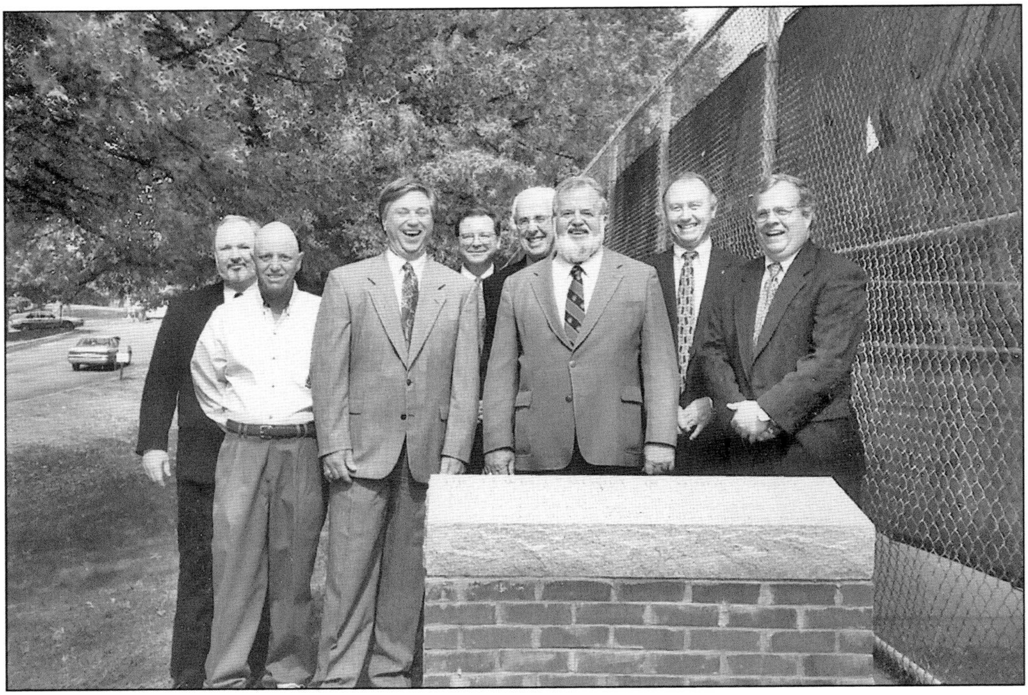

From left to right, Louis Johnston, Roger Demastus, Harvey Fischer, Randy Stevens, Lewis Moore, Arnold Alexander, and Roger Witherow attend the dedication of the Dr. Lewis E. Moore Jr. Tennis Complex in 1996.

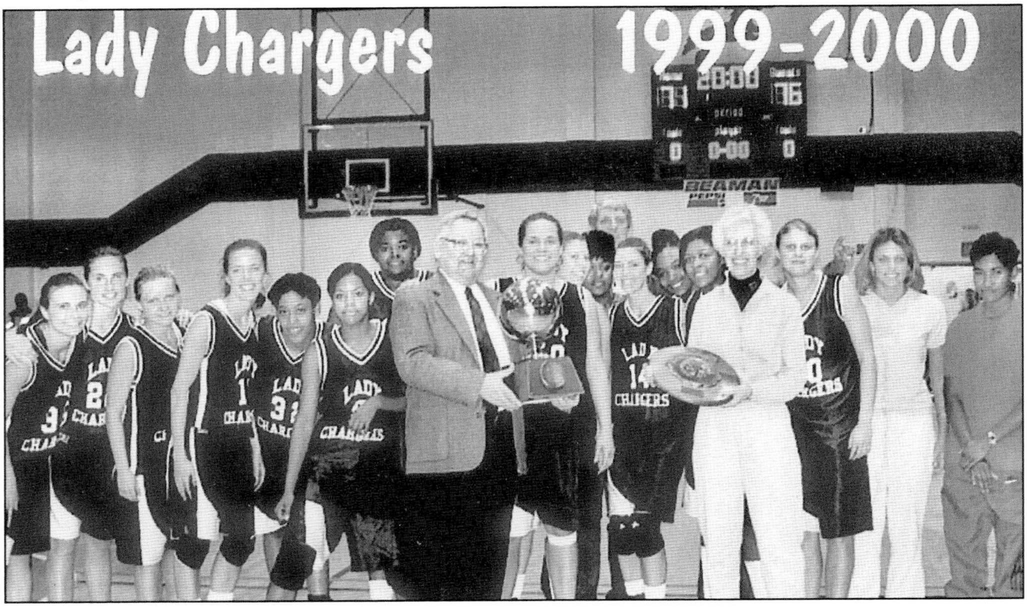

The 1999–2000 Lady Chargers earned eighth place in the NJCAA Tournament. From left to right in this picture are Wendi Hartsfield, Angie Overstreet, Sharon Smith, Rebecca Miller, Jessica Grayson, Haley Webster, Chantee Frierson, TJCAA commissioner Dr. Quinton Lane, Lindsey Wilson, Kelly Opalewski, Robbie McElwee, Coach Larry Brewer, Tabitha Napier, Angie Maxwell, Jaqvilla Pigg, President Hawkins, Cassidy Jenkins, Corey Cravens, and Antionette Armstrong.